The Use of Art in Counselling Child and Adult Survivors of Sexual Abuse

of related interest

Creative Therapies with Traumatized Children
Anne Bannister
ISBN 1 84310 155 6

Play Therapy with Abused Children
Ann Cattanach
ISBN 1 85302 193 8

Creative Group Therapy for Women Survivors of Child Sexual Abuse
Speaking the Unspeakable
Bonnie Meekums
Foreword by Anne Bannister
ISBN 1 85302 453 8

Creativity and the Dissociative Patient
Puppets, Narrative and Art in the Treatment of Survivors of Childhood Trauma
Lani Alaine Gerity
Foreword by Edith Kramer
ISBN 1 85302 722 7

The Artist as Therapist
Arthur Robbins
ISBN 1 85302 907 6

Can You Read Me?
Creative Writing with Child and Adult Victims of Abuse
Edited by Jacki Pritchard and Eric Sainsbury
ISBN 1 84310 192 0

Narrative Approaches to Working with Adult Male Survivors of Child Sexual Abuse
The Clients', the Counsellor's and the Researcher's Story
Kim Etherington
ISBN 1 85302 818 5

The Child's Own Story
Life Story Work with Traumatized Children
Richard Rose and Terry Philpot
Foreword by Mary Walsh, Co-founder and Chief Executive of SACCS
ISBN 1 84310 287 0

The Use of Art in Counselling Child and Adult Survivors of Sexual Abuse

Maralynn M. Hagood

Foreword by Marian Liebmann

Jessica Kingsley Publishers
London and Philadelphia

First published in the United Kingdom in 2000
by Jessica Kingsley Publishers
116 Pentonville Road
London N1 9JB, UK
and
400 Market Street, Suite 400
Philadelphia, PA 19106, USA

www.jkp.com

Printed digitally since 2005

Library of Congress Cataloging in Publication Data
A CIP catalog record for this book is available from the Library of Congress

British Library Cataloguing in Publication Data
A CIP catalogue record for this book is available from the British Library

ISBN-13: 978 1 85302 228 9
ISBN-10: 1 85302 228 4

Contents

LIST OF ILLUSTRATIONS 6
LIST OF TABLES 6
DEDICATION AND ACKNOWLEDGEMENTS 7
FOREWORD BY MARIAN LIEBMANN 9
INTRODUCTION 11

1 Theoretical Issues in the Use of Art in Counselling Child and Adult Survivors of Sexual Abuse 29

2 Developmental Issues in the Use of Art in Counselling Sexually Abused Children 54

3 Therapeutic Issues and Special Problems in the Use of Art in Counselling Sexually Abused Children 74

4 Case Examples in the Use of Art in Counselling Sexually Abused Children 92

5 The Use of Art in Counselling Mothers of Sexually Abused Children 119

6 The Use of Art in Counselling Adult Survivors of Sexual Abuse 146

7 The Use of Art in Counselling Adolescent Sex Offenders 174

8 The Use of Art in Group Work with Adolescent and Adult Sex Offenders 195

9 Diagnosis or Dilemma: Artwork by Sexually Abused Children 223

EPILOGUE 247
REFERENCES 250
INDEX 263

Illustrations

Figure 4.1	Sarah's drawing of the 'Mean Bear'	94
Figure 4.2	Therapist's drawing of the 'Mean Bear'	95
Figure 4.3	'Red Wedges'	96
Figure 4.4	Sarah's painting of the 'Mean Bear'	98
Figure 4.5	'Two Giraffes'	102
Figure 4.6	'My Mother, the Witch'	104
Figure 4.7	'My Mother, the Tiger'	105
Figure 4.8	Mother and daughter painting together while angry	106
Figure 4.9	Mother and daughter painting together after resolution of feelings	107
Figure 4.10	'Power Struggle'	108
Figure 4.11	'A Heart' and 'Hansel and Gretel'	109
Figure 4.12	Comparison of the 'Heart' with the 'Christmas Tree'	110
Figure 4.13	'This is Me'	113
Figure 4.14	'Family Collage'	114
Figure 4.15	'My Mother and Myself'	115
Figure 4.16	'Mixed Feelings'	116
Figure 4.17	'Love and Sadness for My Father'	117
Figure 5.1	'Major Shmuk'	138
Figure 5.2	'Throw Him to the Sharks!'	138
Figure 5.3	'Dilemma'	139
Figure 5.4	'My Mother/My Daughter'	142
Figure 5.5	'Mandala in Flames'	143
Figure 5.6	'Lost in a Storm'	144
Figure 6.1	'Faceless'	165
Figure 6.2	'The Monster'	167
Figure 6.3	'Trapped'	167
Figure 6.4	'The Black Blob'	172
Figure 8.1	'Keep Your Daughter Away from Me'	207
Figure 8.2	'Time Management and Isolation'	208
Figure 8.3	'I Think of Driving Away'	209
Figure 8.4	'Lonely and Unbelieved'	210
Figure 8.5	'Abandonment'	212
Figure 8.6	'My Dad and I Fishing'	213
Figure 8.7	'Monster Molester'	217
Figure 8.8	'Angry and Alone'	218
Figure 8.9	'Lost and Unimportant to the World...No Understanding'	219
Figure 8.10	'I Gave Her More than She Bargained for'	220
Figure 9.1	Children's drawings: Developmental scores increasing with age	239
Figure 9.2	Children's drawings: 'Sex abuse indicators' decreasing with age	241

Tables

Table 9.1	'Sex abuse indicators' as features of normal development	240
Table 9.2	Non-occurring 'sex abuse indicators' in drawings of nonabused children	242
Table 9.3	Rarely occurring 'sex abuse indicators' in drawings of nonabused children	242
Table 9.4	Frequency of genitalia appearing in drawings of nonabused children	243
Table 9.5	Frequency of genitalia appearing in drawings of nonabused children related to age	243

I dedicate this book to all of those children and adults who have suffered the trauma of childhood sexual abuse. It is my hope that the ideas in this book will help them work through their pain and move to a life of success and happiness. It is possible – I have seen it happen many times!

Acknowledgements

I want to express my gratitude to my American art therapy and counselling colleagues with whom I learned about working with sexually abused children and their families in California prior to my move to Scotland in 1989. I am also grateful to my British art therapy colleagues who encouraged me to make the move across the Atlantic and supported me through my adjustment to living in a new country which was much more difficult, yet rewarding, than I had ever imagined. Many British social workers, counsellors, psychologists, art therapists and other mental health professionals have also given me valuable feedback. Cultural and legal issues in Scotland and England are in many ways very different from those I had encountered in the United States. On the other hand, I quickly learned that human nature is the same on both sides of the Atlantic, and that sexually abused children and adults suffer in much the same way regardless of their country or culture. I also appreciate the valuable work that has already been done by my psychology, counselling and art therapy colleagues in the area of clinical work and research into child sexual abuse. A combination of their contributions and my own clinical experience of seventeen years in the field of sexual abuse has been the basis for the writing of this book.

I wish to thank those nonabused Scottish children who faithfully made many drawings for me with which to compare with those of sexually abused children in the never-ending quest to find ways to detect and prevent more damage being perpetrated onto children. I also wish to thank staff at the primary school where I collected the drawings for their ongoing support and assistance. I am grateful to staff and research colleagues at the Edinburgh University Department of

Psychology who supported me through my PhD study into children's drawings relative to indicators of sexual abuse. Dr Boris Semeonoff (now sadly deceased) spent many hours encouraging me in my research and opened doors for me for presenting what I knew about drawings of sexually abused children to other British professionals as well as pointing me in the right direction regarding publishing my work. I am indebted to Professor Robert Morris and Dr Halla Beloff who both offered me considerable support throughout the lengthy research project. I want to acknowledge the American art therapist, Dr Donald Uhlin (also deceased), who inspired me to do research into children's drawings and to pursue a career in art therapy. In particular I wish to thank my mother, Mrs La Jeune Hagood, (recently deceased) who lovingly gave me both emotional and financial support throughout the research. The St Andrew's Society of San Francisco also generously assisted me financially throughout the PhD.

Above all, I wish to express my appreciation to all of those children, adolescents and adults with whom I have worked since 1983 in both California and Scotland, who sadly suffered both the trauma of childhood sexual abuse and its aftermath. Their efforts to overcome their difficulties through the use of art in counselling were inspirational in the writing of this book. They have taught me a great deal over the years in the way of courage and determination to gain a life of victory over victimisation. Without their input, the writing of this book would have been totally impossible. I hope that what they have taught me through their art creations will be passed on to those who work with both child and adult survivors of sexual abuse, enabling them to offer guidance and support to those who make their difficult journey toward greater mental health and happiness. My special thanks go to Sandy who kindly gave me consent to use her artwork for the cover of this book.

Foreword

Thirty years ago there was very little discussion of child sexual abuse; most therapists and counsellors thought it was a rare and traumatic condition that affected only a very few of their clients. Much earlier Freud had bowed to colleagues' opinions and switched from believing his patients' accounts to ascribing them to fantasies. We just could not believe children's accounts of their traumas, so most therapists accepted Freud's views. Now we are wiser, and much sadder.

This book is the product of seventeen years' work in this field, and provides much good sense and advice in working with children who have been abused and their mothers. It is underpinned by a thorough look at theoretical issues and a comprehensive reference section. What also comes over is a warmth and acceptance of clients of all ages and situations, and a pragmatic willingness to adapt the work to some difficult spaces and situations. The many case examples bring the theories and methods to life, and each chapter has a useful summary.

Few therapists have the chance to work on both sides of the Atlantic, and the comparison between the US and the UK (particularly Scotland) is very illuminating. Another unusual bridge is made between work with survivors and work with perpetrators, with the inclusion of two chapters on work with adolescent and adult sex offenders. Working with offenders gives therapists and counsellors insights which are useful in working with survivors. The book takes an unequivocal stance that offending is the responsibility of the perpetrator and never the fault of the survivor.

One of the most debated questions is how far children's pictures can be regarded as showing evidence of sexual abuse. In the US pictures are often presented to courts as such evidence, while British courts are more sceptical, and art therapists and counsellors in the UK do not practise in this way. This book demonstrates how most of the ways of 'reading' children's pictures are based on psychoanalytic views which are derived from adult work, which may not apply to children.

The book provides another dimension often missing from studies of children's pictures: the huge body of work done on developmental aspects of children's drawings. Children draw very differently at different ages and often also from one day to the next. Few studies have included nonabused children as comparisons. Maralynn Hagood has started to rectify this in her research on drawings done by nonabused children, to see how far they do, or do not, include features regarded as 'sexual abuse indicators'. The final chapter draws some initial tentative conclusions, but there remains much more research to be undertaken in this area. The purpose of such studies is to give us the ability to provide protection and help for children who are being abused – an overall aim with which we would all concur.

Marian Liebmann
September 2000

Introduction

The purpose of this book is to demonstrate how the use of art may be incorporated with counselling in therapeutic work with child and adult survivors of sexual abuse. The contents are based on a total of seventeen years of clinical work with sexually abused children and their families, including nine years of research into children's drawings relative to possible indicators of sexual abuse.

Background

I was initially drawn to work with sexually abused children and their families in the early 1980s while working in California. At that time there was an ever-increasing awareness of the high incidence of child sexual abuse across the United States. I assumed that most of the presenting problems that one was likely to encounter in therapeutic work would be experienced by those with a history of sexual abuse. That assumption has certainly been borne out in my experience with this population. As a registered art therapist and Licensed Marriage, Family and Child Counsellor (MFCC) in California, my American work was carried out largely within programmes specialising in the treatment of families of sexually abused children as well as in private practice settings.

During my training as an MFCC at California State University, Hayward, I commuted weekly to California State University, Sacramento, for my art therapy training, working on both qualifications in tandem. I thus had the opportunity to find many ways to integrate counselling and art therapy theories and techniques (Hagood, in press). I became fascinated with the numerous ways both modalities could complement and enhance each other. My work soon became more focused on working with sexually abused children and their mothers, as well as adolescent and adult sex offenders. I found the application of both counselling and art therapy with this population to be well received as well as effective. I was continually impressed by the way that drawings and paintings amplified verbal techniques commonly used in counselling and psychotherapy. Artwork allowed for further expression of feelings, problem-solving and empowering survivors to heal and ultimately to leave their histories of abuse behind.

My first trip to the United Kingdom was to an international conference in 1985 at Goldsmiths' College, University of London, sponsored by the British Association of Art Therapists, where I was warmly greeted by a number of British art therapists. Numerous papers were presented by psychotherapists from all over the world on the use of art in the therapeutic process. I was fortunate to be able to present my master's thesis on Jung's mandala and its relationship to art psychotherapy (Slegelis 1987). I became interested in learning more about the involvement of British art therapists in research (Hagood 1990). My transition from California to Scotland actually began in 1987 when I was on holiday in Scotland and the 'Cleveland scandal' broke in the newspapers. Dr Marietta Higgs, an experienced paediatrician, had reported a very large number of suspected cases of child sexual abuse in Cleveland, northern England. The story was splashed across every British newspaper and on the lips of everyone I met. At that time I became acutely aware of how little professionals in the United Kingdom knew about issues of sexually abused children. I also learned that Parliament was earmarking funding for training of professionals in working with sexually abused children. Since my plan was to pursue a PhD in Scotland, I realised that I could support my research by carrying out such training as well as having the deep satisfaction of knowing that I was making a contribution on behalf of sexually abused children.

In 1988 I was invited by the National Society for the Prevention of Cruelty to Children (NSPCC) in the Greater Manchester area to train and consult with social workers on eight different teams who were involved in child protection work. At that time I approached the Psychology Department at Edinburgh University with my research interests, and in 1989 moved across the Atlantic to Scotland to carry out research into the development of children's drawings relative to possible indicators of sexual abuse. Living in the city centre of Edinburgh after spending my entire life in northern California left me in a very pleasant state of culture shock. Discovering the many nuances of Scottish culture, including the rich art, drama and architecture I encountered, was quite an adventure. I was greeted by many warm, friendly and enthusiastic people who were very supportive of my work. Having ancestors from Scotland made the experience especially meaningful to me.

Over the following years, I was privileged to train many mental health professionals such as psychiatrists, social workers, psychologists, counsellors, art therapists, nurse practitioners, home health visitors and others throughout the United Kingdom in various aspects of the use of art in working with sexually abused children and adult survivors. Because most professionals were only beginning to work in this area, they felt de-skilled and experienced a considerable amount of anxiety. Participants in training workshops which I presented used artwork themselves in order to work through some of their own feelings of inadequacy and helplessness in working with this population. Their paintings and drawings enabled them to be able to empathise to a greater extent with the children and adults with whom they worked, as well as being able to offer support to each other. They were also able to experience the power of art media to elicit memories and express emotions.

I became registered with the British Association of Art Therapists in 1990 and in 1993 my licence in Marriage, Family and Child Counselling from California enabled me to become qualified in the United Kingdom as a Chartered Counselling Psychologist with the British Psychological Society. In 1994, I assisted in the early stages of development of the first therapeutic centre for sexually abused children in Scotland within the National Health Service (NHS) to be housed in a child protection unit. I worked with very severely damaged children who had been grossly sexually abused and again found that they loved being engaged in the art process. At that time the reporting of child sexual abuse in Scotland was doubling each year and unfortunately continues to rise. I have been working since early 1996 for the NHS alongside clinical psychologists in a geographical area in Scotland where the incidence of sexual abuse is estimated to be very high. Since 1996, my focus has moved to working in adult mental health in primary care as well as occupational health. An average of 50–70 per cent of my caseload has consisted of adult survivors of sexual abuse.

When I made my transatlantic move in 1989, I had to roll the clock back by ten to fifteen years as far as work with survivors of sexual abuse was concerned. Therapeutic work had been considerably developed in the United States by that time because awareness of child sexual abuse had surfaced there much earlier. Since 1989, however, I have seen the development of the work on behalf of sexually abused children and adult survivors in the United Kingdom ever-increasing, depending on the geographical area and the amount of resources available for such work.

In 1998, I completed my PhD in psychology at the University of Edinburgh, having longitudinally investigated drawings by ordinary Scottish children assumed to be nonabused to learn how they might differ from those of sexually abused children. I had attempted in my earlier work in California to use children's artwork to substantiate suspicion of sexual abuse with little success. Since I had not worked with ordinary nonabused children, I wanted to learn whether any of the characteristics in children's drawings alleged to be indicative of a history of sexual abuse were actually features reflective of ordinary children's cognitive development. It was impossible, unfortunately, to obtain access to sexually abused children at the outset of the study because of a series of cases of alleged sexual abuse in Scotland (Ayrshire and the Orkney Islands). Constant media coverage and resultant sensitivity over the subject of child sexual abuse throughout the United Kingdom made gaining access impossible. The research therefore had to focus only on drawings by nonabused children. This was nevertheless very important, because it had not been done previously.

It was demonstrated in the research that around one-third of the features in children's drawings previously purported to be indicative of sexual abuse actually were more directly associated with the child's level of developmental maturity. At the same time, the findings revealed that around two-thirds of these features did *not* appear or rarely appeared in drawings by nonabused children, and therefore remain to be further investigated (Hagood 1999, 2000c) (for further discussion, see Chapter 9). The results of the investigation have raised concerns as to what extent children's drawings may be used validly in the detection of sexual abuse. Much more research needs to be carried out before we will know which characteristics in children's drawings, if any, are indeed indicative of a history of sexual abuse. Difficulties in funding to date and continued problems in gaining access to sexually abused children in Scotland have unfortunately made it impossible to continue with the research at this point in time.

Integration of counselling and art therapy with survivors of child sexual abuse

The most concise, yet all-encompassing definition of art therapy I have found is that adopted by the American Art Therapy Association:

> Art therapy is a human service profession that utilizes art media, images, the creative art process, and patient/client responses to the created products as reflections of an individual's development, abilities, personality, interests, concerns, and conflicts. Art therapy practice is based on knowledge of human developmental and psychological theories which are implemented in the full spectrum of models of assessment and treatment including educational, psychodynamic, cognitive, transpersonal, and other therapeutic means of reconciling emotional conflicts, fostering self-awareness, developing social skills, managing behavior, solving problems, reducing

> anxiety, aiding reality orientation, and increasing self-esteem. (American Art Therapy Association 1999, p.3)

It is apparent in reading this definition that the overlap in using art in therapy with a wide variety of models of counselling and psychotherapy is possible. It is the purpose of this book to demonstrate how the blending of verbal approaches with the use of art media can be effectively used with both children and adults who have suffered the unfortunate trauma of child sexual abuse. Ideas from this book should not be used indiscriminately without serious consideration of the unique needs and circumstances of each individual with whom one is working, nor can anyone call themselves an art therapist or counsellor unless they have undergone the rigorous professional training required to become qualified in either field.

Each child and adult survivor of sexual abuse is totally unique and approaches *always* have to be appropriately related to the issues he or she may be dealing with. A thorough understanding of his or her psychological history and developmental level is also necessary. The survivor's needs *always* come first regardless of the need of the therapist to 'try a new approach'. It seems obvious that work in the United States cannot be transplanted directly into other cultures, but many approaches and techniques, I believe, can be incorporated into the evolving work in Britain and elsewhere. Treatment methods in working with survivors of sexual abuse, both children and adults, are currently being developed within the United Kingdom on an ever-increasing basis and many ideas stemming from American approaches to treatment are gradually being adapted to the British system and culture (Pattison 1992).

British art therapists are also developing their work with sexually abused children on an ever-increasing basis (Murphy 1998). Shortly after my move to the United Kingdom, I wrote a paper (Hagood 1992b) for *Inscape*, the official journal of the British Association of Art Therapists, encouraging British art therapists to look seriously at the possibilities for developing art therapy approaches with those who had been sexually abused. I was happy to learn that the article inspired British art therapist Jenny Murphy to compile a collection of articles from a variety of British art therapists illustrating how art therapy with sexually abused children in the United Kingdom has evolved to date (Murphy 2000).

In 1989 a survey of 553 sexual abuse treatment programmes throughout the United States indicated that in more than half of these programmes art therapy was used along with insight therapy, play therapy, behaviour modification, cognitive restructuring and relapse prevention (Keller, Cicchinelli and Gardner

1989). By the early 1990s, a survey revealed that 16 per cent of American art therapists were specialising in working in the area of child sexual abuse (Gordon and Manning 1991). A large number of art therapists in Canada were developing expertise in working in the area of child sexual abuse in the early 1990s (Knibbe 1990; Marrion 1990). Australian counsellors and psychotherapists are also using art in working with sexually abused children (Tsalikis 1998).

A major difference between American and British art therapy is that American art therapists emphasise the use of artwork in diagnosis to a far greater extent than do British art therapists, who tend to focus more on the psychodynamic process itself (Woddis 1986). Such a focus obviously inspired the direction I took with my research into children's drawings. As will be discussed later (Chapter 9), there are numerous problems with this diagnostic approach, in particular with drawings by sexually abused children (Hagood 1992a, 1999). Nonetheless, efforts by American art therapists to use drawings as evidence in child sexual abuse litigation have been increasing (Cohen-Liebman 1994, 1995; Levick, Safran and Levine 1990). Art therapists and other clinicians who use children's artwork need to be *extremely* cautious in using such an approach. It is important to acknowledge that erroneous allegations of sexual abuse have devastating effects on children and their families.

There is a dearth of outcome studies on the efficacy of various treatment methods with survivors of sexual abuse. This creates problems for those practitioners with a strong research background, such as psychologists and psychiatrists, who are fearful of working with survivors until more outcome studies are carried out. It is obviously important to learn which approaches are most helpful for survivors of sexual abuse and eliminate methods which may hinder the healing process, or in some instances harm the person further. It is important to add, however, that a lack of outcome studies also exists for most psychological therapies. This problem is by no means unique to the treatment of those who have been sexually abused, nor to art therapy and counselling research. Until we have more hard evidence, we must continue to reach out to survivors with what skills and knowledge we do possess in order to alleviate their suffering and not repeat the rejection and abandonment that most of them have already experienced.

Incidence of child sexual abuse

Child sexual abuse is not going to disappear by ignoring it or wishing it away. In order to appreciate fully the need to develop therapeutic approaches in working with child and adult survivors, it is important to understand to what extent child sexual abuse is believed to occur. The frequency of child sexual abuse has been debated in the United States, the United Kingdom and other parts of the world. While there are variations in reporting, it is apparent that child sexual abuse is considered a serious matter.

Coulborn-Faller (1995) reported that the number of cases of suspected child sexual abuse in the United States has increased from 6000 reports in 1976 to 330,000 in 1993 (National Center on Child Abuse Prevention Research 1994). The National Committee to Prevent Child Abuse has reported that between 1988 and 1997 child abuse reporting levels increased by 41 per cent, a large percentage involving sexual abuse. In 1997, for example, 8 per cent (84,320) were *confirmed* victims of sexual abuse (Wang and Daro 1998).

The percentage of adults who have been sexually abused has been estimated by a number of researchers. An earlier study by Finkelhor (1979) involved data from 796 students at six New England colleges and universities. He found that 19.2 per cent of women and 8.6 per cent of men had been sexually abused as children with the mean age at onset being 10.2 for girls and 11.2 for boys. Kilgore (1988) estimated that at least 30 per cent of the female population and 10 per cent of the male population in the United States had been sexually abused. Kilgore included in her research different forms of sexual abuse in addition to father–daughter incest, such as sexual abuse by other relatives and forms of extra-familial sexual abuse. It is also suspected that many more male children than previously believed are victims of sexual abuse, but are less likely than girls to disclose such abuse. Faller (1988) found in her study of 144 sexually abused children that approximately one-half of children were sexually abused before age 5. She found that 16 per cent were sexually abused before age 3, 37 per cent between ages 3 and 5, 21.5 per cent between ages 6 and 9, 23.8 per cent between ages 10 and 14, and 1.7 per cent after age 14. Until that time it was commonly believed that the onset of sexual abuse was considerably older. Various studies have reported a range of 2.5 per cent to 10 per cent of male children who have been sexually abused (Vander Mey 1988). The psychological impact of sexual abuse on males has also been noted (Longo 1986).

Similarly, the reporting of suspected cases of child sexual abuse in the United Kingdom has been increasing. Baker and Duncan (1985) conducted a survey of 2019 men and women aged 15 and over and found that 10 per cent recalled being sexually abused before the age of 16 and that the majority who reported a history of abuse felt harmed by the experience. On the basis of such results, the authors estimated that there were over 4.5 million adults sexually abused as children before they were 15 years of age. It was further estimated that potentially 1,117,000 British children will be abused before age 15. The investigators stressed the need for early detection and prevention. While half of the study population were abused with no physical contact (i.e. erotic conversation or exhibitionism), the numbers, nevertheless, were considerable. The study prompted in the late 1980s an acknowledgement of the potential scale of the problem in Britain. These predictions, indeed, have been dramatically confirmed since Baker and Duncan's 1985 study.

The extent of child sexual abuse in the United Kingdom was brought sharply to public awareness by the Cleveland Inquiry in 1987 (see *The Times* (London), 'Cleveland inquiry', 7 July 1988, p.5). A national scandal arose from the reporting of 127 alleged cases of child sexual abuse by two paediatricians in Cleveland and a major investigation followed (Butler-Sloss 1988). This resulted in the traumatic and, in some cases, inappropriate removal of many children from their homes by child protection authorities. The number of reported cases of suspected child sexual abuse in the United Kingdom has increased steadily since that time (see *The Scotsman*, 'Ministers act on child abuse', 7 July 1988, p.1). The NSPCC released figures which reflected twice as many cases reported in England from April 1988 to April 1989 as were reported in the preceding year (Miles 1989). In Ireland in 1988 there were 512 cases of child sexual abuse confirmed in one health board alone (Lawlor 1993). Likewise a greater frequency of reporting such abuse was publicised in Scotland. In one year (1992), for example, Lothian region reported a 65 per cent increase in such reporting (*The Scotsman*, April 1992) and in 1994 Fife region reported an increase of 67 per cent of reporting of child sexual abuse cases in the previous year (*Dunfermline Press*, July 1994).

Symptoms and psychological effects of child sexual abuse

The literature contains a considerable body of publications on the incidence of child sexual abuse and treatment for survivors. In a review of the existing research into child sexual abuse, Finkelhor (1987b) stated that, although there had been few systematic evaluations of large samples of sexually abused children at that time which had assessed the prevalence of various symptoms, nonetheless the weight of the growing number of studies was impressive. It is clear that awareness of the effects of child sexual abuse on psychopathology and problems relative to behaviour, development and relationships continue to emerge on an ever-increasing basis.

Serious consequences are manifested by psychological symptomology listed in the *Diagnostic and Statistical Manual of Mental Disorders* (4th edn – revised) (DSM IV-R: American Psychiatric Association 1997). Symptoms of victims of sexual abuse are frequently clustered to form a diagnosis of post-traumatic stress disorder (PTSD) which stands on its own as an adult psychiatric diagnosis. Two new diagnostic categories of sexual abuse now appear in DSM IV-R.

Briere (1984) suggested that the diagnosis of PTSD was a useful conceptual framework for studying the individual's response to sexual abuse. Its 'essential feature is the development of characteristic symptoms following a psychologically traumatic event that is generally outside the range of usual human experience' (American Psychiatric Association 1980, p.236). Further attempts to describe the effects of sexual abuse were made by Briere and Runtz (1987), who then argued that symptoms resulting from sexual abuse did not fit neatly into the category of PTSD because they also included alcoholism, drug addiction, suicide attempts and revictimisation in adult relationships. They did agree, however, that symptoms of drug/alcohol addiction and suicide attempts are usually linked with depression (also a symptom of PTSD). In a later study, Briere (1989) listed a total of 23 symptoms described in the *Diagnostic and Statistical Manual of Mental Disorders* (3rd edn – revised) (DSM III-R: American Psychiatric Association 1987) which occurred at a significantly higher rate among adult subjects who had been sexually abused than among those who had not. Symptoms included depression, sleeping disorders, flashbacks, dissociation, headaches, stomach problems, temper problems, relationship problems, dizziness, passing out, sexual problems, fear of others, excessive washing, feelings of inferiority, guilt and unreality, out-of-body experiences, memory problems and eating disorders. These comprised only a partial list of manifest symptomology of early childhood sexual abuse discussed by Briere (1989).

Deblinger *et al.* (1989) compared the rates of PTSD symptoms across sexually abused, physically abused and nonabused psychiatrically hospitalised children and found that sexually abused children did indeed exhibit symptoms of PTSD with the significant addition of inappropriate sexual behaviours. In addition, the sexually abused children showed a tendency to exhibit more avoidant/dissociative symptoms as compared with the nonabused children. It is proposed by these researchers that the presence of inappropriate sexual behaviours may be an important factor in differentiating sexually abused victims from other traumatised children.

Kilgore (1988) listed symptoms consisting of depression, guilt and shame, low self-esteem, panic disorders, phobias, somatisation and hysteria. Interpersonal difficulties and social withdrawal were also commonly found. Cognitive-perceptual symptoms including hallucinations, recurrent illusions, nightmares, detailed knowledge about sex, inability to concentrate at school, learning disabilities and language delays frequently occurred in survivors of sexual abuse. According to Kilgore (1988) serious behavioural problems were found in those who have a history of sexual abuse. These behaviours include suicide gestures, excessive masturbation, exhibitionism, sexual abuse of other children, running away, stealing, lying, excessive bathing, self-mutilation, fire setting, promiscuity, prostitution, enuresis and encopresis (wetting and soiling), delinquency, age-inappropriate thumb-sucking, urinary infections, chronic stomach aches and eating disorders. Many of these symptoms satisfy the criteria for PTSD. Freidrich, Urquiza and Beilke (1986) addressed the numerous behaviour problems experienced by sexually abused children. Koverola *et al.* (1993) found that 67 per cent of the children they studied could be classified as experiencing symptoms consistent with a diagnosis of depression.

The findings of the above studies are substantiated by the Canadian researchers McLeer *et al.* (1998) who found that there were significantly more symptoms of PTSD in children who had recently disclosed sexual abuse when compared with clinical and non-clinical groups of nonabused children. Again, it was concluded that sexually abused children are at high risk for PTSD and the need for good treatment planning was highlighted.

Dysfunctional family dynamics are frequently present in families where sexual abuse has occurred, particularly in instances of intra-familial incest. Severe family problems included isolation from the environment, undifferentiation in family members and avoidance of growth and change which would enable children to establish outside contacts and eventually be able to leave home (Alexander 1985). Behaviour problems of these children are exacerbated by families where there was greater family conflict and lower family cohesion (Freidrich, Beilke and Urquiza 1988).

Relationship difficulties, developmental effects limiting the sibling's ability to form meaningful relationships within his or her peer group and dysfunctional family dynamics are evident with these victims. Sibling incest, related to dysfunctional family dynamics, is estimated to occur five times as often as father–daughter incest (Conn-Caffaro and Caffaro 1993).

Further substantiating the damage resulting from sexual abuse, Kendall-Tackett, Williams and Finkelhor (1993) reviewed 45 studies which revealed that sexually abused children consistently had more psychological symptoms than nonabused children. In summarising this review, the authors concluded that the most frequent symptoms were fears, behaviour problems, sexualised behaviours, poor self-esteem and PTSD.

In the United States, where children have been involved in therapeutic programmes for a number of years, there is an increasing awareness of the occurrence of dissociative disorders, especially Multiple Personality Disorder (MPD), in children who have been sexually abused (Putnam 1989, 1993). Even though such awareness also existed in the nineteenth century and was known to Pierre Janet and other clinicians (Carson and Butcher 1992), it is only now that it is being increasingly linked to the trauma of sexual abuse. This disorder is a more serious version of dissociation which can develop with more clear-cut symptoms in adulthood and until recently was believed to be rare. However, evidence is building in support of the occurrence of this disorder among victims of sexual abuse. Ross, Norton and Wozney (1989) found that 79.2 per cent of 236 cases diagnosed as MPD had a history specifically of sexual abuse in childhood. Putnam *et al.* (1986) reported childhood abuse of a sexual nature in 83 per cent of the MPD cases in their study. The term 'MPD' has recently been revised to 'Dissociative Identity Disorder' (DID). There are others on both sides of the Atlantic, however, who question this diagnosis and argue that symptoms of MPD may be created by the suggestion of the therapist.

Developmental maturity is frequently affected by child abuse, whether it is physical, sexual or emotional. It is proposed by Trikett and Putnam (1993) that problems in both psychological and biological processes of pubertal development occur as a long-term result of sexual abuse. Mindfulness of developmental considerations in the treatment of sexually abused children is also stressed by Tyndall (1997), who argues the need for a multi-modal therapeutic evaluation approach.

An increasing awareness of the fact that young sexually abused children in some instances may themselves sexually abuse other children has also surfaced and is referred to as 'abuse-reactive behaviour' (Cunningham and MacFarlane 1991; Gil and Johnson 1993). It is as yet unknown to what extent being a recipient of this behaviour may impact on a child psychologically.

Many of the studies discussed above focused on symptoms of sexually abused children, but when they do not receive any therapeutic intervention, these symptoms are likely to carry over into adulthood. Adult survivors of sexual abuse suffer from the difficulties discussed above, only by the time they reach adulthood, these problems have become seriously entrenched (Ainscough and Toon 1993; Briere 1989, 1992; Gil 1988). Because so many children do not gain protection from their abuser(s), nor receive any therapeutic intervention, many of these symptoms carry on throughout their lifetime, unless they are fortunate to receive help later on.

To undo the serious damage suffered by adult survivors usually requires fairly long-term therapy. With the move by insurance companies in both the United States and the United Kingdom toward brief therapy approaches and the policy of the NHS to offer fewer sessions to patients, obtaining long-term help is difficult for many people. There is a serious shortage of psychologists working within the NHS and only recently have counsellors been employed to help with such work. British employee assistance programmes are also learning that many problems in the workplace are exacerbated by employees with a previous history of sexual abuse. They too are limited in the number of sessions they can offer, thereby being able to offer only superficial treatment.

Therapeutic approaches in working with survivors of child sexual abuse

Recent research utilising brain scan technology is demonstrating that early childhood abuse could result in neurobiological abnormalities responsible for subsequent psychiatric disorders through abnormal development of the cerebral cortex and limbic system (Perry 1996, 1997; Read 1998). Characteristics in artwork of sexually abused children are typically at a lower developmental stage than that of nonabused children (Hagood 1999), also supporting the notion that sexual abuse negatively affects a child's cognitive development. Perry *et al.* (1998) also argue that we may need to rethink seriously how we go about therapy with sexually abused children altogether. Many adults diagnosed as schizophrenic are also revealing a history of severe childhood abuse, and only very recently are researchers beginning to include seriously mentally ill people in their studies of the incidence of childhood sexual abuse (Read 1998). Many such patients are likely to be given only psychotropic medication and not receive any counselling or psychotherapy at all.

The trauma model

My core theoretical approach is based primarily on what has been named the 'trauma model' (Edwards 1998), also known as 'abuse-focused therapy' (Briere 1992; Gil 1987). This approach focuses primarily on the experiences and dilemmas of those who have been seriously abused as children. It is not unusual for survivors of sexual abuse to receive treatment focused only on symptom reduction without addressing the many underlying issues relative to childhood traumatisation. Proponents of the trauma model argue that treatment needs to *include* dealing with past trauma as well.

Children and adults who have been sexually abused have also been severely emotionally abused. A fair number of them in my experience have also been physically abused, and in some cases very severely. It is the working through of these difficulties which is central to my work. Survivors need to learn to give up maladaptive ways of coping learned in order to survive their traumatic childhood and to exchange them for healthier ones. Other theoretical models in working with art and counselling are important, but secondary. They are the means and tools to achieve the much-hoped-for goal of moving survivors from lives of victimisation to reasonable happiness and healthier psychological functioning.

There is a move at the present time to develop the trauma model or abuse-focused therapy. There are still far too many survivors of abuse who have not had the issues of their childhood abuse addressed in therapy, or in many instances, discussed at all. Yet therapists who have specialised in working with abuse survivors realise that the core issues of abuse experiences must be dealt with. As mentioned previously, in the current climate of cost-effectiveness, time-limited therapy and overall lack of resources for therapeutic work, many survivors receive only very superficial intervention, and are not in therapy long enough to develop the degree of trust required to be willing to explore what has happened to them.

The need for knowledge of therapeutic techniques in addressing the many issues of children who have been sexually abused, their mothers, adolescents, adolescent victim/offenders, adult survivors and adult offenders is clearly stated in the bulk of existing literature. I have attempted to use an integrative approach using concepts of the trauma model and current theoretical models in counselling and art therapy which have demonstrated a considerable amount of effectiveness. I have endeavoured to blend aspects of various theories of art therapy, counselling and psychotherapy in ways appropriate to the particular needs of each person with whom I have worked, depending on what they bring to their sessions.

When I began working with sexually abused children and adults in 1983, I, like many others, had little to rely on in developing my own style of working. Little was published at that time in therapeutic approaches with sexually abused adults or children. When I began studying art therapy in 1978 there were extremely few books published on art therapy. I was the only art therapist in most of the treatment programmes where I worked which specialised in working with children and adults who were affected by sexual abuse. I worked alongside many counsellors and social workers; all of us were struggling to learn treatment issues specific to this population. It was necessary to borrow from many existing ideas with the hope of pulling together effective ways of working. Much was also learned by mistakes and feedback given to me by both the children and adults with whom I have worked. Feedback from participants in workshops I have offered has also been invaluable.

Case studies and examples of artwork will be presented in this book which graphically illustrate the pain and dilemmas faced in the recovery process by various child and adult survivors of sexual abuse with whom I have worked. Theories of counselling and art therapy which I have found to be particularly relevant to working with child and adult survivors of sexual abuse will be discussed in Chapter 1. A discussion of the wide variety of art media which can be used will also be included. Chapter 2 will explore developmental issues specific to various age groups of children and which art media are most appropriate for each level of development. The many problems specific to working with sexually abused children and their presenting symptoms are presented in Chapter 3. Ways of handling these particular problems are discussed along with mistakes I have seen made along the way which, while perhaps made with good intentions, are not helpful to sexually abused children. Case studies and examples of artwork of sexually abused children from ages 3 to 11 in both individual and group therapy are presented in Chapter 4. Individual and group work with mothers of sexually abused children will be presented in Chapter 5, including their particular therapeutic issues and illustrating how artwork was incorporated into their treatment. Therapeutic work with male and female adult survivors of sexual abuse who have suffered serious psychological difficulties as a result of their abuse will be explored in Chapter 6 along with examples and possible uses of artwork.

After working for a number of years with sexually abused children and their mothers, I felt that it was important to understand more about sex offenders themselves in order to have a clearer picture about why sexual abuse happens. The many therapeutic issues involved in the use of art in counselling adolescent victim/offenders are discussed in Chapter 7. Chapter 8 includes illustrated group case studies using art in counselling adolescent and adult sex offenders. Many issues on working with adult sex offenders overlap with those relative to young sex offenders. An examination of how these issues present themselves in a more entrenched manner in working with adult sex offenders will also be presented in Chapter 8. This book will also explore the many problems in using artwork in diagnosis with sexually abused children. Chapter 9 will discuss using children's drawings as evidence of a history of sexual abuse and the need to have a thorough understanding of how cognitive development also influences what children put into their artwork. The importance of *not* inappropriately attributing these characteristics to sexual abuse when they may be reflective of the child's stage of development will be stressed. Clinicians have little or no opportunity to work with ordinary healthy children to see characteristics in their drawings upon which to make a comparison.

Problems of chronic depression, alcohol and drug abuse, eating disorders, severe family dysfunction, low self-esteem, history of abuse for both the mother and the offender, and relationship difficulties in all areas are but a few of these issues which must be addressed along with the sexual abuse itself, as they are a substantial part of the problem. Professionals need to become more aware of these issues and desensitise themselves to what actually happens in sexual abuse in order to be able to listen empathetically to survivors and to see their stories unfold in artwork. Unfortunately, in many instances the subject of sexual abuse is so horrendous that some professionals are still not willing to hear patiently what survivors have to say, which only reinforces their helplessness and hopelessness.

This book should be useful for adult and child psychiatrists, adult and child psychologists, art therapists, counsellors, play therapists, child-care workers, social workers, probation officers, mental health workers, school psychologists, special education teachers and other mental health professionals who come into contact with children and adults who suffer the aftermath of child sexual abuse. Survivors *need* to be believed and to be listened to without having their feelings of helplessness and abandonment further reinforced. Some mental health workers who are afraid of the subject of sexual abuse may avoid receiving training – which only exacerbates their fears. By avoiding these issues, a vacuum is created within which the horrendous secret of sexual abuse is maintained and the lives of so many children and adults continue to be traumatised. It is hoped that this book will serve to alleviate some of those apprehensions and to enable workers to more skilfully and empathetically relate to survivors of sexual abuse to aid in the healing process.

Children and families who are affected by sexual abuse on both sides of the Atlantic similarly report feelings of powerlessness, low self-esteem, shame, guilt, fear, embarrassment and anger. These appear to be human issues regardless of culture. While there obviously are cultural differences between the United States and Britain in dealing with the effects of child sexual abuse, it has been my observation that the similarities far outweigh the differences. Sexually abused children and their families are similarly victimised regardless of nationality. The trauma, however, continues to be exacerbated in the United Kingdom because there are still so few therapeutic programmes to help these children and their families. My experience in working with adult survivors of sexual abuse with the NHS in Scotland has made me increasingly aware of the profound psychological damage which is done to many of these people. Treatment required to undo years of victimisation by abuse as well as not receiving intervention is long term and uses tremendous resources. Because of the paucity of therapists available to do this type of work, many still receive no help whatsoever.

The British culture does not yet fully embrace the use of counselling and psychotherapy to the extent that those in the United States do, and financial resources in Britain are more scarce. Americans sometimes are laughed at because they all seemingly have their own 'shrinks'. Because British people are accustomed to having their medical care largely paid for by the NHS, there is considerable resistance to the notion of paying for psychotherapy and counselling. The stigma attached to seeing a therapist is still considerable, much as it was in California in the late 1970s. This situation has changed increasingly in the past few years as counselling programmes have been developed at various British colleges and universities.

The cultural contrast between working in the field of child sexual abuse in the United Kingdom with that of the United States, particularly California, is considerable. In California, discussions of personal experiences of sexual abuse are open and frank, almost to a fault. Most American psychotherapists, whether they be art therapists, marriage, family and child counsellors, clinical psychologists or psychiatrists, are now well aware of the issues of child sexual abuse and have developed approaches to healing the aftermath (Finney 1990; Gil 1988, 1992). The development of such work is gradually evolving in the United Kingdom. The longer I am in Britain, however, the fewer *major* differences I see in basic counselling and psychological theoretical models, political and legal issues, research dilemmas, techniques and approaches. The historical development of art therapy in the two countries has been parallel in many ways. The influence of American therapeutic approaches and mental health research on professionals in the United Kingdom is considerable, with Britain being in much earlier stages of dealing with the problem of child sexual abuse than is the United States. Those who include artwork with verbal approaches are in the unique position to make considerable contributions to the fight against child sexual abuse and the resultant psychological and psychiatric damage done to these children and surviving adults.

The difficulties in working in the field of child sexual abuse in the United Kingdom are discussed by Bentovim (1993). They are also well summarised by clinical psychologist Dr Sue Llewelyn (1994):

> It cannot have escaped the attention of most psychologists that during the past 10 years or so there has been a huge expansion in awareness of the psychological consequences of trauma. Attention has been divided between the public trauma experienced by the victim of earthquake, warfare or train crash and the private trauma experienced by the victim of childhood abuse. Articles have been published, grants awarded and conferences organised. Post traumatic stress disorder has gained a firm place in psychiatric classification systems. Despite this, it appears that we have been applying a double standard: it still is not quite acceptable to talk openly, unsuspiciously or entirely sympathetically about the victim of sexual abuse.
>
> One of the most tragic aspects of our attitudes toward child sexual abuse is the belief that its recent exposure is only a fad or a passing bandwagon which has attracted the wrong-headed or voyeuristic attention of professionals (see for example the Cleveland Inquiry). Further there is often the suspicion (rarely voiced about the plane crash survivor) that the child has been making it up, or even if it is true, has exaggerated its effects for 'attention' ... Furthermore, the shrouding in secrecy and suspicion of sexual abuse has contributed very significantly to the severity of its effects. (Llewelyn 1994, p.171)

I believe that art therapists and counsellors have a unique opportunity to develop techniques especially applicable to issues of sexual abuse. Clara Jo Stember was the first art therapist in the United States to specialise in working with sexually abused children (Stember 1978, 1980) and has been followed by many others.

I see many opportunities for those who use artwork with counselling or other psychological interventions to join in the much needed treatment of child victims of sexual abuse, their mothers, adolescent victim/offenders and adult offenders. Artwork is a very powerful tool and accesses painful issues that sexually abused children and family members frequently want to avoid, but need to address in order to recover. Such an approach not only can be healing to the survivor of sexual abuse, but also may serve as a powerful preventative measure to hopefully minimise the later development of more serious psychiatric problems and the recycling of abuse to future generations.

CHAPTER 1

Theoretical Issues in the Use of Art in Counselling Child and Adult Survivors of Sexual Abuse

This chapter discusses both counselling and art therapy theory which I have found to be particularly useful in working with sexually abused children and adults. This is not to say that theoretical approaches are in any way limited to those discussed in this chapter. I would encourage further exploration into the vast amount that is now written, not only about art therapy and counselling, but also about the treatment of survivors of sexual abuse. The purpose of this chapter is to lay the groundwork for integrating both verbal and visual approaches in the therapeutic process. It will also discuss the use of art in counselling groups. A variety of art media commonly used in the use of art in counselling will be explored along with possible settings for carrying out the work.

Integration of counselling and art therapy

Integrating the use of art in counselling is effective for a variety of reasons (Hagood, in press). The use of counselling skills such as listening, reflecting and reframing along with warmth, genuineness and positive regard serves to enhance art therapy skills. Including art expression within the counselling process can open up feelings and issues in a way which words alone cannot. Exploring each art piece amplifies what has been revealed through talking. Creating artwork is an enjoyable activity for most children. The art process holds children's attention much more intensely than just talking. Young people who have been abused usually have considerable behavioural problems but can become easily drawn into the art process. They are somehow able to concentrate at a deeper level with a cessation of acting-out behaviour. Poor attention span is common with abused children, and artwork appears to help them to focus on issues as they emerge. Artwork encourages sharing and mutual feedback between the survivor and the therapist, or between members in a group, drawing everyone into the group process. Group participants are invited to comment on each other's artwork and to relate it to their own problems. Those who initially resist joining in tend to participate later on in the session if they are not pressured. They do not want to be left out and notice that others are enjoying themselves. Sharing of artwork enables others to realise more easily that they are not alone in their problems or feelings. It also helps them to reduce their sense of isolation and to relate better to each other.

Many adults also respond well to incorporating art expression into their counselling experience. It is not unusual, however, for adult survivors of sexual abuse who suffer from extremely low self-esteem initially to resist the use of art. They are often fearful of what the therapist or others in a group will think of their art ability. Providing reassuring comments and starting out with very non-threatening media such as magazine collage gets them involved in the visual process; as they build their confidence, they are likely to respond to further involvement with art materials. In group work, the use of art also influences the development of group cohesiveness. Because of the openness of the content of the drawings, self-disclosure becomes easier when participants see others creating related images.

Because artwork accesses feelings better than words, it is not unusual to see survivors break down and cry with the impact of looking at what they have created. They may insist that they are happy, but the artwork may reveal otherwise. Paintings and drawings help to retrieve childhood memories and to gain greater insight into the present situation. Creating artwork around a childhood memory usually elicits more memories and can be very powerful. Such an approach needs to be used with caution by not encouraging survivors to uncover more than they are ready to handle. The use of non-directive free art expression within a counselling session provides a place for symbolic resolution of conflicts. Artwork provides a permanent record of the therapeutic process and can be reviewed in order to assess progress. Artwork helps to focus on the issues at hand by externalising problems concretely and facilitating solutions.

In many instances the completion of a piece of art to show to others may instil a sense of pride, contributing to higher self-esteem. Edith Kramer, one of the founders of American art therapy, began her work in a home for delinquent boys, many having been abused. She frequently had them exhibit their artwork in a central location because they felt so much pride in what they had accomplished (Kramer 1971, 1975). Artwork dealing with painful issues, however, most likely would not be appropriate for such a display. Special art projects can be created to display in a central area.

Art therapists typically have training and experience in a variety of theories and techniques. This brief review is not intended to explore all of these theories in depth and readers are encouraged to consult the considerable amount of literature available in art therapy and counselling. A good deal of art therapy training is based on psychoanalytic theory. This approach can be highly beneficial as far as expression of emotions and resolution of conflicts are concerned. It may require interpretation back to the client and anyone who uses artwork in this fashion should have considerable training and qualifications in psychoanalytic theory and art therapy.

Therapeutic work with sexually abused child and adult survivors

Therapeutic programmes specialising in working with sexually abused children and their families have been established in the United States since the late 1970s (Giarretto 1982). This gave American professionals a leading edge in this type of work, with Canada and Australia following closely behind. The development of treatment programmes advanced somewhat in the United Kingdom during the 1990s. A major problem in the United Kingdom continues to be that shortly after disclosure work, the child is not likely to receive long-term therapy, nor are the parents. In Scotland, many children receive short-term counselling by social workers with no qualifications in counselling or psychotherapy. Waiting lists for adults seeking psychology or counselling services on the NHS can be as long as one year in some areas. Art therapy services are rarer still.

Art therapists in Britain are trained primarily in psychodynamic approaches strongly based on the object-relations theories of David Winnicott (1971) and Melanie Klein (1949). After qualifying, however, many go on to develop other ways of working. American art therapists are likewise trained in theories of art therapy relying on tenets of psychoanalysis, in particular Edith Kramer and Margaret Naumburg along with others who have expanded on their models. American art therapists have also developed more recent humanistic approaches as a basis for the use of art therapy, such as Gestalt art therapy as espoused by Janie Rhyne (1984, 1987) and Violet Oaklander (1978). Family art therapy has been developed by Hanna Kwiaktowska (1978) and Helen Landgarten (1987) and is used by a large number of American art therapists. Rogerian person-centred art therapy has been developed more recently in the United Kingdom by British art therapist Liesl Silverstone (1997).

As mentioned earlier, I trained in psychology, marriage, family and child counselling and art therapy simultaneously. I was fortunate to study under the American art therapist and art educator Dr Donald Uhlin (1979), who was the first to publish photographs of artwork created by sexually abused children. He inspired me ultimately to do research into children's drawings relative to sexual abuse just before his death in 1981. At that time I learned that various American art therapists were already bridging theories of art therapy with those of counselling and psychotherapy ranging from psychoanalysis to more contemporary humanistic approaches. In my counselling training I learned the theories of existential, phenomenological and humanistic psychologists such as Carl Rogers and Fritz Perls. At the same time I was studying the evolving ideas of phenomenological art therapist Mala Betensky (1973, 1995) and Gestalt art therapist Janie Rhyne (1984). I was required to learn the psychoanalytic approaches of Freud and Jung, and was amazed to learn that pioneer American art therapists such as Edith Kramer (1979), Margaret Naumburg (1953) and more recently child art therapist Judith Rubin (1984) were developing their approaches in art therapy based on these theories. I was rigorously trained in family therapy focusing on the theories of Bowen (1978), Minuchin (1974) and Satir (1967, 1972). Since then, Landgarten (1987) has developed a method of family art psychotherapy based on their theories. I was delighted to learn that Kwiaktowska (1978) was developing a psychoanalytic art therapy approach in working with families. She was actively involved in research for the National Institute of Mental Health in Washington DC, using family drawings to enhance the understanding of family dynamics.

Directive versus non-directive debate

I continue to be amazed at the ongoing debate about whether one should work directively or non-directively, whether it is in counselling or art therapy circles. In my experience, in some instances, one may be more appropriate than the other and in others a combination of both may be in order. My work on a clinical psychology team has also taught me that there are many directive cognitive and behavioural interventions which can alleviate symptoms much more quickly than non-directive work. Relief of disabling symptoms such as panic attacks, inability to handle anger, depression and so on go a long way to helping the survivor to gain mastery over his or her life and no longer feel like a victim. Much of my experience came from highly structured treatment programmes where directive work was essential. To have the luxury of allowing a survivor of sexual abuse to remain in long-term open-ended treatment where totally non-directive work is allowed to unfold is extremely rare in the present climate. Problems with excess dependency on the therapist also arise if treatment is allowed to go on too long.

Murphy (1998) interviewed 52 British art therapists about their use of directive or non-directive art therapy in working with sexually abused children. She found that 60 per cent of respondents said they continued to work non-directively because of sexually abused children's need to be in control and that direction from the therapist could feel intrusive. I would agree with these concerns and would argue that themes are only suggestions; if the child wants to follow his or her own avenue with the artwork, it should always be allowed. I believe that there is a danger in dichotomising the directive/non-directive debate, however, and would prefer to see more flexibility, using whichever is appropriate at the time. Various writers have demonstrated how art therapy approaches can be integrated in both directive and non-directive ways with various counselling and psychotherapy theories such as Freudian, Object Relations, Jungian, Self-Psychology, Adlerian, Behavioural, Cognitive, Developmental and Eclectic (or Integrative) (Rubin 1987).

The directive versus non-directive controversy has also found its way into debates over how group art therapy should be conducted. British art therapist Marian Liebmann (1986), for example, wrote the first book to be published on group art therapy; it was based on a study of 40 art therapists. She found that most of them had a similar approach. She used a highly structured and somewhat directive format which consisted of an introduction of a theme, the art-making process, and then a discussion of the artwork created. Her book is rich with ideas on themes and media. British art therapist McNeilly (1983), however, was critical of a directive approach, arguing that a totally unstructured approach was preferable. He claimed that being directive did not allow for exploration of interpersonal relationships and that it was simply a didactic process between separate members and the therapist, thereby fostering excessive dependency on the therapist. In my experience, a good group therapist is cognisant of such a possibility and works very hard at *not* obstructing the group process. When a particular group member is needing feedback from the therapist, this is also allowed, as long as the rest of the group is involved. The therapist, however, continually works to be a catalyst for group members to relate to each other.

American art therapist Harriet Wadeson (1980) was also against the use of theme-centred art therapy groups, arguing that the art therapist was merely providing such projects and should be sensitive to the emergence of themes brought into the group by participants themselves. I have found that providing projects indiscriminately is not useful, but when working with the highly sensitive issues of child and adult survivors of sexual abuse, it can be useful occasionally to introduce an art project which is fairly neutral, such as a Mother's Day card, Easter card, special drawings or paintings, and so on. Therapeutic artwork can elicit very strong feelings and if therapy becomes too painful, children will begin to avoid artwork altogether. It became my style to introduce such a 'neutral' project in a session subsequent to a very intense session to give these children a break from their painful issues. By redirecting my therapeutic goal to a creative activity (which is in itself healing), the fostering of self-esteem and improvement of socialisation skills were usually the result. This also provided an opportunity in some instances to create artwork to display in a central area. This is one example of the value in both directive and non-directive approaches depending on specific needs of those who participate in both individual and group therapy. Again, the values of Rogers' person-centred approach is to be paramount at all times (e.g. warmth, empathy, positive regard and genuineness).

British art therapist Diane Waller (1993) has developed a method called 'group interactive psychotherapy' and advocates pursuing themes which emerge spontaneously out of discussion among group members. In some instances she introduces a theme at the outset. It is refreshing to observe how she is not locked into hard 'rules' involved in the 'directive versus non-directive' debate or about the 'right' and 'wrong' way to conduct group art therapy. She also incorporates Yalom's (1975) psychoanalytic curative factors into her therapeutic goals and presents an integrative approach. Both books written by Liebmann (1986) and Waller (1993) are well worth exploring for further ideas in group work with adults and children who have been sexually abused.

Person-centred counselling and art therapy

It is interesting to note that Carl Rogers was very supportive to the development of the profession of art therapy. Silverstone (1997), a registered art therapist in London, has developed a training programme on 'Person-Centred Art Therapy' based on her understanding of Rogerian counselling and art therapy principles. Her work was endorsed by Carl Rogers himself. Before I moved to Scotland, I was fortunate to attend a California conference at Sonoma State University and to hear Rogers' daughter, Natalie Rogers, present her own personal artwork, demonstrating how she used it to help her through a difficult life transition. She has taught creative arts therapies workshops (both within the United States and internationally) where she strongly emphasises the use of artwork in the therapeutic process. I also participated in a workshop presented by Rogers' granddaughter, who is a registered art therapist in private practice in California. Person-centred counselling provides an excellent foundation for verbally processing images made during the art therapy process. When the subject of counselling theory is addressed, the work of Carl Rogers is usually the first to be mentioned, and for good reason. When I observed one of the famous 'Gloria' videotapes during my training, I quickly concluded that his warm, genuine and supportive style was especially appropriate to art therapy.

Rogers spent his entire career endeavouring to integrate the intuitive with the objective and the clinical with the statistical. He continuously applied objective scientific methods but moved away from the notion of using people as 'objects' for research. His primary concern was for a more phenomenological and humanistic approach. Rogers viewed himself as a clinical psychologist. In 1968 he formed the Centre for the Studies of the Person. He was one of the first three psychologists to receive the Distinguished Scientific Contribution Award from the American Psychological Association, having spent 46 years contributing to counselling and psychotherapy research, the empirical study of emotional phenomena, the philosophy of science and the encounter group movement (Pervin 1984). He was also president of the American Psychological Association for twelve years and nominated for a Nobel Peace Prize. The impact of his humanistic approach has been strong in the field of industry and education as well as in counselling and psychology. While it is not within the scope of this book to present a detailed discussion of counselling theory, the major tenets (or core conditions) of Rogers' (1951) theory of 'person-centred therapy' are discussed here to form a basis for the adaptation of counselling and art therapy approaches in working with survivors of childhood sexual abuse. It is important to acknowledge that Rogers' early work was with troubled children (Rogers 1939).

Realness, genuineness and congruence

The counsellor needs to be authentic without putting up a professional front (Mearns and Thorne 1992; Rogers 1951). In other words, to be oneself is both permissible and desirable. A climate of naturalness on the part of the therapist creates the scenario for clients to find resources from within themselves rather than looking to the therapist as being the 'expert' who has all the answers and will take most of the responsibility in the treatment process. Such empowerment is especially essential in working with survivors of sexual abuse who frequently come from a background of both authoritarian and abusive relationships. An authentic, natural approach puts clients at ease and enables them to feel more comfortable about discussing issues that are exceedingly painful and difficult. Trust is especially difficult for those who have been abused. It is important to interact with a survivor in a non-authoritarian manner. Emphasising that the therapist will take a journey *with* them to support them in their recovery and mastery over victimisation is essential. Survivors typically feel helpless and frequently look to the therapist to rescue them. Counsellors and art therapists need to be especially careful in this area not to have their 'rescue buttons' activated and fall into the trap of overprotecting and rescuing. Building in the constant belief that survivors have within themselves the strength to overcome problems and to create a new and healthier life is a constant goal of therapeutic work.

Warmth and unconditional positive regard

Warmth and caring provide the catalyst for therapeutic change. Survivors quickly detect whether or not a therapist cares about them. Total acceptance of a survivor of sexual abuse is absolutely essential, even though sometimes his or her behaviour may be annoying. Both child and adult survivors typically loathe themselves and blame themselves for their abuse. Children often demonstrate their self-hatred with acting-out behaviour to convince others of their belief that they are 'bad'. To like the child genuinely (but not some of his or her behaviour) is challenging, but a necessary component of good therapeutic work. Adult survivors frequently use self-harming behaviour, such as eating disorders, self-cutting, head banging and so on in order to continue to abuse themselves, believing they are unworthy and to be hated not only by themselves, but by others as well. These behaviours serve to numb psychological pain and ultimately may become addictive. They may have learned manipulative behaviour in order to get their needs met in environments where they were neglected. Unfortunately, they are often criticised for such behaviour by mental health professionals who do not seem to understand that it was learned in order to survive as a child. Therapists need to lay the foundation for the development of self-acceptance by demonstrating that the survivor with whom they are working is genuinely liked. When the counsellor is non-judgemental, therapeutic movement is much more likely and the client is more able to feel safe to explore his or her anxiety, depression, fears and concerns. The client is likely to be excessively fearful of rejection or condemnation, and consistent genuine acceptance and warm support by the therapist are very important.

Communication of empathic understanding

A good therapist, whether a counsellor or an art therapist, should be able to reflect back to the client a deep level of empathic understanding. Survivors especially need to feel understood, because they have rarely had such an experience. They are accustomed to having their thoughts and feelings invalidated and disrespected. To be able to put oneself in the client's 'skin' and to perceive the world as the client does enables him or her to feel less lonely and isolated. Knowing basic skills in listening and reflecting are invaluable in facilitating this process. Therapists likewise seek to enable their clients to value themselves, to gain a sense of empowerment and to feel understood. Contrary to popular belief among therapeutic circles, I have found that some self-disclosure may be used effectively as long as it is appropriate and serves to amplify the therapeutic process, *not* meet the needs of the therapist. Limited self-disclosure can enable the survivor to see that the therapist is a real human being and elicit further disclosure from the survivor. Research has clearly demonstrated that appropriate self-disclosure not only elicits further disclosure of the client, but also is likely to enhance the therapeutic relationship (Jourard 1971).

It is important that the emphasis always be on the *person,* not the artwork, which is simply a vehicle for the person to work through his or her issues. Concerns among art therapists about 'Where is the art in art therapy?' are published on both sides of the Atlantic. I would counter this question with 'Where is the *person* in art therapy?' It is essential not to get caught up in whether we are using 'art as therapy' or 'pure art therapy', or to debate which theory is the 'only' one. In any kind of therapeutic intervention, the primary focus should *always* be on the child or adult before us who has lived a life of pain and tragedy and ask ourselves how artwork might be used to facilitate his or her recovery.

Any survivor of child abuse should never be forced to create a piece of artwork, but gently encouraged. Refusal to paint, draw, sculpt or create a collage most likely stems from fear of painful feelings and a high degree of self-hatred and anxiety. Survivors have been forced to do acts which were both physically and emotionally painful and respect for their boundaries is paramount. They *always* have the right to say no.

Virginia Axline's play therapy

Over 50 years ago Virginia Axline (1969) began to develop her theories around the same time that Carl Rogers' ideas were becoming well known. She advocated a non-directive approach in working with children based on the same assumptions as Rogers, namely the belief in the child's ability to solve his or her own problems. She adapted the same principles in working with very young children by using reflective comments on what they are doing with toys and/or art materials and emphasising warmth and acceptance.

Axline summarised her approach in what she called 'The Eight Basic Principles'. These are:

1. The therapist must develop a warm, friendly relationship with the child, in which good rapport is established as soon as possible.
2. The therapist accepts the child exactly as he or she is.
3. The therapist establishes a feeling of permissiveness in the relationship so that the child feels free to express his feelings completely.
4. The therapist is alert to recognize the feelings the child is expressing and reflects those feelings back to him in such a manner that he gains insight into his behaviour.
5. The therapist maintains a deep respect for the child's ability to solve his own problems if given an opportunity to do so. The responsibility to make choices and to institute change is the child's.
6. The therapist does not attempt to direct the child's actions or conversation in any manner. The child leads the way; the therapist follows.
7. The therapist does not attempt to hurry the therapy along. It is a gradual process and is recognized as such by the therapist.
8. The therapist establishes only those limitations that are necessary to anchor the therapy to the world of reality and to make the child aware of his responsibility to the relationship. (Axline 1969, pp.73–74)

Axline repeatedly stressed (as did Rogers) the importance of complete acceptance of a troubled child and stated that this is of primary importance to the success of therapy. In working with children who have been sexually abused, the challenge is immense. Many of these children have lived in an environment of chaos and abuse and may have learned a great deal of obnoxious behaviour, expecting to be abused again. It is not unusual for counsellors and therapists to feel intense anger and an urge to be critical. Finding ways to reassure the child that he or she is likeable, but that the behaviours are not always acceptable, is an important part of treatment. Axline (1969) also argued that limits to destructive behaviour need to be set to establish healthy boundaries, but that it needs to be done in a way not to undermine the child. Destructiveness of toys and art materials, and attacking the therapist or other children are obviously some examples where the therapist needs to become more 'directive'. Some sexually abused children actually sexually abuse other children or are physically abusive. To place no restrictions on such behaviours would obviously be non-productive. As discussed in other parts of this book, failure to address these behaviours may result in these children becoming abusers in later life.

Axline advocated the use of a variety of toys and art materials in working with disturbed children. While she does not discuss in great detail her use of art materials, she includes several illustrations and case examples in her well-known book *Play Therapy* using painting and drawing materials including ink pens, felt-markers, watercolours and tempera paints (Axline 1969). She did not distinguish between art and play therapy, but used artwork as a continuum of the play therapy process. She clearly demonstrated how working with children with the use of art can be effectively used based on sound principles of counselling theory.

Phenomenological art therapy

Betensky (1973, 1995) has developed a method of art therapy called the 'Phenomenological Approach'. Betensky's approach is especially appropriate for those using a person-centred counselling approach. The child or adult's responses to the artwork are paramount. Betensky writes:

> The centrality of the artmaker is one of the most essential factors in the method. The clients in art therapy, whose first-hand experience goes into artmaking, are the chief beholders of their own art expressions. They are the ones who then experience the process of looking at the self-made phenomenon as it appears to their senses and consciousness. Thus, the artmakers themselves arrive at subjective meanings, not the art therapist.
>
> This aspect of freedom from predetermined judgments is most needed for the treatment of art expression in art therapy. (Betensky 1995, p.21)

Very basically, Betensky's methods include several stages:

1. 'Phenomenological perceiving' where after the artwork is completed, a physical distance is created between the client and the artwork. A period of time is then spent with concentrated attention to the

painting, drawing or sculpture followed by an invitation to explain the artwork in detail to the therapist.

2. An informal 'phenomenological' discussion is then carried out between the client and the therapist. After the client has exhausted all possibilities of meaning for the artwork, the therapist may make comments about what he or she observes, but any interpretations are left with the client. There are no authoritarian interpretations with the meaning of the artwork specifically belonging to the client.
3. 'Phenomenological accounting' takes place where the client is asked to recall the process of art-making, look at the relationship of the artwork with any previous artwork, and explore how the artwork relates to the client's current or past life circumstances.

I have found Betensky's methods to be especially useful in processing artwork of survivors of sexual abuse, child and adult alike. It is an easy-to-learn and non-threatening approach and provides a framework for thoroughly exploring artwork to gain the maximum amount of understanding and insight.

Gestalt approaches to the use of art in counselling

The influence of Fritz Perls' (1969a, 1969b) Gestalt therapy on American art therapy theory was considerable. American art therapist Janie Rhyne (1984), a colleague of Perls, developed a method of using a variety of art media working on the 'here and now' theme of Perls' work. She began working with troubled adolescents in a high school setting in San Francisco and developed her ideas from this initial work (Rhyne 1984, 1987). She also presented a great number of workshops for highly functioning clients, including professionals, to help them explore themselves and their relationships, and to work toward personal growth. She used a wide variety of media, including stones, feathers, sequins, coloured paper of all sorts and odd-shaped boxes, encouraging a high degree of creativity. She worked metaphorically with both individuals and groups with a focus on the 'here and now', expression of feelings and self-awareness. She introduced the idea of using cartooning, a technique greatly enjoyed by older children and adolescents. She carried out her PhD research into the symbolic expression of various emotional states and went on to lead American art therapists in the development of research methodology.

Perls was instrumental in developing Gestalt therapy (Perls 1969a, 1969b). He trained as a psychoanalyst, but was unhappy with analytic theory. His theory was an attempt to fill the theoretical gaps of psychoanalysis and to emphasise integrating or re-integrating our 'split-off' parts into a whole person. He also viewed dreams as reflections of 'split-off' parts of the dreamer. The time focus in Gestalt therapy is in the 'now' with no concern about past events. What is going on in the present moment was Perls' main concern.

Perls' personal style was abrasive and directive and sometimes very upsetting for his clients. He gave less attention to warmth; confrontation was used freely. For this reason Gestalt therapy has been frequently criticised. This style may be more effective in some confrontive aspects of work with adolescent and adult sex offenders, but caution should be emphasised because many fragile survivors of sexual abuse would experience this approach as emotionally abusive. It is important that any use of Gestalt therapy techniques needs to be carried out with caution, because there is the danger of pushing a survivor into a psychotic episode if therapy is too confrontive. An empathic, supportive and warm approach is *always* in order. According to Ivey and Simek-Downing (1980):

> A confrontation is defined as... *he pointing out of discrepancies between or among attitudes, thoughts, or behaviors.* A confrontation is *not* telling a client that he or she is in error or a bad person. (p.102)

I have found that it is quite possible to use aspects of Gestalt therapy in a warm and supportive manner with survivors of sexual abuse. I have seen, for example, the 'empty-chair' technique used very effectively in helping adult survivors to gain a sense of empowerment in working with relationship difficulties and rehearsing more assertive styles of behaviour. I have also found Perls' concept of 'staying with the feeling' to be especially helpful with survivors who tend consistently to avoid their painful feelings. I have found many of Rhyne's ideas to be useful in working with both children and adults who were sexually abused. Her methods of identifying emotional states, using cartooning and creatively putting together art materials have been particularly useful. Caution is needed because artwork is very powerful and can access unconscious material before a person is ready to deal with it. Very sensitive timing on the part of the therapist is essential in order to avoid the client becoming overwhelmed with his or her own imagery. Unlike Perls, Rhyne was much gentler and more supportive with clients.

Violet Oaklander, another Californian, is a licensed marriage, family and child counsellor who also trained in special education, working with emotionally disturbed children with learning disabilities. While not an art therapist herself, she developed many ways of using art and toys in working with troubled children in what she called the 'Gestalt approach'. Many of her ideas, however, do not fall strictly within the concepts of Gestalt therapy. Oaklander's (1978) classical book *Windows to Our Children* is a compendium of many approaches borrowed from a variety of art therapy concepts. It is rich with ideas on working with sexually abused children, and many clinicians on both sides of the Atlantic have found it valuable for their work, including myself.

Oaklander informally uses ideas from projective drawing instruments, such as the House–Tree–Person Test (HTP) (Buck 1948), and Kinetic-Family Drawing (KFD) (Burns 1982), the Thematic Apperception Test (TAT) (Murray 1943) and others. She used them only as projective tools to aid in communicating with children and not in any systematic way. Most of these projective instruments fare very poorly when assessed empirically, having little validity or reliability (Buros 1972; Hagood 1999). Oaklander's book is, however, a valuable resource for ideas in working with sexually abused children, provided there is a solid rationale and clear understanding of the appropriateness of each exercise for sexually abused children.

Behavioural approaches in the use of art in counselling

Behaviour therapy has been derived from behavioural psychologists such as Pavlov (1927) and Skinner (1953). Roth (1987), an American art therapist, describes the integration of behaviour therapy with art therapy, making a case for its use in modifying undesirable behaviours. She explores the common ground between behaviour therapy and psychodynamic approaches and states:

> Behavioural techniques, however, are used by psychodynamically oriented art therapists, usually without being labeled as such. For example, an art therapist who encourages a blocked or inhibited patient to make a scribble in order to involve the patient with media, and then praises the individual for his/her participation, is using a behavioural approach (e.g., reinforcement).
>
> ...All forms of psychotherapy and behaviour therapy, with or without art, share fundamental commonalities, to the extent that they all are attempts to help human beings who have problems. (Roth 1987, p.217)

Roth describes her work teaching troubled children to use art materials and through 'reality shaping' to create recognisable art objects. She demonstrates how she uses reinforcement, intermittent reinforcement, rewards and modelling along with the person-centred concepts of establishing a relationship with the child based on trust and acceptance. While her work is highly directive, it was found to be useful in helping children to create objects which could then be explored from a more psychodynamic perspective.

Incorporating behaviour-modification techniques in working with sexually abused children during the counselling and art-making process can be highly useful. Intermittent reinforcement can help children with extremely poor attention span to stay 'on task' with their art projects. Undesirable behaviour in therapy sessions can be extinguished by refusing to reward it and by focusing on positive behaviours using a good deal of praise. While I was collecting drawings over a long period of time from nonabused children, for example, I used the behavioural technique of rewards by telling the children that if they would do initial pencil drawings for me, they could then do coloured drawings of whatever they wanted. For further discussion of ways that behavioural approaches might be used with sexually abused children, see Chapter 3.

Cognitive approaches in the use of art with counselling

Cognitive therapy has been increasingly demonstrated to be highly effective in the treatment of anxiety, depression, anger management and many other psychological disorders common to survivors of sexual abuse. The work of Aaron Beck (1976) and Albert Ellis (Ellis and Harper 1975) has been highly influential in the development of cognitive therapy. It is now widely used by mental health professionals. The basic approach with cognitive therapy is to address irrational thoughts which are automatic and cause feelings of depression, anxiety or anger. It is often easier to gain control over our thoughts than our feelings. These thoughts constitute black and white thinking, sweeping generalisations and erroneous conclusions about the future (Burns 1980). While little, if anything, has been written on the use of art therapy with cognitive restructuring, there is no reason why artwork cannot be used to further amplify this approach. Having a survivor identify an automatic irrational thought and then create a piece of artwork depicting how he or she feels when such a thought is believed is a useful way to elucidate the situation. Rewriting it with an appropriate and rational thought and then illustrating the change in feelings when the rational thought is believed is likely to prove very revealing. The survivor can then be encouraged to keep a regular art journal in order to identify these thoughts and work on changing them. One young woman with whom I worked said that her negative thoughts were like a 'Cuckoo Bird' sitting on her shoulder shouting in her ear. Working metaphorically with her, I asked her to create a three-dimensional 'Cuckoo Bird' out of coloured sugar paper. She placed it on top of her refrigerator at home to remind her of how irrational these thoughts were. She spontaneously envisioned knocking the bird off her shoulder each time she had a negative thought and reported that this somewhat unorthodox (and humourous) approach helped her a great deal.

Psychodynamic theory in working with sexually abused children

Most art therapists are trained to a certain extent in Freudian psychoanalytic theory and the subsequent theories of Carl Jung, the first psychiatrist to introduce the use of artwork with adult psychiatric patients. Freud initially believed his patients when they told him they had been sexually abused. He presented eighteen case studies at a medical congress in 1896 (Freud 1896). He was ostracised by his colleagues for such a 'far-fetched' theory. He unfortunately ended up retracting his claims, stating that the so-called experiences of his patients were merely 'Oedipal fantasies' and created what has been known as the 'Oedipal Complex' (Masson 1984a, 1984b). Melanie Klein (1949) modified Freud's theory of the Oedipal Complex stating that its resolution began in infants as early as 6 months old.

British art therapists working with children are trained primarily in Kleinian psychoanalytic theory (Klein 1949; see also Case and Dalley 1990) and the analytic theories of Winnicott (1971). Like the theories of Freud and Jung, Kleinian theories about infant sexuality have been highly influential in the development of psychodynamic therapy not only in the field of art therapy, but other areas of psychotherapy as well (Case and Dalley 1990; Kramer 1979; Rubin 1984). It is important to note, however, that these theories are now outdated in many ways and have not stood up well to a good deal of empirical investigation. It is important for art therapists on both sides of the Atlantic to look at more recent work in object-relations theory rather than to continue to adhere to aspects of theory which are more than three-quarters of a century old.

I personally have a great deal of difficulty with some aspects of Klein's theories of sexual fantasies in very young children (Hagood 2000b), especially when it comes to working with sexually abused children. Klein argued that the penis is 'introjected' and forms the basis of the superego in infancy. She postulated that the phase of oral aggression was responsible for the child's unconscious knowledge of its parent's sexual activities. She also largely discounted the influence of the environment on the child's development. She claimed that little girls, even under the ages of 2 and 3, were governed by the 'primacy of the penis and were desperately driven to possess the coveted male genital' (Chassequet-Smirgel 1970). Her theory unfortunately tended to encourage the interpretation of phalluses in children's artwork as a reflection of

Oedipal fantasies and not the possibility of sexual abuse (Kramer 1979; Sagar 1990). Klein also claimed that children had an unconscious knowledge of their parents' sexual activities and they developed aggressive impulses to 'stick' something into their mother's body long before they knew what a penis was (Wyss 1966). There is no empirical basis for her theories. One obvious danger in using this approach is that of neglecting signs in children's artwork reflective of a history of sexual abuse and interpreting them as 'normal' fantasies seen in all children. Such a view unfortunately contributed to the tendency to ignore the possibility of sexual abuse along with psychoanalysts who for years dismissed patients' reporting of sexual abuse as mere 'Oedipal fantasies'. This can feed into the victimisation of many survivors desperate to obtain psychological help. I have actually heard adult survivors of sexual abuse say that their stories were dismissed as fantasies by mental health professionals and as a result they needlessly suffered many more years of being unable to come to terms with what happened to them. It was no different from when their mothers or others refused to believe them when they were children and their sense of victimisation was again reinforced. It is possible that some aspects of Klein's theory are useful, but these particular aspects of her theory concern me where sexually abused children are concerned.

I also have difficulties in the concept of allowing sexually abused children to be involved for long periods of time in chaotic mess making which is sometimes interpreted as wanting to get 'filth' out of their system due to the abuse (Sagar 1990). I might be accused of having my own 'control issues', but in my considerable experience with sexually abused children, I have found that they need some sort of secure containment to prevent them from regressing into chaos and resultant acting-out behaviour which can be very frightening. I would argue that encouraging them to make messes with no containment encourages them to regress and is counterproductive. Edith Kramer advocated fairly non-directive art therapy with disturbed children, but intervened whenever she felt that the end result would be damaging to a positive therapeutic outcome. However, she too tended to dismiss children's artwork containing phalluses as 'Oedipal fantasies' (Kramer 1979).

Expression of feelings is important, but in working with sexually abused children, it is essential to weave in current ongoing issues around personal safety, lack of guilt for what happened to them, working through their feelings of anger toward the abuser and/or their mother, self-esteem issues and the assurance that they will no longer be abused. It is also essential to address any sexual abuse they may be perpetrating onto other children in a cognitive-behavioural approach to diminish the likelihood of them becoming adult sex offenders (Ryan 1988).

More recent writers in object-relations theory, such as Masterson (1976), Mahler, Pine and Bergman (1975) and Kernberg (1975), have made considerable contributions to working with child and adult survivors of sexual abuse who suffer from borderline personality disorder and provide an object-relations theoretical framework very useful to the working through of developmental issues. The incidence of borderline personality disorder is most strongly linked with a history of sexual abuse, and newer methods of working with these survivors has recently been developed involving cognitive and behavioural approaches (Linehan 1993).

Individual work using art and counselling

My use of art with counselling in individual work with sexually abused children has proved to be very rewarding. Working with children as young as 3 years old and watching them work through their conflicts and feelings about what had happened to them was facilitated when art expression was included. I watched many of the therapeutic issues of survivors of sexual abuse unfold before my eyes. Talking directly to abused children about their problems is usually very difficult and anxiety producing for them. The use of art materials, however, proved otherwise. Individual work with older children using drawings, paintings and clay sculpture provided rich material enabling me to understand their problems and feelings to a much greater extent. Children metaphorically portrayed what had happened to them. They were able to paint or draw some of their nightmares and family drawings revealed a good deal about what was going on at home. In counselling older children and adolescents I found that sometimes simply providing a small easel and paints created a more relaxed environment and they were more easily able to talk about their problems. Case examples of working with some of these children will be presented in Chapter 4.

Group counselling using art with child and adult survivors of sexual abuse

Rogers strongly advocated the use of groups in therapeutic work. He was a forerunner of the encounter group movement in the 1960s and 1970s (Rogers 1961). He began shifting his emphasis from individuals to groups and society. He stated that changes occur more rapidly and clearly in small, intensive groups. My experience in group work has led me to the same conclusion.

Art therapists on both sides of the Atlantic have relied heavily on the concepts of Irvine Yalom (1975), an American psychoanalyst who emphasised that there are several curative factors at play in group therapy. These are:

1. Instillation of hope
2. Universality
3. Imparting of information
4. Altruism
5. The corrective recapitulation of the primary family group
6. Development of socialising techniques
7. Imitative behaviour
8. Interpersonal learning
9. Group cohesiveness
10. Catharsis
11. Existential factors (such as inevitability of death).

Advantages of using art in group counselling

One of the major advantages in using art in group counselling is that everyone can join in at the same time. Participants are not left out and more often than not are eager to be involved. Art is an avenue of communication where words fail. The old adage 'a picture is worth a thousand words' is clearly demonstrated with the addition of art materials. Artwork facilitates the creative process, which many believe in itself is healing. It is an enjoyable activity and encourages play, which is very therapeutic. Many survivors of sexual abuse were not given the opportunity to play during childhood because of their constant struggle for survival.

Art products are tangible and may be reviewed at a later time. They are a useful adjunct to written case notes and should be stored confidentially along with case notes to amplify and clarify issues arising during group therapy sessions. Children can be involved in creating their own special file folders with coloured sugar (construction) paper and be encouraged to decorate the front of the folder with drawings or magazine collage. These drawings or paintings, however, need to be used wisely and are not available to anyone else to interpret out of context, which can create serious problems such as confidentiality issues and loss of trust (for further discussion, see Chapter 3).

Review of media

Generally speaking, there is a wide variety of art media which can be effectively used in art in counselling with both children and adults who have been sexually abused. The appropriate choice of media for children is largely dependent on their age and developmental stage, as will be discussed further in Chapter 2. There is a world of difference, for example, in using fine-pointed pencils versus large paintbrushes and watercolours. Chalk, for example, feels very different from oil pastels, and clay feels very different from fingerpaints. Choice of paper will make a difference as well as how various media interact with different types of paper. Paper with no texture at all will feel very different from paper with a lot of 'tooth'. Certain types of paper will not handle paints and may easily dissolve when paint is applied. The way media interacts with different types and colours of paper is valuable to know. Low-cost potter's clay will be very brittle when it dries unless it is fired in a kiln. Plasticine (or modelling clay) does not dry at all. Fast-drying clay does not require firing, but is more expensive than potter's clay. It is strongly recommended that mental health professionals with no previous art training who are using artwork involve themselves in art classes so that they can become familiar with various media and how it feels to use them.

The degree of control afforded by various media is also important to understand. Fine-pointed pencils and felt-markers provide much more control than do soft-leaded pencils and wide-pointed felt-markers. Oil pastels provide less control than pencils and markers, but more control than paints, and so on. The use of media with more control are less likely to elicit emotions but may be encouraged where a high need for control is important. When encouraging survivors of sexual abuse to express their feelings, usually looser media are more effective. Abstract art tends to elicit feelings more strongly than realistic artwork. Encouraging survivors to use shapes, patterns and symbols is likely to help them to get in touch with their feelings more easily than having them draw realistic pictures with media which require a great deal of control, such as pencils or felt-markers.

It is possible to find art materials in a variety of locations. Shops that specialise in children's toys and art supplies, art supply catalogues, Sunday markets, garage sales and thrift shops are some possibilities. Supermarkets or low-cost department stores may have bargains on basic art materials. Do-it-yourself stores often have end rolls of wallpaper which may cost nothing, and newspaper printers may be able to provide end rolls of newsprint for very little or no expense. Shops that specialise specifically in art supplies are likely to be more expensive. For most professionals working with survivors of sexual abuse, cost of materials is an issue, but it is possible to find ways to find a wide variety for very little expenditure. Art supply catalogues contain a wide variety of art media which can also be adapted to therapeutic use.

Various types of paper can be used in artwork such as newsprint, poster paper, ordinary photocopy paper, special sketching and watercolour paper with various degrees of 'tooth', cartridge (butcher) paper, coloured sugar (construction) paper, crêpe paper, coloured tissue paper, sandpaper, cardboard and so on. Again, it is important to understand what types of media are appropriate for each type of paper used.

Drawing materials requiring more control include graphite pencils, coloured pencils and felt-tip markers (fine, medium and wide-pointed). Crayons which have a high wax content are less likely to result in intense colours. Cray-pas (oil pastels), having little wax content, are softer, and result in bright, intense colours which can be blended and mixed. Various colours of chalks or pastels can be used to blend a variety of effects. Very young children benefit from using 'chubby stumps', which are short thick crayons, and 'chubby chalks' (also short and thick).

Tempera paints which come in palettes of six colour blocks including the primary colours are especially useful for portability and easy clean-up. A variety of different hues can be created with colour mixing. Clean-up is easier than with bottled paints. Tempera paints come in liquid and powdered forms but require a larger storage area and are more difficult to clean up. Those art therapists who have the luxury of a studio area and work with a larger number of children may prefer to go the latter route. Watercolours come in both tubes and blocks, but many inexpensive palettes of watercolour are actually tempera blocks. For purposes of therapeutic work, expensive watercolours used in fine art are not recommended. Fingerpaints, which are to be used with caution, can be cheaply made by adding tempera paint to diluted wallpaper paste. Poster paints and acrylic paints also are available. Oil paints are not recommended because they are expensive, slow-drying and require thinners and solvents which are flammable. Oil paints and acrylics require a considerable amount of art experience to know how to handle their properties appropriately.

Three-dimensional sculpture can be created with various types of clay. Potter's clay, plasticine and play dough, bread dough for small children, wire, papier mâché, pipe cleaners, boxes of various sizes and shapes, polystyrene (styrofoam), aluminium foil, cardboard and folded paper can be used to create interesting sculptures. Collages can be created out of tissue paper, crêpe paper, metallic paper, coloured sugar paper, gift-wrap paper, old greeting cards, wallpaper samples, cotton, wool, sequins, beads, flannel, felt, silk, lace, feathers, yarn, string, buttons, leaves, shells, ribbons, seeds, pebbles, various forms of pasta, old calendars and so on. Magazine collages are extremely useful and revealing, but also very time-consuming. When working with adults, I have frequently suggested that they be created at home and brought to the counselling session or group for discussion and exploration.

Sandtray therapy

Another medium very conducive to working with sexually abused children is that of the sandtray, also known as sand play (Kalff 1980; Lowenfeld 1979; Ryce-Menuhin 1992). Sand play is largely based on Jungian psychodynamic theory, and further study in this field is recommended before engaging in any sort of interpretative work. Allowing a child, or adult for that matter, to create various 'worlds' is considered to be therapeutic and healing on its own. It provides a nonverbal medium for resolution of unconscious conflicts.

I have often included a sandtray along with other art materials, as have many of my art therapy colleagues working with these children. Sandtray therapy involves the use of miniature toys representing human, animal, plant and mineral life. These should include small people, trees and other vegetation, cowboys and Indians, farm animals, wild animals, dinosaurs, fantasy animals, cars, lorries, trains, aeroplanes, boats, fences, bridges, small buildings, pebbles, seashells, and so on. A waterproof box painted blue is filled with sand which can be sculpted to make rivers and lakes. Because of the limitations of many of the places where I worked, I adapted the idea to a smaller scale by using a blue plastic cat-litter box and rice instead of sand. Again, for me, easy clean-up was always an issue. For those able to work in larger studios or play therapy rooms, using the standard size sandtray advocated by Kalff would be preferable.

Sandtrays can be used similarly to drawings. A child is likely to be telling a story which indirectly deals with his or her feelings, concerns or problems. Asking the child to tell the story, what was happening to various people or animals, and what they were saying or doing to each other, provides more insight. Asking if they could be someone in the story, who would it be is also a useful way to learn which toys the child identifies with and to gain more understanding of what the child may be experiencing.

Puppets

Puppets are very useful for engaging very young children. They enjoy playing with them on their own, or may want the therapist to join in with them. Sexually abused children are often better able to talk about some of their problems when a puppet is involved. Oaklander (1978), for example, noted that it is easier for a child to talk through a puppet than to say directly what is difficult to express. A collection of puppets can be created by buying inexpensive stuffed animals at Sunday markets, thrift shops and so on. It is important that their arms do not have a closed seam, because it will be impossible to insert fingers to move the arms about. By tearing out the bottom seam of soft toys and removing some of the stuffing, they can easily be converted into puppets of all sorts and are much less expensive than ready-made puppets. Children can be involved in making their own puppets with papier mâché techniques, paper bags or even coloured pieces of felt. Many ideas can be found in children's art activity books and magazines. By creating mini-dialogues, puppets may be used to help these children to work through their feelings of self-blame and guilt and to come to terms with the fact that the abuse was *not* their fault.

A word of caution about the selection of toys for sexually abused children is necessary. A safe environment for these children is absolutely essential and including scary toys like snakes, witches or toys which in any way remind them of their abuse is *not* advised. These types of toys are upsetting to many of these children, and in my experience when I have seen them introduced, I have heard children insist that they be locked up. Scaring children is *not* therapeutic, even if it is believed that these toys will get children to talk about their abuse. The goal of therapy is always *healing*, not inadvertently creating further emotional trauma.

Summary

The fear that other mental health professionals will learn art therapy approaches and inappropriately use them without adequate training in art therapy is one that has been widely debated in art therapy circles in both the United States and Britain. Art therapists have consistently borrowed from other psychological therapies to establish their own body of knowledge. In my view, the more that art therapists, counsellors and other mental health professionals are able to learn from each other by being exposed to a variety of models, the greater the likelihood of continuing to develop more sophisticated methods of working to help those who have been sexually abused.

In my training of many mental health professionals from various backgrounds, it has been apparent that many of them are already using art in working with sexually abused children. It has been my role to offer guidance as to appropriate ways to use artwork and to remind them of their limitations and ethical responsibilities in not using any modality beyond the scope of their training and experience. I strongly encourage those counsellors and other mental health professionals using artwork to gain further training in art therapy and to develop their own personal experiences with art materials and art expression. Those who incorporate ideas from this book cannot properly call themselves art therapists or counsellors without comprehensive training and qualification in either field (or both).

This chapter has reviewed various theoretical issues relative to the use of art in counselling child and adult survivors of sexual abuse. Counselling and art therapy theories which I have found particularly useful in this type of work have been briefly outlined and discussed. The reader is encouraged to study these various theories and approaches in much more depth. The advantages of including art in the counselling process with individuals and in groups were also discussed, as well as an exploration of various art media. Chapter 2 will present how cognitive development influences characteristics in children's drawings. It will more thoroughly discuss art materials appropriate to various age ranges and the importance of understanding child development in selecting media and working with these children. Other chapters will discuss therapeutic issues to be addressed as well as case examples of both individual and group work with those who have been affected by sexual abuse. The use of art in counselling not only sexually abused children and adult survivors, but also adolescent and adult sex offenders will be addressed in more detail.

CHAPTER 2

Developmental Issues in the Use of Art in Counselling Sexually Abused Children

One of the themes woven throughout this book is the importance of understanding child development in working with sexually abused children. An understanding of how various stages of child development are reflected in children's drawings is essential in using artwork as an additional tool for communication. Selecting developmentally appropriate art media is a necessary aspect of therapeutic work with these young people.

This chapter will focus on cognitive developmental theory and argue that a consideration of psychoanalytic theory alone is inadequate to understand fully aspects of children's drawings. This is a particularly important issue in the interpretation of drawings relative to possible indicators of sexual abuse and the use of children's drawings in the detection of such abuse. Cognitive developmental theory focuses on the child's ability to think at an internal conscious level and seeks to understand the way in which such thinking develops. There is no focus on unconscious mental processes and associated imagery. Interpretations of such imagery are not an integral part of cognitive developmental theory.

A good deal of credit for the theory of cognitive development of children is given to Jean Piaget (1926, 1953), a Swiss biologist and naturalist. Prior to Piaget's work, a considerable number of researchers attempted to explain and categorise the development of children's art-making. Other theorists subsequently either have been inspired by the concepts of Piaget, or have largely borrowed from them. Nonetheless, Piaget's account of intellectual development still dominates our current understanding of the development of children's drawings (Piaget and Inhelder 1969). This chapter will review and discuss the historical evolution of the understanding of children's drawings from a cognitive developmental standpoint.

Art therapists are trained primarily to interpret artwork within a psychodynamic framework. In working with adults, one typically gets direct feedback regarding what their artwork means. The therapist also reflects back what he or she sees in the client's paintings, drawings, collages or sculptures (as discussed in Betensky's phenomenological approach in Chapter 1). The final interpretation, however, *always* lies with those who create the artwork and their interpretation is always to be respected. The therapist may have hunches about possible unconscious material surfacing in artwork, but needs to use great care in how and when any such interpretations are relayed back to the client.

Working with children's artwork is very different. Because many children do not respond to direct interpretations due to their early stage of mental development, therapists working with children may silently interpret their artwork relying on psychoanalytical symbolism (Kalff 1980; Kramer 1971, 1975, 1979; Uhlin 1979). A big problem with this approach is that much of the symbolism discussed by both Freud (1953) and Jung (1935) was based on work with adults and it is questionable whether these interpretations are appropriate for children. Children not only are at a different developmental level cognitively than adults, but also have had far fewer life experiences which might be buried in their subconscious (Jung's concept of the 'personal unconscious'). Jungian therapists rely on symbolism alleged to come from the 'collective unconscious', a composite of primitive images common to all people from all cultures. While Jung alleged that 'archetypes' were also found in the psyche of a child, he provided no evidence to support this claim.

Many therapists who use art in working with children make interpretations without any feedback from the child, and most case studies do not reflect a serious consideration of the child's stage of cognitive development and how that might be affecting their artwork (Case and Dalley 1990; Kramer 1979; Tsalikis 1998; Uhlin 1979). Compound this problem with the fact that therapists also see their own projections in artwork and the groundwork is laid for a good possibility of mistaken interpretation. For further discussion on interpretation of drawings of sexually abused children, see Chapter 9.

Art therapists on both sides of the Atlantic tend not to get rigorous training on the effects of child development on children's artwork. A list of references of literature to be covered in the national examination by the American Art Therapy Association to become a fully credentialled art therapist (ATR-BC) includes only three books on the development of children's drawings (Art Therapy Credentials Board 1994). The bulk of literature art therapists are held accountable for in this qualifying examination is psychodynamically oriented.

Writers included in the list such as Lowenfeld and Brittain (1957) and Gardner (1980) have a good basic understanding of child development and children's drawings, but Lowenfeld and Brittain's work has been revised numerous times since 1957 and includes references to a considerable amount of research carried out since that time. The third book listed is by Machover (1949) and is notorious for its extremely poor validity and reliability. More rigorous researchers into children's drawings relative to cognitive development, such as Goodenough (1926), Harris (1963), Koppitz (1968) and Naglieri (1988), are not included at all. While Kellogg's work was not systematically accounted for (Kellogg 1955, 1969), her writings on her vast collection of 1 million children's drawings collected from all over the world are also worthy of the attention of art therapists who are qualifying. Such a strong emphasis on psychoanalytic theory and a weak one on cognitive development have unfortunately resulted in spurious attempts by American art therapists to carry out systematic research into drawings by sexually abused children (Hagood 1999 2000b, 2000e, 2000g). (For more detailed discussion, see Chapter 9.)

The need for a thorough understanding of how ordinary cognitive development affects what children draw at various stages of mental maturity cannot be more strongly emphasised. In my research into drawings of ordinary nonabused children (Hagood 1999), I observed 34 children from ages 4 to 10 making over a thousand drawings for me over a period of two years. These drawings consisted of the Draw-A-Person Test (DAP) (Naglieri 1988) which includes one drawing each of a Man, a Woman and a Self; the Composite House–Tree–Person Test (HTP) based on Buck's (1948) original work is one drawing including three items within the same drawing: a house, a tree and a person. Family drawings were collected including both the Draw-A-Family Test (DAF) (Hulse 1952) and the Kinetic-Family-Drawing Test (KFD) (Burns 1982). I also collected a large number of 'free' drawings where the children were told they could draw whatever they wanted.

When I saw characteristics in these ordinary children's drawings which were supposedly indicative of certain psychological symptoms, including sexual abuse, according to much of the art therapy literature, I queried the children about why they had drawn them. They responded to my questions in utter amazement. Their explanations for what they drew were extremely simple and logical, making my questions sound foolish. When I told them what some writers have claimed about some of these features in their drawings, they laughed loudly. I thought of the many times that I myself had jumped to erroneous conclusions about what young sexually abused children were drawing without having worked with ordinary healthy children for comparison. My psychoanalytic interpretations, in hindsight, must have sounded ludicrous to the investigative police to whom I often sent children's drawings along with my 'interpretations' without hearing the child's explanation or taking it seriously. The artwork was *never* taken seriously as evidence. Yet I was closely complying with the extensive training in art therapy which I had received.

The danger of interpreting troubled children's drawings without an understanding of what ordinary children draw was emphasised a long time ago by Harris (1963) and Lowenfeld and Brittain (1987), all well-known experts on children's drawings.

Lowenfeld and Brittain discussed the dangers of interpretation of children's scribbles:

> Some individuals...look at children's drawings as an indication of inner feelings and inhibitions. When an adult looks at an ink blot, he can often see within this blot figures or forms that remind him of certain aspects of his own life. Adults can also look at scribbles in the same way and see certain forms or shapes, but this has very little to do with the child's meaning. Some of the circular motions and longitudinal lines may seem to tie together to make a person in the child's drawing, but adults should not try to find a visual reality there or try to give scribbles their own interpretation. (Lowenfeld and Brittain 1987, p.193)

Harris (1963) emphasised the value of looking at the developmental process in ordinary children as a basis upon which to judge so-called 'pathology' of certain groups. He stated:

> Another major step ahead has been the growing recognition that a knowledge of the usual is essential for the recognition of the unusual. Many reputedly abnormal or unusual features in the drawings of individual children or of small, selected groups lose their apparent significance when the age and sex of the subjects and the conditions under which the drawings were made become known. All this serves to emphasize how valuable were these early descriptive studies of drawings by large groups of school children as a basis for more recent work. (Harris 1963, p.19)

My research has strongly substantiated the views of Harris, Lowenfeld and Brittain. As discussed in Chapter 9, I have seen the consideration of cognitive development repeatedly ignored in the literature on drawings of sexually abused children and among many of my co-workers who also used artwork with sexually abused children. The literature on drawings of sexually abused children, for example, tends to discuss developmental factors briefly and superficially. The research simply did not control for the ages of the children involved. The need for a thorough understanding of how normal cognitive development affects what children draw at various stages of maturity cannot be more strongly emphasised (Hagood 1999, 2000g).

History of research into the development of children's artwork

A considerable amount of interest in classifying the development of ordinary children's drawings existed at the end of the nineteenth century and the beginning of the twentieth century. Large samples of children's drawings have been collected by numerous researchers over the years and various theories have been developed to explain how and why children's drawings change as they mature.

The first research into children's art was carried out by Ricci (1894). Ricci, an Italian poet, began by observing the drawings of children under an archway where he had sought shelter from the rain. His subsequent reports encouraged the study of children's art as a means of better understanding children's experiences and development. Ricci observed that the child starts drawing with an interlacing network of lines and then moves on to simple representational forms becoming more and more detailed as the child grows older.

Sully (1895), an English philosopher and psychologist, was the first to use the term 'schemata' or 'schema' for the child's simplified drawing concept. He was highly influenced by the work of Ricci and emphasised the mental concept of the child expressed by a simple representational symbol which stood for the object drawn. At the same time Barnes (1893) seriously organised, conducted and reported scholarly studies of children's artwork, noting a definite sequence of development according to chronological age. He regarded children's drawings as symbolic language. Lukens (1896) described the development of children's drawing in terms of chronological age and was followed by yet other investigators interested in such an approach.

German researchers Lichtwark (1887) and Baldwin (1898) subsequently began investigating parallels between the child's development in drawing and popular evolutionary theories emerging at that period of time. They compared the development of children's art in the early years to palaeolithic cave drawings which were believed to reflect the early stages of the development of humankind. Anthropologists and psychologists continued to be fascinated with such comparisons for many years thereafter, further encouraging an interest in the stages of development in children's art.

Levenstein (1904) developed the concept of storytelling relative to children's drawings, noting that in the early years it was somewhat fragmentary. He found that as the child grew older, his or her drawing involved linear, panoramic and time-sequence factors to elaborate on the storytelling. Kerschensteiner (1905) studied thousands of drawings made by German school children and roughly classified these into three basic areas relative to the content of children's artwork. These categories included schematic drawings, drawings in terms of visual appearance and drawings which attempted representations of three-dimensional space (Thomas and Silk 1990).

Verworn (1907) attempted to describe an integrative process bridging the development of unconscious and conscious processes with kinaesthetic experience in artmaking. It is interesting to note that this effort was made so early in the twentieth century, but the subsequent development of theory relative to children's drawings continued to split between these processes arguing an either–or stance. The concepts of *ideo plastic* and *physio plastic* were introduced by Verworn (1907) to describe children's art development where the emphasis was on kinaesthetic experience. Around the same time, Stern (1908) argued that young children experience themselves as the centre of space in their drawing and that an attempt is made to subordinate the environment to themselves. According to Stern this motivates the child increasingly to organise the space of the drawing surface. Stern (1908) noticed a relationship between drawing and language development and drew the analogy that 'scribbling is to drawing what babbling is to speech'.

Efforts continued to be made by numerous other researchers to observe and classify the development of children's drawings, resulting in a variety of different, but overlapping categories of varying numbers. Rouma (1913), for example, studied drawings of school children over time and classified these into ten developmental stages. At the same time Luquet (1913, 1929) was working to classify children's drawings into five stages. His work has been especially important because it embodied a unifying theory and subsequently influenced the work of Piaget. Luquet made the assumption that children's drawings were based on an internal mental model and postulated that children's drawings were essentially realistic in intention. He believed that children made an initial attempt to portray a recognisable representation of an object. He proposed developmental stages in organisational and graphic skills, including the child's realistic intentions (Thomas and Silk 1990). Burt (1921) described a gradual growth from pure motor activity to linear storytelling. In the transition to maturity, realistic tendencies are initiated as well as the discovery of spatial depth and motion. Burt claimed that there was a general tendency for discarding of art in adolescence. He argued, as did Lukens much earlier, that only a few children remained involved in art and that further development of their artistic capabilities occurred only if they had received encouragement and guidance.

While Piaget did not place much emphasis on children's drawing development, he nevertheless laid the foundation upon which subsequent drawing theories were based. Piaget borrowed extensively from Luquet's (1929) earlier work and adopted his classification of stages in children's drawing development (Thomas and Silk 1990). Piaget's concept of assimilation is borrowed upon heavily by psychotherapists who use art in their clinical work. They have observed that children appear to use their drawing to recreate personally important incidents and that the drawing serves an assimilative function (Rubin 1984). Sexually abused children tend to draw symbols of their trauma over and over again in an attempt to come to terms with what has happened to them and to gain a sense of empowerment (see Chapter 4 for a case example).

Piaget basically regarded drawing as a representation of the real world. He was interested in children's drawings principally as a source of evidence to support his theories of the child's developing representation of the real world and especially the conception of space. Piaget argued that children's drawings are convenient illustrations of their comprehension of three-dimensional space and a reflection of the child's developing representation of the world. Piaget, however, did not seriously attempt to investigate the development of children's drawings. Thomas and Silk (1990) summarise Piaget's use of children's drawings as follows:

> While Piaget sometimes used children's drawings to illustrate his theory (especially those aspects concerned with the representation of space), studies of drawings were never central to the development of his theory, nor did they offer crucial tests of his propositions. Consequently, neither Piaget nor subsequent investigators influenced by his theories devoted much attention to children's drawings. By the 1970s, many contemporary textbooks on cognitive development and child psychology scarcely mentioned children's drawings. (p.29)

Development of children's drawing tests to measure cognitive development

Florence Goodenough (1926) published her well-known book on the measurement of intelligence by the use of children's drawings. Her work developing the Draw-A-Man Test established a long tradition of using drawings to assess intellectual development. Her research methods were rigorous and her findings have been replicated by more recent researchers who have built on her work. Harris (1963) elaborated on Goodenough's work, revising and extending her children's drawing test to use a drawing of a Man and a Woman. He too used sound and rigorous methodology.

Machover (1949, 1953) developed a similar drawing test based strictly on psychoanalytic interpretations. Her work has been strongly criticised for lacking in objectivity, and having poor validity and reliability (Buros 1972). Harris (1963) and other writers (e.g. Blum 1954) challenged many of Machover's analytic interpretations. Koppitz (1968) attempted to bridge the concepts of cognitive development and analytic interpretations in her Human-Figure-Drawing Test. She questioned many of Machover's interpretations in some instances, but sadly still relied on Machover's invalid work in others. There are also considerable problems with Koppitz's methodology (Hagood 1999). Naglieri (1988) developed a Draw-A-Person Test, attempting to refine and expand on the work of all of the preceding writers. It includes drawings of a Man, a Woman and a Self, with good correlations with other recognised measures of intellectual maturity. His test is the most contemporary and has been well standardised with good reliability and validity. It is interesting that art therapists have not acknowledged Naglieri's contemporary Draw-A-Person Test, which is now widely used in research by psychologists.

Lowenfeld and Brittain (1987) have contributed to the understanding of the development of children's drawings beginning with Lowenfeld's (1939) earlier work, following through with several revisions. They have combined many of the concepts of the previous writers discussed above along with more recent research findings. As a result they have been able to summarise succinctly the developmental stages of children's artwork regarding drawing characteristics, space representation and human figure representation. They have attempted to relate their theory closely with Piaget's stages of cognitive development as well as to include consideration of art media commonly used by children at different developmental levels.

Kellogg's research into early development of children's art

Rhoda Kellogg (1969) analysed the early development of children's art between the ages of 2 and 4 in greater detail than have other writers. She focused more on the actual structural evolution of children's drawings than on internal thought processes. Her conclusions were drawn from studying a collection of over 1 million drawings from nursery school children in California, as well as children from all over the world. At age 2, according to Kellogg, the child begins to create *combines*, where two diagrams are joined together, and then *aggregates* (units of three or more diagrams). Between ages 3 and 4, line formations described as *mandalas* (symbols formed from a circle divided into quarters) begin to appear. She discussed the appearance of *suns*, consisting of circles with lines crossing the perimeter. At this age, she noted the occurrence of *radials*, defined as a formation with lines radiating from a point or a small area. She believed that the mandala, sun and radial evolved out of the combines and aggregates.

Kellogg differed from Lowenfeld and Brittain (1987) in that she claimed that children do indeed begin to make human faces at ages 3 and 4 appearing as aggregates. The development of the human figure progresses from humans with head-top markings and arms attached to the head, to humans without head-top markings, to armless humans, to humans with varied torsos, to humans with arms attached to the torso, and then to relatively complete human images. According to Kellogg the appearance of animals emerges at this stage. At around 5 years of age children's drawings are done in such a way that it is frequently difficult to tell whether they are humans or animals.

Golomb (1990) challenged Kellogg's work and argued that only a small percentage of the children in a formalised study drew the forms that Kellogg described. Malchiodi (1998) also disagreed with Kellogg's findings by observing drawings of 100 pre-school children. While Kellogg (1969) catalogued at least 1 million children's drawings, she unfortunately did not do it systematically. I myself have occasionally observed sexually abused children from ages 3 to 4 draw mandalas. Research into this area is very much needed, particularly in order to gain further understanding on how children's drawings might be used for protection from sexual abuse and other trauma. It appears that the observations of Golomb (1990) and Malchiodi (1998) need to be replicated on a much larger scale.

It is important to note that Kellogg's observation of very young children's aggregates, combines, mandalas and radials are part of *normal* development and those working with sexually abused children must not get carried away with various interpretations of these components of children's drawings. While it is true that sexually abused children frequently draw below their normal developmental level, interpretations of these characteristics as being 'bizarre', and thus a possible indicator of sexual abuse, need to be made with extreme caution. Such characteristics in drawings of very young children are entirely normal.

Developmental stages of children's artwork

Lowenfeld and Brittain agreed with Piaget and Inhelder (1969) that the period between 1 and 2 years of age is the time when children develop symbolic play and begin pretending. Their classification of the development of children's drawings, however, begins from ages 2 to 4.

Scribbling Stage

The first subcategory of the Scribbling Stage is the Disordered Scribbling Stage (occurring around age 2) where there is no attempt to portray the visual environment. Children have little visual control over their scribbling. Lowenfeld's and Brittain category of Disordered Scribbling corresponds with Piaget's sensorimotor stage. The child sometimes scribbles beyond the paper and tends to ignore previous marks on a page. The child's motor activity utilises large muscles with movement from the shoulder and kinaesthetic pleasure is experienced. The child grasps tools with the whole hand and makes lines by swinging the arm, looking away while scribbling. No attempts are made to draw a human figure at this phase of the stage.

The Controlled Scribbling Stage follows when the child discovers that there is a connection between motor activity and the marks on the paper. This may occur as early as six months after the child has started to scribble. As the child discovers the coordination between visual and motor activity, he or she is stimulated to vary the motions. Children at this stage tend to become engrossed in their scribbling activity and begin to add to it. As the child progresses through this stage, he or she is better able to stay within the drawing area, draws around previous marks on the page, and may concentrate on certain parts of the drawing. The child's intentions at this stage do not go beyond the movement of the crayon and enjoyment is essentially from the kinaesthetic sensation and feeling of control.

Moving on to the Named Scribbling Stage at around the age of 3½, the child places scribbles purposely, utilises previous marks on the page, and may begin to give empty space some sort of meaning. The child's lines are now becoming edges of shapes. The child relates marks to things known but may change the identification of the subject in the process of drawing. The child uses a greater variety of line, begins to hold the drawing tool between his or her fingers, and now has a longer attention span. A scribble may be pointed out by the child as being a person. The child also begins to name actions such as running, jumping and swinging. The child's thinking is changing and he or she starts to name the scribbles, even though the images are not recognisable to others. Scribbles are now connected with the world and the child moves from kinaesthetic thinking to imaginative thinking. The space between lines begins to symbolise substance, but communication is more with the self. It is quite clear that although parts may have some intent as they are being drawn, the child still has no preconceived notion as to what the finished scribbling will look like. A line that is drawn at the top of the page may be called a tree but may end up being given a different name before the picture is completed. The wavy line may depict a dog running, or the child making giant steps. The scribbles and lines that appear meaningless to adults do in fact have a real meaning to the child who is making these drawings . An understanding of how very young children use scribbles is especially important in working with sexually abused children to avoid unduly projecting our own fantasies of genitalia or other so-called pathology into scribbles and jumping to the wrong conclusions.

Pre-Schematic Stage

The next stage in Lowenfeld and Brittain's system is the Pre-Schematic Stage between the ages of 4 and 7 years. At this stage occurs the greatest variety of form symbols representing one and the same object. Gradually, the child creates its own expressive symbols for every form. Schematic drawing begins to predominate and to become the means of expression and communication for the whole of the child's experience of form. In this stage first attempts at realistic art are made. The characteristics of human drawings at this stage are as follows:

1. the head–feet symbol grows out of the scribble
2. symbols are flexible, constantly changing
3. people are looking at the viewer, usually smiling
4. the gradual inclusion of arms (often from head), body, fingers, toes
5. expectation of distortion and omission of parts
6. expectation of clothes, hair and other details at the end of this stage.

Shapes for things are geometric and lose their meaning when removed from the whole, placement and size of objects are determined subjectively, and objects drawn are often not related to one another. Art becomes a communication with the self. Known objects seem to be catalogued or listed pictorially. As far as space representation is concerned, objects seem to float around the page and the size of objects is not in proportion to one another. Objects are distorted to fit space available and the child sometimes turns or rotates the paper while drawing.

Schematic Stage

Lowenfeld and Brittain's category for the artwork of children from 7 to 9 years old is the Schematic Stage. Here the child develops a form concept which is repeated again and again. The schema is altered only when special meaning is conveyed. There is a bold, flat and direct representation; drawings increasingly reflect the child's knowledge of the environment. The organisation of objects is two-dimensional and there is little or no overlapping of figures. X-ray drawings are common at this age, fusion of time and space, and often there are multi-baselines. Human figure drawings are usually made up of geometric shapes with arms and legs showing volume and more correctly placed. Proportions depend on emotional value and there is a repeated schema for a particular person. The child establishes a baseline on which objects are placed and often a skyline, with the space between representing air.

Gang Age

Lowenfeld and Brittain's next stage in the development of children's artwork is the Gang Age representing 9 to 12 years of age. The human figure is now portrayed with greater stiffness and there is a growing awareness of clothing details. There is less exaggeration, distortion and omission of body parts. Body parts retain their meaning when separated from each other. Greater awareness of details and physical environment extends to drawings in general. Events are characterised rather than drawn realistically and there is still no understanding of shade and shadow at this point. The baseline disappears and the sky now comes down to the horizon. Overlapping of objects increases and interrelationships between objects are depicted. Attempts to depict proper perspective are now made by showing depth through size of objects.

Pseudo-Naturalistic Stage

The Pseudo-Naturalistic Stage is Lowenfeld and Brittain's category for artwork of children ages 12 to 14. At this stage children become increasingly self-critical in their ability to do artwork. The ability to focus on selected parts of the environment is present and this stage marks the end of spontaneous art activity. Projection of non-literal, personal meaning into objects and events takes place at this stage. The awareness of the environment continues to increase, but only the important elements are drawn in detail, as well as illustrative of action. The human figure representation now is closer to the correct proportions and there is a greater awareness of joints and body actions. Facial expressions vary for meaning and sexual characteristics are overemphasised. Cartooning is very popular at this age and a person can be represented by less than the total figure.

Adolescent Art

The final category in Lowenfeld and Brittain's classification system is Adolescent Art, representing children from ages 14 to 17. Here, without further instruction in art, drawings still tend to resemble the 12-year-old level. There is a more conscious development of artistic skills, mastery of art materials, and more control of purposeful expression. Perspective is now fairly well learned and there is an increasing awareness of atmosphere. The human figure includes exaggerated detail for emphasis and the use of satire is now incorporated into drawings with ever-increasing attempts to create more realism. Awareness of proportion, actions and visible details increases. Statements about society, religious themes, individual justice, or the expression of love and hate often preoccupy the adolescent. This reflects Piaget's theory that children at this age begin to develop the capacity for abstract thinking. The search for personal identity is a main developmental task for the child at this age (Erikson 1950) and is now increasingly reflected in his or her artwork.

Developmental theory relative to sexually abused children

According to Piaget, the developmental level of a child has a considerable effect on how the child interprets abuse. Young children are likely to interpret the abuse in an erroneous way and blame themselves. For example, children around 8 years old at the level of concrete operations will tend to interpret what has happened at face value without being able to think in abstract terms. They will be unable to understand that what has happened to them is not their fault, and hence be reluctant to reveal what has happened to them out of a sense of guilt. Such observations have obvious implications for the difficulties in therapeutic work with children at this stage of development who have been abused and typically do carry a heavy sense of guilt. Such feelings of guilt set the scenario whereby they are less likely to verbally disclose such abuse. Drawings thus become particularly important in revealing the possibility of sexual abuse when a child is unable to verbally disclose the trauma.

In symbolic play during therapy children relive events and experiences in order to make sense of them (Thomas and Silk 1990, p.62). In the same way that a child uses dolls or toys to recreate a previous experience and to arrive at a happier solution (Piaget and Inhelder 1969, p.60) a child may use art materials to work through traumatic experiences in graphic form. Painting, drawing and sculpture serve as an assimilative function and this idea provides much of the basis for the use of art in therapeutic work with children (Rubin 1978).

Appropriate art materials for sexually abused children

It is important to realise that not only do the characteristics of artwork change and evolve as the child matures, but also his or her ability to handle art materials changes. Not only children's mental development, but also their physical development and fine motor skills determine which types of media are most appropriate at each age level. Involvement with appropriate art materials aids in the child's creative growth, development of characteristics of flexibility, imaginative thinking, originality and his or her emotional growth. It enables the child to express feelings whether negative or positive.

A variety of media is especially useful in using art therapeutic approaches with very young sexually abused children. It is important, however, to be aware that because of some of the sexual experiences these children have had, they may react with revulsion to certain types of art media. Very young sexually abused children may have been exposed to their abuser's ejaculate and may recoil if given white glue, clay or other sticky media to use in the art process. There also may be a fear of getting their hands dirty. A great deal of sensitivity and understanding is needed if this occurs.

Ages 2–4

Lowenfeld and Brittain (1982) wrote that during the Scribbling Stage (ages 2–4) children need art materials which will facilitate free expression without the intrusion of any technical difficulties. Proper materials and the development of a child's skills play an important part in the expression of art. Any material used with children must fit their needs for expression as well as their skill level. The child's skills will assist him or her in the maximum expression of feelings and emotions.

Lowenfeld and Brittain pointed out that many ordinary small children also react to media over which they have no control (e.g. fingerpaints) as a matter of normal development. They stated that research experiments have demonstrated that the use of materials such as fingerpaints and watercolours tended to remind children of their earlier stage of development and might cause them to regress, thus retarding development temporarily. Such a reaction may or may not have anything to do with the child's sexual experiences. Axline (1969), however, used fingerpaints with very young troubled children and appeared not to have any problems with it. It is important, in any case, to emphasise that any time a young child refuses to use *any* art media he or she should *never* be forced to use it.

Watercolour at this stage of development is also considered to be inappropriate because the colours tend to run and flow easily. Young children are unable to gain control over their movements on the paper and may become easily discouraged by the material. If the child attempted to scribble with watercolour, the lines produced with the wet brush would have to be interrupted frequently. The paper would fill with brush strokes and the lines would run into one another, merging into a blur, which would be frustrating to the child. Thicker paints such as tempera or poster paints, however, are enjoyed by young children. Lowenfeld and Brittain recommend the use of a fairly large paintbrush and paper at least 18 × 24 inches (45 × 60 cm) in size, or larger. Children at this age enjoy creating 'abstract' paintings using bright colours, again mostly for the kinaesthetic pleasure it brings.

Children between 3 and 4 years old have undeveloped motor skills and should be offered art materials which easily fit into their small hands and allow them to experience kinaesthetic pleasure. Ordinary pencils are unsuitable because sharp points prevent smooth gliding along the paper and the points break easily. In my experience, fine-pointed felt-markers are also not useful for this age because young children frequently stab at their artwork, quickly breaking the points. I have found washable 'Crayola' felt-markers with a thick base and a strong broad point narrowing gradually toward the tip to be very effective. There is also no worry about clothing become stained. It is important to avoid 'smelly pens' – those with various 'flavours' – because these children are especially vulnerable to later glue-sniffing addictions and it is important not to encourage them inadvertently along these lines. Lowenfeld and Brittain encouraged the use of large unwrapped crayons and sheets of blank white paper around 12 × 18 inches (30 × 45 cm) for crayons. Good examples are 'chubby stumps', which are short unwrapped crayons with a diameter of approximately

¾ in. 'Chubby chalks' are similarly shaped pieces of coloured chalk. They are easily grasped and have no sharp points to break off.

Puppet-making is especially enjoyable for young children. Lowenfeld and Brittain strongly discouraged many art projects, such as Mother's Day cards, May baskets and so on, for children at this early stage, stating that they are not developmentally ready to perform on such a level which is foreign to their understanding and ability. It is well known that sexually abused children tend to be developmentally immature; fostering their normal healthy development should be a primary goal of therapy.

Ages 4–7

As children change and mature into the next phase of development, which Lowenfeld and Brittain call the Pre-Schematic Stage (ages 4–7), the materials which are appropriate begin to change as well. The continued use of tempera or poster paints with larger brushes as discussed above is still appropriate at this stage. Smaller paintbrushes may be gradually introduced as the child becomes better able to manage detail. Children in this age group still enjoy thickly prepared tempera paints used with a bristle brush on absorbent, large and heavy paper. Watercolours are still difficult for children in this age range to handle.

Clay is an excellent three-dimensional material for the Pre-Schematic Stage, but if a sexually abused child is fearful or resistant, it is important to offer reassurance.

Moist clay can be easily stored in plastic bags and water can be added to maintain the proper consistency. Plasticine or clay with an oil base is much more expensive than ordinary potter's clay; it may stain and the consistency cannot be altered. As discussed earlier in this chapter, the child at this stage will be making first attempts at representation of objects and storytelling. Stories are likely to be told in very indirect ways because abusive events which the child has experienced will be too anxiety producing. Finding ways to enable young sexually abused children to express their feelings about the abuse is especially helpful, along with providing a warm and accepting environment.

Ages 7–9

Children between ages 7 and 9 (the Schematic Stage) are increasingly concerned with more realism and detail in their artwork. Objects such as green grass and trees, blue skies, blue water, houses and animals appear with increasing detail. Using a loose medium like watercolour would prove to be very frustrating and would not facilitate the child being able to carry out what is developmentally appropriate. Good-quality coloured crayons which can be mixed and blended into interesting effects are appropriate. The quality of crayon can be determined by the amount of surplus wax that can easily be scratched off the paper. Oil pastels contain much less wax and are more likely to produce brilliant colours which can be mixed and blended into interesting effects. Larger sheets of paper (12 x 18 inches or 30 x 45 cm) are still best for children of this age to allow for freedom of expression. Coloured pencils may now be gradually added if the child is seeking to make a drawing with more detail. Coloured chalk, coloured papers and collage materials now become useful to give the child an opportunity to explore and manipulate his or her environment.

Ages 9–12

Children at the Gang Age, according to Lowenfeld and Brittain (1987), have a greater need to fill in spaces. For this purpose, it is useful to peel and turn crayons on their sides to fill large areas. Tempera paints can be thinned a bit more because the older child has greater natural control over the medium. There is now a greater concern with detail and children at this age begin to seek media which offers greater control, such as pen and ink, felt-markers or coloured pencils. Having a limited number of paints at this age encourages children to mix their own colours creatively. Coloured paper, such as tissue paper and sugar paper, is a basic material for this age and it provides a natural means of overlapping.

Children in the Gang Stage have their fine motor skills much more developed and find craft work to be useful involving materials such as wood, papier mâché, wire, cloth, straws, buttons, boxes and anything else that looks interesting. Children at this age enjoy collecting bark, rocks, pieces of wood, seashells, seed pods, feathers and other objects commonly found in nature. Sexually abused children may find these kinds of projects helpful for their low self-esteem or useful as projects when it is necessary temporarily to stay away from more emotionally loaded art expression related to their trauma.

Another useful material for children at the Gang Age is ordinary potter's clay, which can be used for many three-dimensional projects. Lowenfeld and Brittain criticise the making of objects such as ash trays and plaques as 'busy-work' and do not encourage their use at this age. I have seen sexually abused children, however, benefit from making such objects because of their poor attention span. Their fragile self-esteem can actually be improved when they have produced an object to be proud of or to give to a family member.

The flowing, merging quality of watercolour becomes more suited to children as they approach age 12. As children mature into adolescence, they are increasingly interested in experimenting and more likely to find an accident in watercolour painting to be exciting instead of frustrating. A colourful sky will be made more dramatic by the introduction of a variety of colours which can be easily blended with watercolours. Fingerpaints can be used at this age for expression without the concern that children will be too involved with the textural consistencies and tend to regress.

Adolescents

All of the art materials discussed for younger children are appropriate for adolescents, who are now able to mix and experiment with various media. Ink drawings are especially enjoyed by adolescents and ordinary black ink or felt-markers provide more control. They have developed sufficient muscle control at this age to be able to create a considerable amount of detail in their drawings. There is now an increasing ability to work with more complex materials and mixed media. Not all adolescents enjoy watercolours; for some it may be frustrating and for others it may be an excellent art medium. Again, involvement in art classes is helpful where special techniques such as 'wet-on-wet', overlapping edges (fencing) and the use of mastique to keep areas of a painting white can be learned. The merging, flowing quality of watercolour produces atmospheric effects that can be quite pleasing. In working with watercolours and other more advanced media, participation in art training is particularly important for the therapist.

Adolescents who have been sexually abused may not have the ability to concentrate well enough to learn more difficult media and may make better use of more basic art materials. In using art in counselling with sexually abused adolescents the choices of art media will also depend on the setting and potential problems with cleaning up and storage. The bulk of therapeutic work, however, will be addressing various aspects of having been abused and problems and feelings resulting from the abuse. Choices of art media should be made accordingly. There are special problems encountered when working with sexually abused children frequently involving the use of art materials. These problems will be explored in greater detail in Chapter 3.

Settings appropriate for the use of art in counselling

Appropriate settings for the use of art in counselling vary depending on one's place of employment. I have worked in play therapy rooms where a mixture of toys and art materials was available. In one setting in Scotland, I worked in a child protection unit and was required to use the same room where disclosures of sexual abuse also took place. The room contained a variety of toys, games and a sink for clean-up of art materials. The children with whom I worked, however, had not disclosed their abuse in this room, so were not upset by it. It may be inappropriate to use the same room where a child has made such a disclosure because of the necessity of providing a safe, warm environment for therapeutic work. Disclosure of the abuse is usually traumatic and the child may want to avoid the room where it occurred. Sensitivity to the child's needs in this area is obviously important.

I worked in several play therapy rooms in counselling centres. I have discovered that if too many toys are available, the child may become distracted from doing artwork and jump around from one toy to another. I have often found it more useful to move to an ordinary counselling room. It was possible to keep the carpeting clean by placing a plastic shower curtain on the floor and carrying a basic supply of art materials in a fishing tackle box offering portability. In this situation, I used materials which required very little clean-up because of time constraints.

Some art therapists are privileged to have an entire art studio in which to work. Many art projects can be carried out in this setting including potter's wheels and kilns for firing clay and glazes. In this situation, storage usually is not a problem and a wide variety of paints, glazing materials and other media are easily available. There may be room for display areas and tables specially set up for art projects. This type of situation is usually found in hospital settings or residential children's homes.

Summary

It is clear that the development of children's drawing falls into a progression of changes with time. Content, clarity, detail, accuracy, colour choices, composition, perspective, structure and so on – all are influenced by the growth of children's understanding of their world. Various aspects of their drawings are influenced, beginning with the earlier focus on themselves (egocentricity) with motor ability and kinaesthetic pleasure strongly influencing their artwork through an increasing awareness of their environment and relationships as they advance in years. At the other end of the spectrum is the adolescent child who is now more aware of values, justice versus injustice, identity issues and so on.

The number of influences on a child's drawing that have little to do with their 'unconscious' are considerable. The question of how developed a child's 'unconscious' is appears to be another key consideration and obviously difficult to measure in any sort of objective way. Children have enough difficulty discussing the problems they are aware of. To assume 'interpretations' of what they have 'unconsciously' drawn can be dangerous at best. Nowhere is this more true than when dealing with children where the results of erroneous conclusions about possible sexual abuse based on artwork can result in disastrous consequences for both the child and his or her family.

It must be said, in summarising various views of the development of children's drawings relative to cognitive theory, that there is a danger in assuming literal categories of children's art, i.e. that characteristics of children's drawings always occur at certain age levels. Children who have demonstrated a mastery of a certain skill level linked with an older age may within the very same drawing revert to characteristics of drawings of much younger children (Lowenfeld and Brittain 1987; Thomas and Silk 1990). These categories are *not* fixed, as such, and in some instances, characteristics of an ordinary nonabused child's drawing may reflect different stages even within the same drawing. It has been my clinical observation that this is particularly problematic with sexually abused children who may vary considerably in their so-called developmental level within a one-hour therapy session. Artwork may appear age-appropriate during initial drawings, but later on during the same session may become more infantile and 'regressed', particularly when the child illustrates more traumatic issues. The child may even revert to scribbling or stabbing, which are similar to characteristics of children's drawings at the earliest phase of development.

This chapter has explored various developmental aspects of working with sexually abused children. It is apparent that the effects of cognitive development on the content, quality and characteristics of children's drawings are considerable. The importance of taking into account the effects of cognitive development on the characteristics of children's drawings was emphasised. The various investigators reviewed above have added immensely to the understanding of children's drawing development in ways considerably different than that of psychoanalysts who focus on symbolic interpretations. Problems with interpretations of children's drawings were also addressed along with the need for art therapists and others who use children's artwork in their clinical practice to have a greater and more in-depth understanding of the influences of cognitive development. The history of research into the development of children's drawings was reviewed along with stages of development in children's artwork. Children's artwork changes and becomes more complex as the child matures. Art media appropriate for various stages of a child's development changes with age and the use of these materials were also explored. Chapter 3 will discuss behaviour problems and therapeutic issues specific to working with sexually abused children, including special problems with art media. Actual case examples of using art media with sexually abused children from ages 3 to 12 will be presented in Chapter 4.

CHAPTER 3

Therapeutic Issues and Special Problems in the Use of Art in Counselling Sexually Abused Children

There are numerous complex issues and dynamics involved in working with sexually abused children. While it is essential to have a foundation in counselling and/or art therapy theories and skills, it is equally important to know these issues and dynamics in order to address them properly. Many aspects of working with younger sexually abused children also apply to the treatment of older children and adolescents who have been sexually abused. If therapists have already worked with other troubled children and/or adolescents, many skills are easily translated to working with young people who have been sexually abused. While the focus of this chapter is on working with children, it is useful to imagine what it must have been like for adult survivors when they were children in order to understand better how these problems have been carried over into adulthood. Working with sexually abused children offers a good deal of insight into helping adult survivors. Using art with adult survivors of sexual abuse will be explored in Chapter 6.

Symptoms and problems commonly experienced by sexually abused children were reviewed in the Introduction. This chapter will elaborate on these symptoms and offer ways to help children cope with them. It will focus on emotional and behavioural problems likely to be encountered in working with sexually abused children. Various treatment issues will be explored as well as potential problems in using art materials. Specific case examples of both individual and group work will be presented in Chapter 4, which will illustrate how these therapeutic issues were addressed incorporating artwork.

A word of warning

If working with a case which has not yet gone to trial or is still in the investigative process, the therapist must be *extremely* careful not to use leading questions when working with sexually abused children. In this situation, unless the child discloses directly to the therapist, it is best not to ask specifically about sexual abuse, leaving any questions about the abuse to those more directly responsible for the investigative process. It is necessary to remain totally non-directive at this stage, allowing the child to go at his or her own pace. Appropriate limit-setting on destructive behaviour, however, still needs to be maintained. If the child is still in the investigative stages of disclosure, it is important to be very careful not to use art themes which may be considered to be influencing the child. Otherwise, the work can undermine the efforts of the legal system to gain protection for the child and the therapist may become guilty of contaminating the case. In these days of false memory syndrome allegations where therapists are blamed for putting ideas of sexual abuse into children's minds, a cautious approach is absolutely necessary. If it has been substantiated that the child and/or children with whom you are working have been sexually abused, it is still important not to make comments alleging that someone other than the known offender has abused them as well. If there is suspicion that there are other abusers involved with a child (which sometimes is the case), concerns must be reported to the appropriate authorities for further investigation and left to them. Sadly, this may not be enough to protect the child. I have observed police investigations where the child was clearly stating details about sexual abuse, but because he or she had seen a recent television programme on sexual abuse, the story was dismissed because of the possible influence of the programme. Gaining evidence in sexual abuse cases is extremely difficult to do, and tragically many children continue to be abused even while they are undergoing therapy, if the abuser still has access to the child. The emotional turmoil for the therapist in these situations is considerable. It is extremely painful to work with a child when a therapist has strong suspicions that the abuse is continuing. Gaining emotional support from a supervisor or peers is crucial.

It is important *not* to get caught up in details of the sexual abuse itself by insisting that the child talk about it repeatedly. Talking *directly* about sexual abuse is frightening to the child and often elicits acting-out behaviour or resistance to coming to therapy. Insisting that the child recite details of the abuse only places him or her in another emotionally abusive situation. Eliciting details about the abuse is appropriate during the investigation process and should be carried out by those trained to do so. Threatening children that they cannot leave therapy unless they have talked openly about the details of their abuse (which I have actually witnessed) is extremely abusive to the child and under no circumstances should be tolerated. To scapegoat one child into telling his or her story because others in a group have told their story is creating the same scenario as the original abuse. Either the child complies or is emotionally abused. The major purpose of therapy for these children is to *protect* them from abuse and to enable them to heal and learn to trust and like themselves, *not* place them in anxiety-producing situations from which they cannot escape.

Working with sexually abused children

It is crucial to remember that a sexually abused child needs to be respected in the same way as any other child. Children will readily pick up on therapists' feelings of discomfort and awkwardness. Therapists need to be careful *not* to treat them with 'kid gloves', or as though they are contaminated or so fragile they will fall apart. Therapists' own attitudes toward victims of sexual abuse need to be examined and they must make certain that they themselves are not guilty of common societal attitudes such as intense curiosity, pity, disgust or hostility. Many people who work in the mental health field have histories of various types of abuse themselves, and working with these children can cause strong emotional reactions (known in psychodynamic theory as counter-transference). It is essential to have access to support, supervision and personal counselling if such intense reactions do occur; otherwise a therapist may be unable to create enough emotional distance to be sufficiently objective in working with the child.

It is important to let sexually abused children know that they are genuinely liked and cared about. Simply being enthusiastic and happy to see them goes a long way toward helping them to realise that they really do have worth. One child actually said to me that he liked me because he knew I liked him. Abused children are especially sensitive and will readily pick up any nonverbal cues that may suggest that a therapist, or anyone for that matter, does not like them. Acting-out behaviour is to be expected and should be viewed as an attempt to see whether they are liked, in spite of their negative behaviour. They expect negative feedback and often have a hard time accepting anything positive. Acceptance and positive regard for these children is one of the most important aspects of therapeutic work. When therapists become 'stuck' not knowing where to go with the child relative to their issues, remembering that just being there for the child in a dependable way goes a long way toward teaching him or her to trust again. Unconditional positive regard is absolutely essential if the child is to be helped to overcome his or her extreme low self-esteem. His or her behaviour may be extremely difficult, but the *child* is always valuable.

Sexually abused children may try to alienate the therapist for several sessions. Fears of abandonment and rejection are very strong and the child may be afraid of getting attached to the therapist and then having him or her leave. The child may try to drive the therapist away at the outset to avoid having this happen later on. Be prepared for obnoxious behaviour with some children at the outset and try not to overreact. It is important to watch one's own angry feelings and how they are handled. When the therapist 'weathers the storm', the child will gradually begin to develop trust and to open up a bit more about his or her problems. One boy with whom I worked exhibited obnoxious behaviour, waiting for me to criticise him and reject him. When I did not, he wanted to know if I was going to leave him like everyone else did. When I reassured him, he brought a chocolate cake to our next session and our relationship remained very positive throughout our sessions together.

Being a positive role model demonstrating nonabusive behaviour is paramount in working with these children, as well as teaching them that problems can be solved in healthy and nonabusive ways. It is important, for example, for therapists not to allow a child to hit them. The child will quickly lose respect for the therapist as well as feel afraid of his or her own loss of control. Firmly and gently taking the child's hands and telling him or her that it is not acceptable to hit anyone is one way to handle the situation. The child will most likely be feeling a good deal of anxiety and anger from time to time. Asking 'Why do you feel that way?' or saying 'I don't know why you feel that way', or worse still, 'You shouldn't feel that way' make the child feel judged and criticised.

Sometimes sexually abused children become extremely passive. They may be excessively compliant with little or no sense of their own identity or their own wishes. They may wear drab clothing in neutral colours in order not to be noticed. They are overly eager to please and to avoid conflict at any cost. They may be smiling constantly and have serious difficulties in asserting themselves. They have learned to accept abuse silently and are unable to stand up for themselves. These children need to learn assertiveness skills and to realise that they are worthy of having what they want. The 'too good child' needs a considerable amount of help and is often overlooked when other children are more defiant and angry.

I have found as a therapist that it is useful to get in touch with one's own playfulness. Recalling one's own childhood events such as special fun times, playful times and even painful times can enable one to be more empathic with these children. Appropriate self-disclosure such as sharing childhood memories with the child, such as 'I remember when I went fishing when I was little and I really loved it', or comments such as 'My favourite ice-cream is chocolate ... what's yours?' may facilitate the child to feel more comfortable. It is necessary, however, to be able to set boundaries if the child asks too many personal questions. It is important to kneel or sit at eye level with a small child, rather than standing over him or her. This is usually less threatening to the child. On the other hand, therapists of the same sex as the child's abuser need to be extra careful not to replicate scenarios which were similar to the child's environment when he or she was abused. For example, a male therapist lying down on the floor with a child who had been sexually abused by his or her father may be very frightening. Again, while the therapist may have all the best intentions, caution is essential not to replicate any situation where the child was abused.

It is important to allow children to take the lead in individual sessions as much as possible, avoiding excessive control. There is a fine line, however, between too much control and providing enough structure to make the child feel secure. The child should never be forced to talk about or paint, draw or sculpt anything he or she does not want to. The child is likely to refuse to do artwork altogether if it becomes too threatening. If the previous art session elicited feelings about the abuse which were frightening or painful, the child may resist using art materials during the following session. Playing games or using toys may be a better option in order to provide the least threatening situation and to enable the child to learn to trust again.

Because these children fear abandonment so much, it is essential always to keep appointments with them on time. To leave children sitting in the waiting room for a long time before they are seen (which I have frequently observed) is basically telling them that they are not cared about. It is also essential to make every effort to inform the child of any absence if it is impossible to go to work because of illness. On one occasion, when I requested that a child be told why I was unable to make the appointment, the message was not relayed and the child became hysterical. Leaving very small children alone in the play therapy room while making telephone calls or doing other business is also a form of abandonment and is *not* acceptable. These children look forward to coming to see a caring therapist, and such treatment is only a reiteration of the abuse and neglect they have already suffered. Unfortunately because of the frequent staff changes in mental health settings, therapists do move on to other jobs or placements. If a therapist knows he or she will have to leave, it is essential to spend time with the child well in advance. The child will need help to come to terms with the end of the therapeutic relationship and reassurance that it is not his or her fault that the therapist is leaving. I have seen children react very strongly when I have had to change jobs and giving them a good deal of reassurance that I was not rejecting them was necessary. Managing my own feelings also proved to be difficult and gaining support from other colleagues was important.

Damaged Goods Syndrome

The term 'Damaged Goods Syndrome' was coined in early treatment programmes which specialised in working with sexually abused children. This is the unfortunate phenomenon whereby a victim of sexual abuse feels damaged by his or her experiences, even if no force was used and no physical trauma occurred as a result. The child is likely to feel emotionally damaged and degraded. Where there has been physical injury or fear of physical damage, however, the child has a concrete reason to believe that he or she indeed was damaged. If the child experienced pain as a part of the sexual abuse, it is easy to understand why he or she is likely then to believe that a physical injury must have occurred. Correcting this misperception is essential to prevent the idea of permanent damage from remaining in the child's mind. Society's response to sexual abuse creates further difficulties. A sexually abused child, for example, is likely to be viewed by others with intense curiosity, pity, disgust or hostility depending on the perceptions and hang-ups of the people who learn about the abuse. These children can be particularly vulnerable for further sexual exploitation by those who perceive them as 'fair game'.

Guilt

The guilt experienced by children (and adult survivors as well) who have been sexually abused is one of the most difficult issues to treat. Intense guilt feelings following disclosure of sexual abuse are practically a universal victim response. The child is likely to feel responsible for the sexual behaviour, for disclosing the abuse, and for the disruption such a disclosure has created. It is essential to convey consistently to the child and all family members that a child cannot under *any* circumstances be held responsible for initiating sexual activity with an adult or older person. Likewise, a child cannot be held responsible for the disruption to the family which a disclosure elicits. The message needs to be that the child had a right to expect protection, not abuse, from the perpetrator, and the right to be protected by other family members. He or she also had the right to disclose the secret of the inappropriate sexual activity. The perpetrator *alone* is responsible for initiating the sexual activity and for any and all negative consequences which may result, including family disruption following the child's disclosure.

Fear

Fear is another emotion commonly experienced by children who have been sexually abused. They are fearful of not only the consequences of the sexual activity, but also the possibility of subsequent incidents of abuse if they are not in an environment completely safe from the offender. Fear and anxiety usually affect other parts of their lives as well. Difficulties in making friends, concentrating on schoolwork, nail-biting and shyness are other manifestations of fear. These fears may be expressed consciously or may be manifested by sleep disturbance, especially in the form of nightmares, bedwetting (enuresis) and soiling (encopresis). The shame the child feels when he or she wets the bed or soils is considerable. Frequently this problem is not handled effectively and parents' anger and frustration may lead to further shaming of the child feeding into an already fragile low self-esteem. Dreams and nightmares may focus more closely on the sexual abuse itself, as well as fears of physical abuse for having told someone. They sometimes express the child's fear of separation from his or her family, or family members. The child's home or living situation needs to feel safe. Some of these children are also at risk for Attention Deficit and Hyperactivity Disorder (ADHD) and should be referred for appropriate assessment and treatment.

Depression

Depression is experienced by nearly all child victims and symptoms will be exhibited both before and after the disclosure of the abuse. There may be overt signs of depression with the child appearing sad, subdued or withdrawn. Sometimes the depression may be masked and expressed as complaints of fatigue or physical illness. Self-mutilation or suicide attempts may be acted out. Therapists need to anticipate that these children will be depressed to some extent and be alert for signs of possible suicidal ideation. Asking the child directly about ideas of self-harm or suicide in a gentle and sensitive way is important, because he or she is not likely to disclose such thoughts or feelings easily. Depression usually results when angry feelings are repressed and turned inward. Providing these children with appropriate opportunities to ventilate their anger in a safe environment where they are believed and supported is essential. More severely depressed children may need referral for further psychiatric assessment for the possibility of hospitalisation or the need for medication.

Anger

Sexually abused children are angry children, and understandably so. While many times the anger is turned inward resulting in depression, these children may also have frequent temper-tantrums and poor impulse control, and may become abusive (emotionally, physically and sometimes sexually) toward their siblings, other children and adults as well. Defiance and disobedience are common. If asked directly why they are acting out, they usually answer 'I don't know' and seem to be unaware of the connection between their anger and their behaviour. Punishment usually serves to reinforce the situation. Teaching these children how to manage their anger in healthy ways is an important goal of treatment. Cognitive-behavioural approaches are especially useful in this area. Helping them to identify when they are angry and to learn to talk about it rather than acting it out is beneficial. Usually underlying the anger is a great deal of psychological pain, but anger gives them a greater sense of control and avoids dealing with the pain. Children need to learn that acting out their anger toward others is likely to set them up for more abuse.

Low self-esteem and poor socialisation skills

Low self-esteem is reflected in acting-out behaviour. Abused children typically seek to confirm the negative view of themselves by acting out and provoking others to reject, abandon or abuse them, thus validating that they are indeed worthless. This type of behaviour is so commonly seen in child sexual abuse survivors that therapists should anticipate its occurrence. Low self-esteem and poor socialisation skills are experienced by the majority of survivors of sexual abuse. Sexually abused children often feel helpless and are rarely assertive on their own behalf. They basically feel unworthy and undeserving of anything. Fear, guilt and depression as discussed above all feed into a sense of self-loathing. The feeling of being spoiled or damaged in turn tends to undermine the child's self-confidence. Poor socialisation skills are often the result of living in dysfunctional families where children are not allowed to have healthier relationships outside of their own family circle. The frequently unsatisfactory experiences which may result when victims attempt to make friends among age-mates and to initiate outside social relationships further tend to decrease self-esteem.

Poor boundaries

Setting appropriate boundaries for sexually abused children is important in working with them. Some therapists believe that under no circumstances should a child be touched at all. In my experience, an example of an appropriate touch after I have worked with a child for a considerable amount of time might be to guide the child gently to one's office with a touch on the shoulder. If the child pulls away, it is a clear signal that it is not an appropriate touch. To avoid touching the child totally, however, may feed into his or her feelings of being contaminated and damaged. Sexually abused children are usually starved for affection or have learned to get it by sexualised behaviour. They may have little or no concept of appropriate boundaries. Small children may climb up into the therapist's lap as early as the first session, showing little respect for either their own body space or that of the therapist. One way of handling this situation might be by saying something like 'I have an idea – you sit here and I'll sit over here', placing the child next to the therapist. It is also common for some children to want to hug the therapist at the end of a session. However one chooses to set boundaries, it is essential not to do it in a way that makes the child feel rejected.

Sexually abusing other children (abuse-reactive behaviour)

In therapy groups, child-care centres or at school, these children may act out sexually with other children. It is a learned behaviour and does not make the child bad. Very firm limits need to be set in this area and the child must understand that such behaviour is *not* acceptable in the therapy room or anywhere else. Not only are other children badly affected, but also these children may be severely punished, further reinforcing their negative view of themselves. It is important to reinforce continually that the child is OK but *not* the abusive behaviour. Behaviour modification techniques using rewards for positive behaviours and cognitive techniques such as distraction are useful. Punishment tends to reinforce negative behaviours and these children usually have been punished excessively anyway. Even if one is experiencing feelings of revulsion toward the child's behaviour (which is natural) it is important to watch one's own reaction to the child. Overreacting reinforces negative behaviour and children learn to act out just to watch the therapist or others' reactions. As experience is gained in working with sexually abused children, therapists usually become somewhat desensitised to the negative aspects of these children's behaviour.

If sexually abused children are known to act out sexually with other children, they are commonly known as 'abuse-reactive' (Cunningham and MacFarlane 1991; Gil 1987; Gil and Johnson 1993; National Children's Home 1992). Several programmes have been established to develop work in helping these children to cease from such behaviour. Further reading in this area is strongly recommended. Cognitive-behavioural approaches are used to help these children recognise what they are thinking and feeling when they are tempted to act out sexually with another child. Usually feelings of loneliness, anger, anxiety and so forth are triggers, just as they are with older sex offenders (see Chapters 7 and 8). Teaching the child to go to his or her carer, whether it be a parent, guardian or foster parent, and seek comfort rather than to hurt another child is one of the main strategies.

It is possible to incorporate various art approaches to help these children learn to identify the situations where they are most likely to abuse others. These can all be addressed with artwork. Drawing pictures of situations where they are tempted to abuse another child along with appropriate expression of anger and anxiety through art materials are possible approaches. Having the child illustrate the thoughts and feelings he or she experiences before abusing another child would be a useful method. Some children may draw sexually explicit material in graphic detail from a very young age. It is important that whatever these children depict in their artwork, one's feelings of revulsion are managed and there are no reactions with disgust. No matter how revolting the child's artwork or behaviour, inside is a scared and damaged child who needs to be loved.

Verbally and physically abusing others

Abused children often become defiant and may have serious behaviour problems. It is important not to get caught up in power struggles and to watch out for polarisation. It is more useful to 'join' the child and not get caught up in arguments which only escalate. Firmly saying 'I expect you to...' rather than giving a direct order may help to defuse oppositional behaviour. It is important, for example, for therapists not to allow a child to hit them or to call them or others abusive names. If allowed to do so, the child will quickly lose respect for the therapist as well as feel afraid of his or her own loss of control. The child will most likely be feeling a good deal of anxiety and anger. Reflecting back to the child comments such as 'It seems that you are very angry today' or 'You're upset – can you tell me what happening?' is helpful. Helping the child to recognise when he or she is being verbally or emotionally abusive is important. Reducing abusive behaviours is a primary goal of therapy. The use of behavioural approaches such as rules, rewards, limit-setting and time-outs (if working in groups) is usually productive.

Provoking abuse from others

Abused children know how to evoke abusive feelings in others. If one feels abusive toward the child, it is a *normal* reaction and it is important to accept it as such, rather than feeling guilty. However, it is continually essential to watch one's own behaviour. Such children may be inadvertently setting themselves up to be a victim because they are used to it but it reinforces their negative self-esteem. For a therapist to lose his or her temper, shout at the child or slip into the trap of emotionally abusing him or her is *not acceptable.* Working with sexually abused children is very stressful; it is the responsibility for therapists to take care of their own needs and stress management. Hearing horrendous stories of how children are abused or seeing graphic sexual content in their artwork can also feed into vicarious traumatisation and burnout.

Personal safety and self-protection

In an ideal world children should not have to learn self-protection issues because the responsibility for sexual abuse is *always* on the offender. We are becoming more aware, however, that sex offenders deliberately and consciously seek out children who are vulnerable (for further discussion, see Chapter 8). Because so few offenders obtain treatment, and it is questionable how many of them truly respond to therapeutic change, we still need to teach children skills so that they are not so vulnerable and likely to be abused. It is important in working with sexually abused children that they become aware of unsafe situations and are empowered to go to someone if they are approached. We do not know how much of such training with young children is actually useful, because the manipulation and conning of which sex offenders are capable may override any efforts of the child to resist abuse. Children at various developmental levels will also have differing abilities in taking such training on board. In my opinion, however, we still need to make every effort to make children aware of situations where they might not be safe. Even if the abuse of only one child is prevented, it has been a worthwhile effort.

Many children who are sexually abused have parents with poor ability to be protective. In my experience with these children, many of them were allowed to play completely alone in parks, school playgrounds or in other children's homes where they were unsupervised. Offenders are clever at picking up on anything that might identify the child's first name, such as T-shirts, lunch boxes and so on. It is then easy for the offender to call the child by his or her name, giving the impression that he knows the child. Offenders are known to hang out in parks, school grounds, playgrounds and any other place where vulnerable children might be found. I worked with one offender, for example, who was found roaming the fairgrounds in California looking for a teenage victim. Fortunately, he was spotted by one of the therapists who worked where he was in treatment. I have also worked with foster carers who have allowed young boys to play alone on construction sites, seemingly unaware of their vulnerability to further abuse. Some of these children learn many seductive behaviours, and if they are not receiving enough attention, they may seek contact with others with whom they are at risk. While there may be a fine line between scaremongering and teaching sensible protection strategies, educating these children and their carers is nevertheless extremely important. Identifying specific people these children might go to, such as a neighbour, a school teacher or a trusted relative, if someone approached them was also useful. It was sometimes difficult, however, to get very young children to take such teaching seriously. Young boys with whom I worked, for example, would jokingly say they would 'beat the person up'. It required a great deal of effort to help these children identify seriously what they would do or to whom they would go for help. Reviewing who they went to when they were abused and how it felt to be protected was another useful avenue. Helping them to be clear on what actually constituted sexual abuse by teaching them the parts of their body that no one has a right to touch (except, perhaps, their doctor) was also important.

The art process

The child is *always* the expert on his or her drawing or comments about playing. If symbols or clues are seen in the artwork that would be interpreted contrary to what the child is saying, it is essential not to argue with the child. Young children typically do not understand interpretations. If a therapist works psychodynamically, it is essential to exercise a good deal of caution in order not to make erroneous interpretations. For further discussion of specific problems in interpreting artwork of sexually abused children see Chapter 9.

Using open-ended questions is one of the main techniques advocated in person-centred counselling (Mearns and Thorne 1992; Rogers 1942, 1951) and encourages the child to continue giving information. Closed questions lead to short answers, and the child will wait for the therapist to take the lead. It is more effective to give observational feedback to what the child is doing as advocated by Virginia Axline (1969). Making comments such as 'I see you are playing with the clay', 'You've got the crayons', 'You're looking for the paints', 'You've made a red painting' and so on are examples of this approach. On the other hand, finding ways to weave in gently themes of what it must be like to have been abused is also important. Saying 'I know someone who was hurt by a grown-up and he felt very, very sad' may pave the way for the child to begin expressing his or her feelings, either verbally, with toys, or in artwork.

As discussed in Chapter 1, using puppets is another highly effective indirect approach with young children. I used to take a basset-hound puppet (named 'Bosco' – a favourite American chocolate drink) to a group of sexually abused boys from the ages of 4. The puppet talked, for example, about how he had been sexually abused and was afraid to come to the group. This prompted the children to take other toys and puppets in the play therapy room and spontaneously to re-enact putting the offender in prison. I continued to use 'Bosco' at the beginning of each group to introduce various themes about abuse and self-protection. I have found an appropriate integration of non-directive and gently directive approaches to be very productive.

When looking at a child's artwork it is helpful to use expressions such as 'I have a hunch – correct me if I'm wrong', 'I'm wondering about – what do you think?', 'Sometimes it's very hard to talk about, isn't it?' or 'Tell me about your picture – is there a story to it?' These approaches facilitate the child to be able to talk more freely. Saying 'Sometimes I have a hard time figuring things out, can you tell me more about that part of your drawing?' is more effective than bluntly asking 'What's *that*?' Such a direct question will usually cause these children to come to the conclusion that either you are not very clever, or they may feel insulted that you could not see what the object in the painting or drawing was.

It is important to remind the child that all feelings in themselves carry no judgement; to be emotionally healthy, we need to be able to experience a wide range of feelings, both 'good' and 'bad'. It is useful to help children to identify their feelings, which are all OK; abusive behaviour, however, is not. Colouring books on emotions are also useful ways of helping the child to learn that all feelings are acceptable, but that behaviours need to be managed appropriately. Using art materials to identify feelings is especially useful by directly asking the child to make an angry picture, a scared picture or a happy picture. If the child does not wish to follow this directive, he or she will usually express in artwork the most immediate issue at the moment and may ignore you. This is not to be discouraged, because the child's immediate needs always come first. To lecture the child on not doing what he or she is told is *totally* counterproductive.

Artwork can be especially useful in enabling children to express their feelings. Asking children to draw a picture of how it feels to be angry or whatever other emotion they may be feeling is useful. Helping them to learn to manage their angry feelings in a positive way is especially important. Using art materials and toys to express hostility toward the abuser is to be used with extreme caution. It is important to understand that *constant* expression of anger is self-reinforcing. Very young children have a great deal of difficulty in discriminating between fantasy and reality. Using stand-up inflated clowns for them to punch is questionable with very young children, because again they are being taught that physical violence is an acceptable way to solve problems. A child needs to know that if he or she hits a toy that it is not appropriate to hit real people. Some children unfortunately are not able to distinguish the difference. Use of art media such as filling a balloon with red water, painting the offender's face on it, and then hitting it with darts watching the 'blood' run, or making the offender's face with clay and throwing it on the floor to destroy it is not advisable for that reason. This may seem obvious, but I have actually seen sexually abused children encouraged to do these things in the name of treatment. One needs to ask constantly when using art materials for expression of feelings whether the child is being encouraged to re-enact abusive behaviours onto others. Clay pounding, pounding pillows, scribbling, tearing catalogues or phone books are much more appropriate. It is important to reinforce to the child that it is all right to feel angry but *never* acceptable to hurt others.

It is important to exercise caution in which art media are used if a child is upset and acting out. Ideally, the use of art in counselling children provides a wide variety of media which the child is allowed to select as he or she prefers. With abused children, however, they can become very destructive if allowed free rein with certain art materials. This is to be discouraged for two reasons. The first is that to condone violent behaviour is not therapeutic. The second is that losing total control over art materials can be frightening. In using art materials with group art therapy with children, this is an especially important consideration. I would argue that to allow children to destroy their art projects and end up in a regressed, upset and angry state is *not* productive. They are likely to end up having little sense of pride in their art products, thus affecting their self-esteem. Allowing free rein may encourage them to destroy each other's artwork which again is abusive behaviour. Ruining another child's art project is hurtful to that child and tells the destroyer that it is all right to be abusive. They need to be taught respect for themselves and for others. I have found it useful to ask other children in such a group to tell how they felt about their work being destroyed. They have always said that they did not like it at all. Limit-setting is very important in these areas.

If children are agitated, it may not be an appropriate time to get out messy paints or clay, unless the situation is monitored closely. Again, it is important to remember that clay, fingerpaints and watercolours are regressive and difficult to control. Crayons, felt-tips or coloured pencils where the child has more control over the media may be less frustrating and more appropriate. Giving the child art media which will help him or her gain control and mastery helps to overcome feelings of helplessness. If the child is unusually agitated, it may be that it is time to play a game with the child and not address any more therapeutic issues at all in that session. There are no black and white rules, and some children may be able to manage regressive art materials with no problem. Being aware, however, of the special problems of sexually abused children and using one's best clinical judgement in working with them are extremely important.

There are various theories on the issue of allowing children to destroy their own artwork. It is not unusual to see sexually abused children want to tear up their artwork and throw it away. Insecurity about their ability to paint or draw may be part of the reason. Low self-esteem may be demonstrated by discarding their artwork. I usually try to discourage children from destroying their work because I see it as an attempt to be self-destructive. I have told children that their work is important to me and valuable and that I would very much like to keep it in a special place. Other therapists believe that the artwork is the property of these children (which it is) and that they should have the right to do with it whatever they want. Using coercion to stop them destroying their artwork would obviously be inappropriate, but reinforcing their self-destructiveness is to be avoided.

The proper storing of artwork is very important. The child needs to be reassured that it will be kept in a safe place and is confidential. Only in instances where the protection of the child is at stake should the artwork be shown to others. Caution is needed because other staff members with no knowledge of one's therapeutic work with the child may use the artwork in destructive ways. Colleagues have sometimes taken the artwork without my permission and used it with the child to confront him or her on a particular issue. Needless to say, the child's ability to trust in me was seriously damaged. A thorough discussion with other staff members on the safeguarding and proper use of children's drawings is vital to avoid any such abuses. I usually had the child make a special folder out of coloured sugar paper and decorate it with drawings or colourful stickers. At the end of each session, I reassured the child that the artwork would be kept safely in the folder. There are obvious problems with paintings which have not dried at the end of the session and cannot be filed immediately as well as with three-dimensional work such as clay sculptures. Proper storage of the artwork and confidentiality are just as important as maintaining case notes.

Some artwork might be displayed in a central area, which tends to enhance self-esteem. One child I worked with helped me to paint a colourful mural of giraffes and she was so proud of it, I hung it in a central area of the counselling centre (see Chapter 4 case example). Each week she made a point of seeing if it was still there. Her self-esteem was obviously enhanced by this process. This, however, was a special art project and did not reveal any of the more therapeutic issues that were later reflected in her artwork. It is important to make the rule at the outset that most artwork will be kept in the special folder unless it is agreed beforehand that it is a special project to be taken home or displayed. Understanding the child's situation at home is also important before allowing artwork to be taken home. Children are accustomed to taking artwork home from school, but I have experienced artwork being destroyed by careless parents or resentful siblings and these children were considerably distressed as a result. Artwork containing therapeutic material does not belong at home or on display. A drawing, for example, of how a child sees her non-protective mother may be upsetting and inappropriate for other family members to see. Good clinical judgement is to be used at all times.

As sexually abused children begin to express their feelings and issues using art media, it is likely to elicit painful or anxiety-producing feelings and these children may resist using art materials. I made a practice of always introducing a very non-threatening art project for a session following one where this occurred, or simply played games or used other toys or puppets. While Lowenfeld and Brittain discouraged special art projects such as Mother's Day cards, Easter cards, Christmas cards or other projects beyond the developmental skill of the very young child, it is still possible to introduce other art themes which are totally non-threatening. For younger children, making puppets, masks, stringing beads or any number of other art activities might suit the situation. Older children enjoy making flower collages from pictures out of seed catalogues or collages from wallpaper samples. There are many excellent ideas in art education books, occupational therapy journals and children's magazines appropriate for various age levels.

Directive versus non-directive therapy

The debate between using directive and non-directive therapy reverberates through both counselling and art therapy circles. I have consistently found that if children do not want to create artwork around a suggested theme, they are likely to go ahead and create whatever they want to anyway, totally ignoring the therapist. I have found it unhelpful to *force* pre-planned agendas on children. A therapeutic strategy (or treatment plan) may be intended before each session, but it is essential to be prepared to 'go with the flow'. If the child is preoccupied with another issue, it is necessary to be flexible and follow his or her lead. If he or she does not seem to be dealing with a certain issue in a particular session, it is reassuring to know that it is likely to come up again later on until it is resolved. If the child overreacts or resists issues, it is most likely because he or she is not readily to deal with it yet. It is important to respect the child's resistance and it is helpful to say something like 'I know it's hard to talk about', demonstrating empathy and an understanding of the difficulty the child is having. If the child continues to resist, however, the therapist must honour his or her choice at all times.

In my experience, to be totally non-directive with sexually abused children at all times is not useful because it is very easy to avoid dealing with the subject of sexual abuse altogether. I have found it useful to remind the child gently why she or he is coming to counselling from time to time so that the sexual abuse is not totally forgotten. If a therapist continues to avoid the topic of sexual abuse, this may tell the child that it is a taboo subject and feed into their feeling that they need to keep it a 'secret'. On the other hand, it is important to avoid making the child tell his or her story over and over again. It is better to encourage these children to deal with their issues indirectly with toys or puppets, or by having them draw a story, asking who they would like to be in the story. One little boy aged 4, for example, repeatedly drew pictures of an elephant trying to eat a little bird. He identified with the bird and was trying to master his feelings about having been sexually abused. I reassured him and encouraged him to draw more pictures about how to protect the little bird so that the elephant could never hurt him again. Working indirectly is especially important with very young children because it is too threatening to talk specifically about their own abuse.

Artwork reflecting progress in therapy

It has been interesting in my work with sexually abused children to observe changes in the content and style of their paintings and drawings as they begin to feel better about themselves. There are several ways that recovery may reflect itself graphically. The child's artwork may become more age appropriate, reflecting what normally would be expected from children his or her age (see discussion above for age-appropriate characteristics of children's artwork). Many children who have been abused create very chaotic and disorganised artwork (but this is not always the case). If the child has been doing so and you notice that the drawings become more integrated with time, it is usually a validation that the child is making gains. Less scribbling and stabbing at the artwork also indicates a developmental advance, as well as the possibility of less anger and confusion. Depressed children (and adults for that matter) tend to use a great deal of black, brown, dark blue and grey and to avoid the use of bright colours. This is often a diagnostic clue as to the possibility of depression, and further investigation is usually advisable. But as depression lifts, the child may begin using a greater variety of colours and the themes may change to become more positive and happy. Flowers, birds, butterflies and themes of growth and metamorphosis may begin appearing. Themes become more positive and have happier endings. There is usually less aggression depicted such as in war themes with guns and bombs, cowboys and Indians fighting, volcanoes exploding, and so on.

Kellogg (1969) noted that 'mandalas' appear in younger children's artwork as a matter of normal development. Those with a more psychoanalytic background believe that a circle with a cross in the centre symbolises integration, wholeness, completion and resolution (Slegelis 1987; Pasto 1965). Children may draw these spontaneously or sculpt them in a sandtray as they improve. Children of 3 and 4 years old may draw them because they are developmentally appropriate for that age or because they are feeling more centred, or both.

Summary

This chapter has elaborated on the many complex issues and dynamics involved in working with sexually abused children which were reviewed in the Introduction. Emotional and behavioural problems likely to be encountered in working with sexually abused children have been discussed along with possible approaches in their treatment. Emphasis has been placed on the use of unconditional positive regard for these children, regardless of their negative behaviours. The use of observational feedback and other person-centred skills was discussed.

Examples of integrating cognitive and behavioural counselling approaches with the use of art were presented. Strategies for self-protection and better protection by carers was also discussed. Potential problems and possible solutions in using art materials were explored. Case examples of both individual and group work with sexually abused children will be presented in Chapter 5, illustrating some ways that these therapeutic issues were addressed incorporating artwork.

CHAPTER 4

Case Examples in the Use of Art in Counselling Sexually Abused Children

This chapter will present several case examples illustrating how the use of art was integrated with counselling in individual, dyadic and group work with sexually abused children ranging from ages 3 to 11. Issues which arose in each therapeutic situation will be discussed along with art approaches that were used in working with these children, and in some instances their mothers. While the theoretical background relative to working with sexually abused children has been discussed in Chapter 1 and therapeutic issues and special problems were addressed in Chapter 3, this chapter will focus on examples of direct therapeutic work.

Moving from talking about problems to the use of art materials often provides a safer way to express feelings, especially at the outset. The artwork becomes a mediary, so to speak. Seeing the problem depicted graphically adds a visual dimension and enhances the therapist's insight into the situation. In dyadic work the therapist might give feedback or interpret what he or she sees after the mother and daughter have exhausted all of their ideas. In working with sexually abused children and their mothers, the creativity of the art therapist is called upon on an ongoing basis, much as it is for the verbal therapist.

Individual work and the use of art in counselling

There are many advantages in working individually with a child. The entire session provides undivided attention for the child and an opportunity for warmth, genuineness and positive regard from the therapist to rebuild the child's faltering self-esteem. When the child senses that he or she is genuinely liked, in spite of what has happened, the 'Damaged Goods Syndrome' can begin to be overcome. The child can pick and choose from a variety of art media, or in some instances the therapist may judge that a particular medium is most appropriate at the time. The reliability of the therapist in always being there helps to develop the child's ability to trust. Establishing trust usually takes a considerable amount of time and is absolutely essential before the child is likely to begin to deal with what has happened to him or her. Reassuring the child constantly that he or she is valuable is the bottom line in therapy.

Reflecting back to the child what is seen in the artwork and encouraging the child to communicate about it are useful approaches. Many children cannot talk about their abuse at all and may try to use artwork to communicate nonverbally with the therapist. When relying only on artwork to interpret what is going on, one must proceed with a considerable amount of caution and always remember that one's interpretations are very subjective, and may not actually be the case at all. Finding indirect ways to get the child to elaborate on what he or she has created is important, but if the material is emotionally upsetting, it is likely to be very difficult for the child. Forcing an explanation is *never* appropriate, and is likely to create a considerable amount of resistance in the child to using artwork in future sessions.

Case example: Individual work

Sarah, age 3, was referred to me by the District Attorney's office in California. She had been rushed to the University of California hospital with major vaginal lacerations allegedly after having been raped by her grandfather. Her 25-year-old mother was also referred to me for counselling, having a considerable amount of psychological disturbance herself. I was working at that time in a small counselling room within a large building where a variety of professionals leased their offices. I had a small table which was easily accessible for artwork and kept art supplies in my cabinet, along with puppets, a small sandtray which I had made from a blue plastic cat-litter box, and miniature toys. There were sinks for clean-up of art materials readily accessible in the toilet area. I found a palette of six basic colours of tempera paints to be very useful for a variety of approaches to painting with cleaning up being fairly quick and easy. The paint could be mixed into many different colours and thinned down for more watery effects. An array of colours of washable wide-tipped felt-markers and other drawing media were also useful, being easily cleaned up and stored. I had a plastic shower curtain which could be unfolded and placed on the floor for artwork, or to protect the carpeting from any spilled sand.

Little Sarah was immediately amenable to being involved in artwork and enjoyed playing with the puppets and sandtray. She was an extraordinarily beautiful child and very precocious for only 3 years old. She had an effervescent personality and it was easy to see why she could become a target for sexual

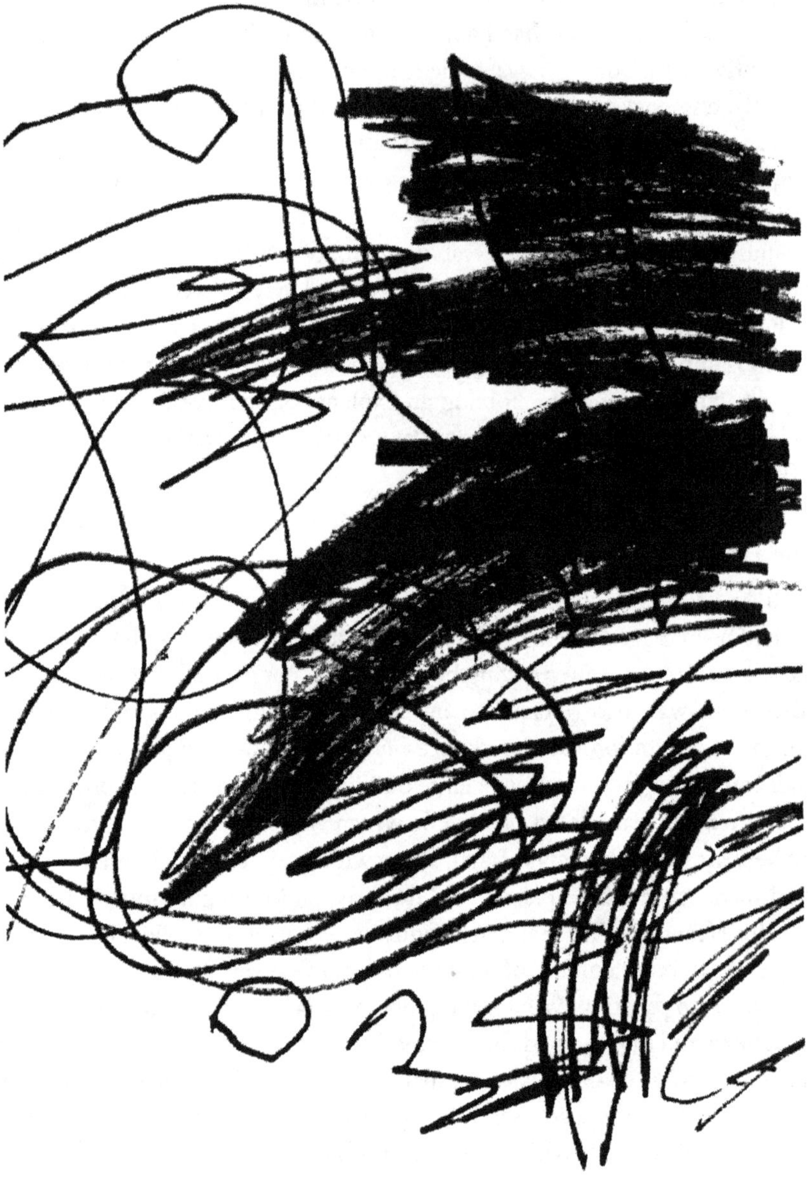

Figure 4.1 Sarah's drawing of the 'Mean Bear'

abuse. She eagerly looked forward to her sessions and confidently would walk up to the receptionist and insist on seeing 'My Maralynn'. When I began working with Sarah, it became immediately apparent that she exhibited very poor personal bodily boundaries. Contrary to many sexually abused children who have lost their ability to trust, Sarah trusted me far too easily and on the first session climbed up into my lap with her face pressed close to mine. I believed it was important to set appropriate physical boundaries with her and gently lifted her up and sat her more appropriately next to me on the sofa, taking care not to reject her in any way. Healthy 3 year olds would most likely be more reserved and take more time to be able to trust.

Sarah was preoccupied with a 'Mean Bear' and all of her attempts at artwork and playing with puppets were around this theme. It was clear that she was afraid of the 'Mean Bear' and wanted to destroy him in order to feel safe. She would routinely look for the bear puppet, which she would angrily throw on the floor. She would jump up and down on it and then throw it behind the rocking chair. She and I would routinely chase an imaginary 'Mean Bear' behind the rocking chair and tell him never to hurt Sarah again. Sarah attempted to draw the 'Mean Bear' on ordinary white paper with felt-markers (Figure 4.1).

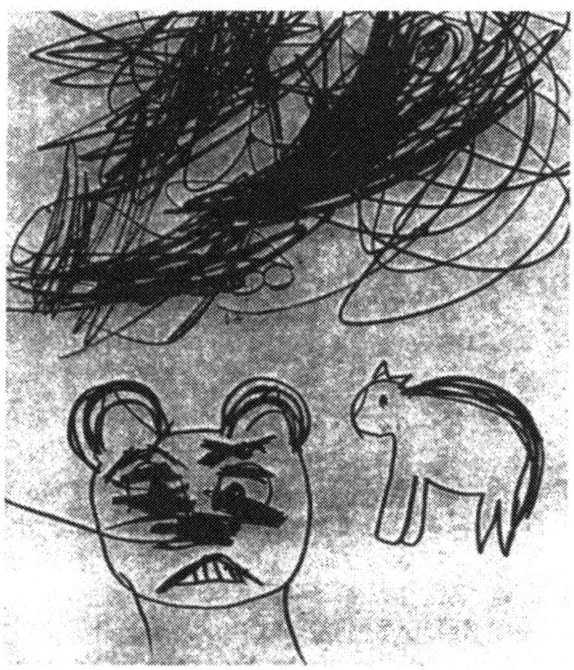

Figure 4.2 Therapist's drawing of the 'Mean Bear'

She consistently picked the colour red and in each drawing would scribble and stab at her attempts to draw a bear. It is interesting to note how her crude drawing appears to represent an erected male phallus, which she stabbed at and scribbled over. She would become frustrated, because developmentally she was not capable of drawing a bear. She finally asked me to draw a bear for her (Figure 4.2) and then took felt-markers and began to scribble over the bear's eyes and nose. Session after session, she repeatedly continued the process, both in artwork and with puppets. It was apparent that she was attempting to master and assimilate what had happened to her and to gain a sense of empowerment.

When Sarah played with the small sandtray, the themes once again were of protecting herself and eliminating threatening toys such as snakes and alligators; she would periodically throw them out of my letterbox (much to the amusement of others who worked in the building). She would also bury the

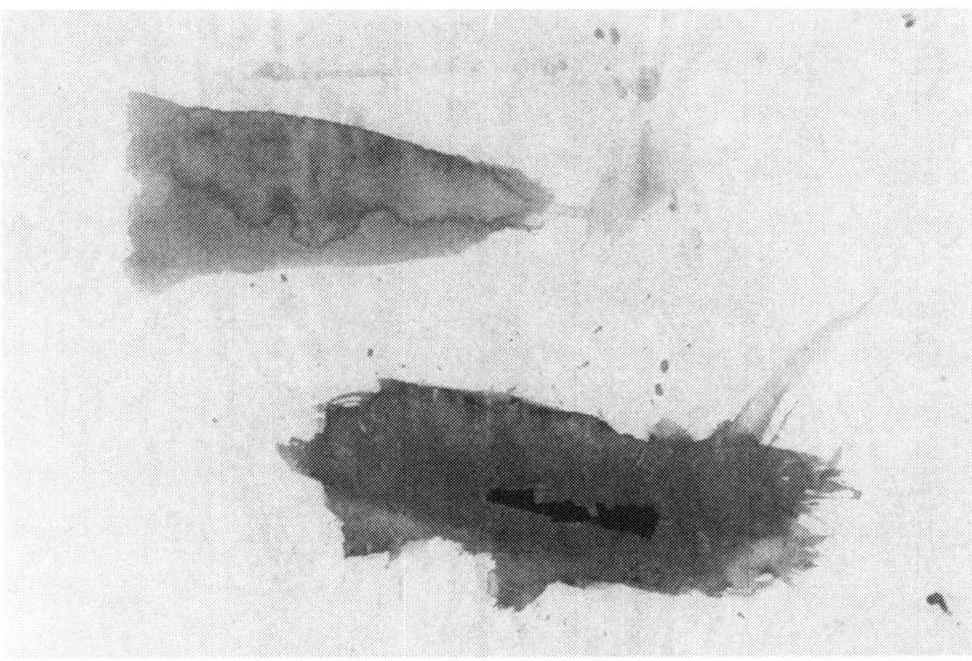

Figure 4.3 'Red Wedges'

snakes and alligators in the bottom of the sand, taking a small doll and placing it at the far end of the sandtray, protecting it with piles of surrounding sand. The metaphors for what she was doing appeared obvious, but again were only my interpretations. I felt that it might be too threatening to ask her more directly about what she was doing, and since the case was still under investigation, I did not want to ask any leading questions.

She then wanted to learn to paint, so I gave her a palette of six blocks of tempera paint and water. Using a one-inch-wide paintbrush, I taught her how to mix the water and paint. She became thoroughly engrossed in the process and began painting large bright-red phallic wedge shapes (Figure 4.3). She dipped into red, then white, and again into red paint, stabbing and rubbing the brush as hard as she could, in some instances tearing through the paper. It is interesting to note that Spring (1985) observed that adult survivors of sexual abuse frequently included large wedge shapes in their artwork. I have observed this phenomenon in paintings of other very young children who were sexually abused.

Sarah continued to paint and stab at these red wedges for another two sessions. I then asked Sarah to try to paint the 'Mean Bear' for me. What she painted actually looked like life-sized male genitals, and it became clear to me that in the eyes of such a small child, the genitals of her perpetrator might easily look like a 'Mean Bear' (Figure 4.4).

As therapy progressed, Sarah no longer brought up the subject of the 'Mean Bear' but began talking more openly about her grandfather, the alleged offender. She appeared to feel safer and more ready to deal with her trauma directly. She said that her grandfather had put his fingers in her bottom and 'mushed it up'. She told me that he was a mean man and then wanted to make him out of clay. She was making it quite clear what her preoccupation with the 'Mean Bear' had meant. She then spent time pounding the clay. During the next session she refused to talk about it any further, saying that it made her stomach hurt. I totally respected her resistance and did not push her any further, moving to less threatening activities such as reading books or playing with toys. She continued, however, to work through her trauma metaphorically with puppets. She selected a monkey puppet one day and told him not to eat any more bananas. Her mother had told me that she had been forced into orally copulating her grandfather. This could also help to explain her painting of the 'Mean Bear' (Figure 4.4).

During my work with Sarah, I saw her mother separately for counselling sessions and tried to help her with serious coping problems she was having with

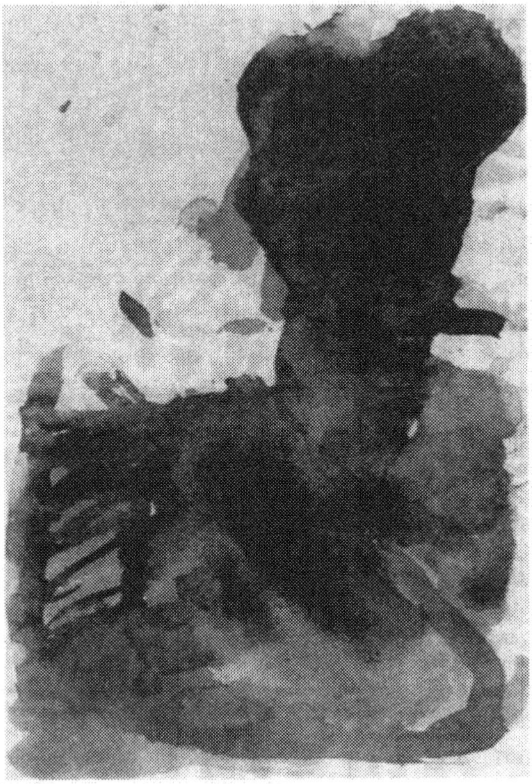

Figure 4.4 Sarah's painting of the 'Mean Bear'

her ex-husband, who was consigned to a drug rehabilitation programme in a nearby town. I used only verbal counselling approaches with her because she was not interested in doing any artwork. Her husband had been consistently violent with her and she had moved house several times. She was extremely tense and anxious, and it did not take long to learn that she too had been sexually abused when she was very young. She was preoccupied with the impending court case to prosecute her father-in-law, the child's alleged perpetrator.

I worked with Sarah and her mother for a total of three months. Her mother had asked my advice about allowing Sarah to visit her father, who had a one-day pass from his rehabilitation centre. I strongly advised her against leaving either Sarah or her 18-month-old sister with their father, who had a history of violence and drug abuse. The grandfather, the alleged offender, was out on bail and could easily visit the children's father as well. The following week her mother very anxiously brought Sarah to see me, stating that Sarah had told her that her 'bottom' was sore. She begged me to get Sarah to tell me what happened during the session, hoping to have more evidence against the grandfather. Sarah, however, told me in that session that she had been abused by three people, and one of them was actually her father. Upon further exploration with her mother, I discovered that she had in fact allowed both Sarah and her 18-month-old infant to spend a day with their father. When I told the mother that Sarah had confided that her father had abused her, the mother refused to bring her in for therapy any longer. I had to file a written report immediately with the Child Protective Services about my suspicions regarding the father's abuse, and that there might be other possible abusers.

Six months later I received a telephone call from Sarah's social worker to consult with me about the case. She sent me a copy of the mother's written consent for me to discuss the case. She queried whether I believed the mother was capable of protecting the children. When I expressed my concerns and relayed to her what had happened, she informed me that the mother was a cocaine addict and was totally dependent on Sarah's father for her supply of drugs, which is why she kept allowing the children to visit him. It also came to light that the father was involved in a prostitution ring. Because of my additional input, appropriate protective measures for both Sarah and her little sister were subsequently carried out.

Mother–daughter dyadic work and the use of art and counselling

Dyadic sessions with mother and daughter appear to be highly beneficial (Faller 1988; Rubin 1973), especially when focusing on the relationship and dynamics between the two. In cases where more than one child in the family has been sexually abused, family sessions with the mother and more than one child may also be fruitful. Some clinicians prefer to have the mother and daughter seen by separate therapists, holding conjoint sessions with both therapists, the mother and the daughter present. In private practice, however, this can be very expensive. Many agencies specialising in the treatment of child sexual abuse have the flexibility to provide such an approach. If the same therapist works with both mother and daughter in individual sessions, ground rules need to be clearly set regarding confidentiality. Information disclosed in individual sessions should not be shared with the other party without prior consent. The mother and child should be encouraged to directly express their concerns to each other in conjoint sessions whenever appropriate. Involving art materials in working with both mother and child can be highly revealing.

My experience with mother–daughter dyadic work is heavily based on the family systems theory (Minuchin 1974; Satir 1967, 1972). My involvement of art therapy was inspired by Rubin (1973). Again, it is important to clarify that my approach also took into account the dysfunctional dynamics occurring when a family includes a sex offender with his own destructive pathology. Regardless of how frustrating it might be to work with some of these mothers, she was *never* to be blamed for the abuse (except in very rare cases where she had actually been the offender). Regardless of theoretical preference, however, it must again be stressed that a thorough awareness of the many issues involved in treating families where sexual abuse has occurred is crucial. The choice of techniques and theoretical models may vary with different clinicians. A thorough knowledge of developmental stages of the child is also essential because issues between mother and daughter will largely depend on those stages. The problems a mother might have with a 5 year old and a 13 year old, for example, would vary considerably. Many times the mother's expectations of the child are much more than the child is capable of delivering at that stage of development, and educating the mother on what is normal behaviour at that age can be very helpful. Taking into account the mother's developmental and personal issues is equally important. A mother in her mid-twenties with small children, for example, will be coming from a very different place than an older mother approaching menopause with adolescents ready to leave home.

Including art with counselling sexually abused children and their mothers has many advantages in dyadic work. Many of these mothers, for example, have a difficult time playing with their children. They often grew up in families where they were forced to assume an adult role very early in life and were not allowed to be children themselves. Teaching the mother and child to play together creatively helps to strengthen the bond between them. The mother also needs to learn ways to spend more quality time with her child at home. Communication skills can be enhanced for both the mother and the child as they learn, perhaps for the first time, to express feelings toward each other and more effectively resolve issues of conflict. The use of artwork, again, brings to light issues that might easily be overlooked. Resultant feelings can be expressed through a variety of art media within the therapeutic session. The mother needs to learn to be more nurturing and supportive toward her daughter. She must be encouraged to meet her emotional needs with peers and supportive relatives instead of leaning excessively on her daughter. Sometimes these mothers have adopted a highly critical stance with their daughters, due to their own lack of self-acceptance, and exhibit excessively controlling behaviour. Such critical and controlling behaviour becomes more obvious as the mother and child work together on art projects. Sometimes it may be more appropriate to address the subject by gently coaching the mother. As she becomes more aware of her behaviour, as well as where she learned it, she can begin to gradually unlearn and change it. As she takes more responsibility, and learns to blame herself less, feelings of guilt are minimised and she is likely to begin feeling more hopeful and empowered.

Planning a specific art approach for each session in advance is good practice, but the therapist must maintain the flexibility to change to a different strategy depending on what the mother and child bring to the session. For example, if the mother and daughter come to the session after a serious argument, it would be far more effective to focus on the current situation rather than rigidly adhering to the pre-planned approach which might have been appropriate under different circumstances. In this hypothetical example a ready-made opportunity presents itself to work on problem-solving, expression of feelings and communication skills. Having a variety of art materials on hand to adapt creatively to the more immediate problem is important. The planned intervention can always be used at a later time, because problems are likely to reoccur until they are resolved.

Some possibilities for adapting art techniques to the issues presented above might be to ask the mother and daughter each to draw how they see a given situation. They then might explain the content of their drawings to each other and the therapist. Feelings might be shared not only verbally, but also by moving into a subsequent art technique expressing emotions through painting, clay or another drawing. Family drawings are especially useful in revealing different perspectives on how the family is seen by the mother and the child. Having the mother and child create joint murals with drawing, painting, collage or scribble drawings where they find 'pictures' in the drawings together are additional possibilities. Painting or drawing a problem as they each see it along with possible solutions, making pictures of how they want things to be, or setting goals for a better relationship are all possible ideas for art projects together. Proper timing is always important, because if traumatic issues are addressed too soon, the mother might not return or the child may refuse to do any more artwork. While the mother and child are involved in the artwork, the therapist can observe the interactions between them, such as power struggles, the mother's ability to nurture and be supportive, role-reversals, problem-solving and communication skills.

Case example: Mother–daughter dyadic work

Marie, a 5-year-old girl, was referred to me by a family therapist working in the same counselling centre as myself who was working with the child's mother and stepfather. Marie's parents had divorced two years earlier, and the mother had remarried. Because the child's stepfather had become violent towards little Marie, it was felt that she would also benefit from therapy. The stepfather had lost his temper with her and threw her toys at her, hitting her so severely that she was covered in bruises. Her school teacher reported suspicion of the abuse to the authorities. The stepfather admitted what he had done and was willing to enter treatment with his wife. There was no suspicion of sexual abuse at that point and nothing was disclosed by the child until much later in treatment.

I began working with Marie by asking her to join with me in painting a mural together, using tempera paints. My strategy was to use the mural-making as a means of establishing a therapeutic alliance. She began by painting a lovely, whimsical giraffe along one side of the paper. When the giraffe's neck proved to

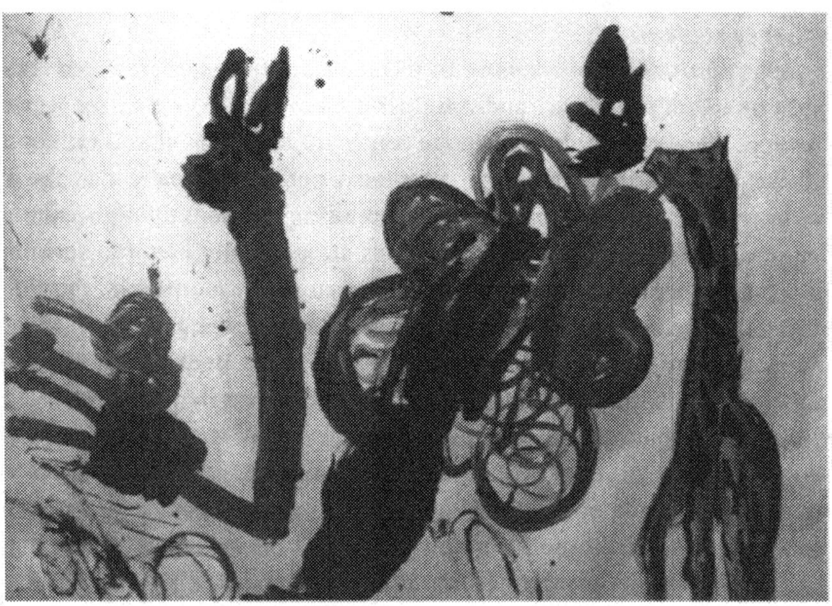

Figure 4.5 'Two Giraffes'

be too long, she creatively turned it around to another side of the paper. She insisted that I paint a giraffe on the mural as well, which proved to be rather dull and plain compared to the charming one she had painted. Marie began complaining that I could paint better than she could and no amount of persuasion to the contrary did any good. We completed the painting by adding trees, birds and a blue sky. I then suggested that because she did such a good job, we might hang it up in a central place in the counselling centre (with the goal of boosting her self-esteem). She was very pleased with the idea, and each week she methodically checked to see that it was still hanging there (Figure 4.5). I was later to learn that Marie's relationship with her mother was highly competitive and that she had assumed that I was trying to compete with her as well.

Marie had problems with bedwetting and felt very guilty about it. Her mother tended to be punitive toward her whenever it occurred. The child would work through her feelings about her enuresis with several dolls in a pram. She identified the doll with black hair as being a 'bad girl' and would mercilessly smack the doll and call it names. I indirectly worked with her by telling her that the doll really was not bad and that maybe she wet the bed because she was scared or worried. I began to encourage her to cuddle the doll and to treat it more lovingly. One session, I brought scissors and hair curlers to the session and we washed the doll's hair, cut it and curled it. Marie was finally able to be reassured that she was not such a bad girl after all, and the mother reported that the bedwetting had become more infrequent.

The mother revealed a history of childhood difficulties and said she could remember absolutely nothing prior to age 7, but she did not report any history of sexual abuse. I worked in individual sessions with the mother from time to time to explore the stressors in her life. She was slightly obsessive-compulsive, working as an accountant for a major airline. She appeared regularly in her airline uniform and had a great deal of difficulty relaxing. Her second husband, the child's stepfather, was childlike and passive in demeanour; it was clear that she controlled him as well as Marie.

Marie's subsequent drawings depicted her mother as a witch and herself as a little kitten in a cage. Children who are victims of abuse often have very hostile feelings toward their mothers. Marie told me that the witch was her mother, and then taking scissors, cut out the kitten and taped it to the top of the paper high above the witch (Figure 4.6). The theme of the witch was incorporated into this child's artwork throughout the duration of treatment. When the child showed the pictures to her mother, her mother laughed and said she was aware that the witch represented herself. Unfortunately, this mother was not able to

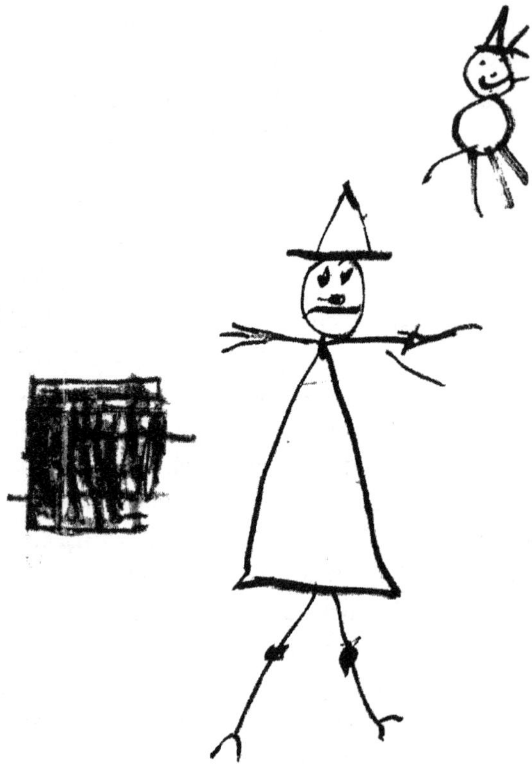

Figure 4.6 'My Mother, the Witch'

understand the impact of her critical and competitive behaviour on her small daughter, much less to empathise with the child's feelings. The story of 'Hansel and Gretel' was a favourite with Marie, and several pieces of her artwork were variations of this favourite fairy tale. Again, she always stated clearly that the witch was her mother.

Marie also drew pictures of her mother as an angry tiger and illustrated herself as a frightened child at the bottom of the page, where she used oil pastels on white cartridge paper (Figure 4.7).

During dyadic sessions, it was easier to learn about the dynamics between this mother and child by seeing how they worked together. Observing the intense competition between the two of them at firsthand proved to be very revealing. For example, as the mother and daughter began using tempera paints together, the child immediately painted a heavy red line down the centre of the art paper to define her territory (Figure 4.8). Her mother began carefully painting a pretty landscape on the left side of the picture. The child began copying her mother's drawing, but began adding more and more red paint to the green foliage in her tree. The tree soon turned into brown mud. While the mother was still painting her picture, the daughter picked up a separate piece of black paper and began smearing bright red paint on it with black spots, continuing to express her rage. Finally, when she was asked what was happening, her lower lip protruded and she began crying profusely, saying: 'Mommy always does everything better than me.' It was then possible to coach

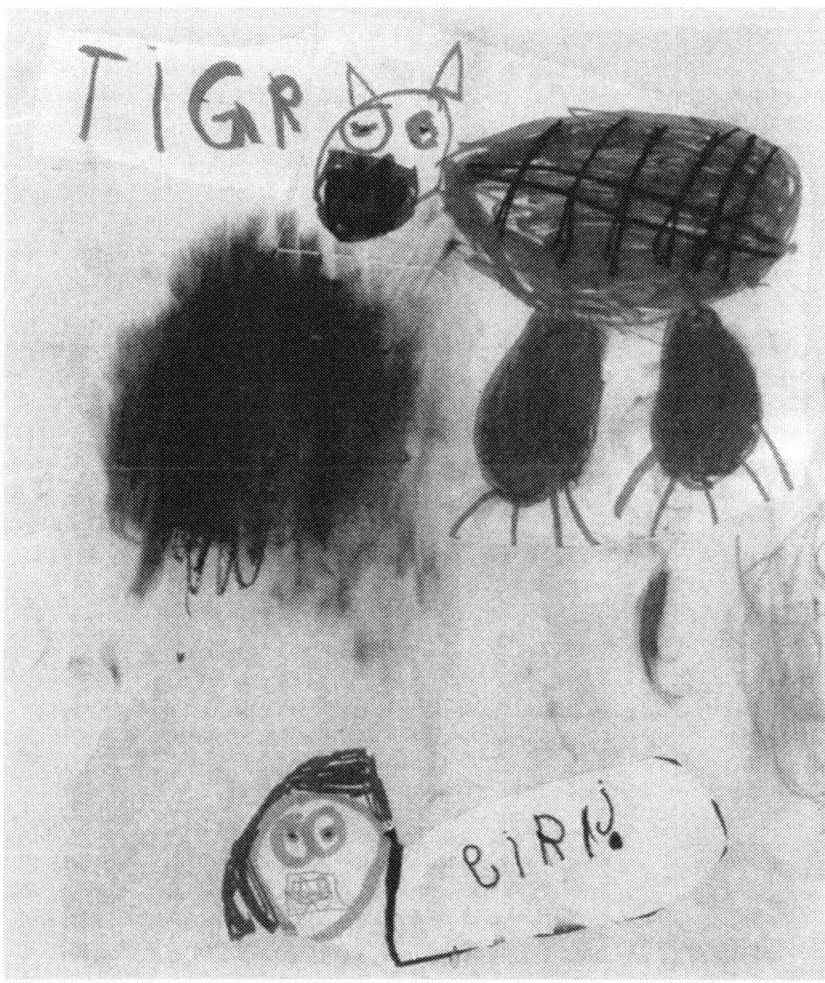

Figure 4.7 'My mother, the tiger'

the mother into providing nurturing for the child, which she was better able to do once she understood what was going on. After several minutes of the mother cuddling and consoling her daughter, they were asked to do another painting together. They were then able to work together much more harmoniously. In the second painting, the child painted no line of separation, nor did she obliterate anything in her half of the picture (Figure 4.9).

When the mother and child appeared for their session the following week, however, competition and power struggles were again evident as they argued throughout the entire joint execution of a large collage made of white paper

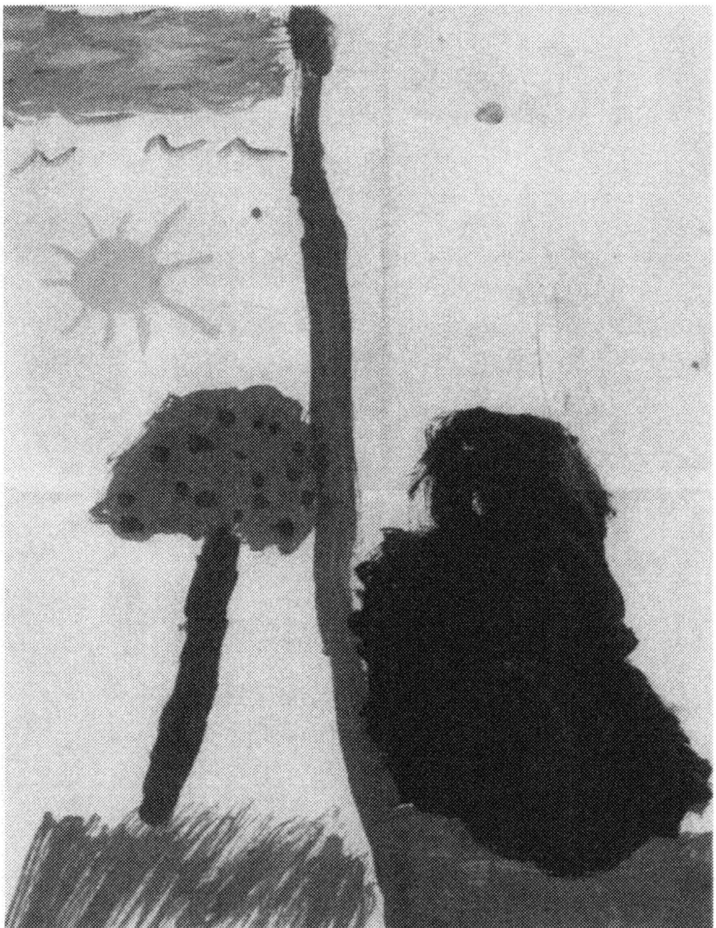

Figure 4.8 Mother and daughter painting together while angry

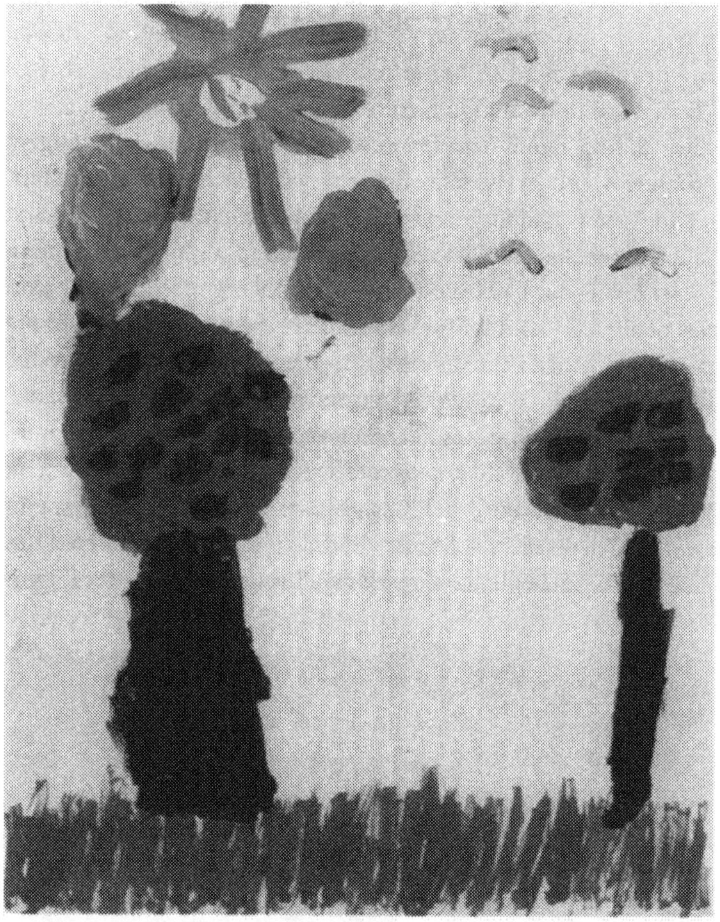

Figure 4.9 Mother and daughter painting together after resolution of feelings

with smaller bits of paper. The mother incessantly attempted to control her daughter's placement of collage materials, and vice versa. The two of them cut the paper into small geometric shapes, which Marie filled in with various coloured crayons. The two of them argued throughout the project, ordering each other where to paste the bits of paper. The final product was chaotic and neither mother nor daughter exhibited any joy in the finished art production (Figure 4.10). Even though progress had been made in the preceding session, this session illustrated the difficulty in effecting a change in behaviour in a short period of time.

My work with Marie proceeded in individual sessions over the next few months because the mother regularly found excuses not to attend further sessions with her. Later on, Marie returned from a two-week visit with her natural father and drew a large picture of a life-sized male phallus while with her parents during family therapy. Marie insisted that the drawing was of a 'Heart' (Figure 4.11). In the same drawing with the 'Heart', Marie had drawn 'Hansel and Gretel' standing next to each other, neither with any clothes on, with male and female genitalia respectively, along with genital penetration of 'Gretel'. Her behaviour had become considerably regressed and she exhibited a good deal of anxiety. The family therapist gave the picture to me and I reported my suspicions of sexual abuse to the authorities. I sent the drawing to the Police Department along with my required written report of suspicion of sexual abuse. Unfortunately, the drawing was not taken very seriously and it was at this point that I made the decision ultimately to do research into children's drawings as possible clues to sexual abuse. In hindsight, when comparing the drawing of the 'Heart' with a Christmas tree Marie had drawn earlier, I discovered that Marie had imbedded the same phallic shape (as well as size) into the tree (Figure 4.12).

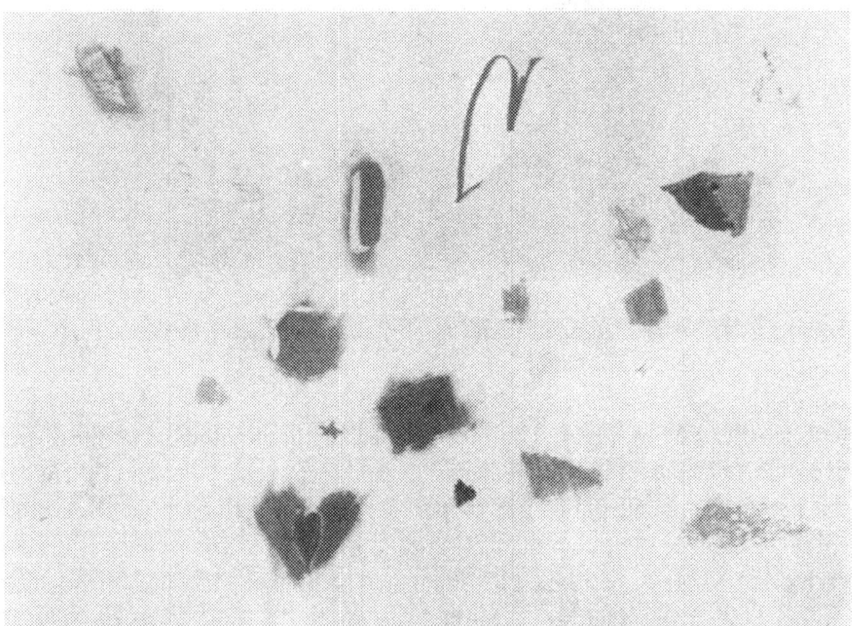

Figure 4.10 'Power struggle'

It is also interesting to note that she drew the Christmas tree on the same day she was to visit her natural father.

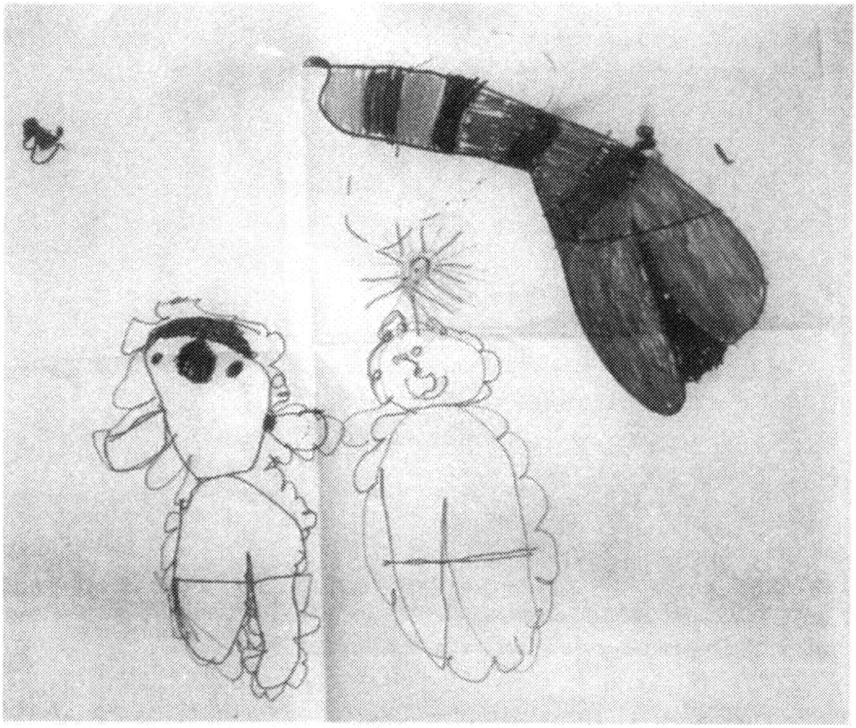

Figure 4.11 'A Heart' and 'Hansel and Gretel'

Marie's mother became hostile toward me at that point and failed to bring her for any more sessions for another two months. The family therapist was finally able to coax her into bringing the child back for further therapy. Marie, however, refused to do any more artwork for me from that point on. I proceeded to work with her using play therapy techniques with toys and puppets.

As my work with Marie continued, I knew that I would be moving to another city within the next two months and discussed with Marie's mother and stepfather the possibility of turning the case over to my supervisor, who was an expert on child sexual abuse cases. The stepfather became highly anxious and said he did not think that would be a good idea. Around the same time Marie had come to therapy sessions twice with a discharge on the back of her dress, but with no recent visits to see her natural father. I began to suspect that her stepfather might now be a possible offender. I again reported my suspicions to the Police Department, leaving the investigative aspects of the case entirely in

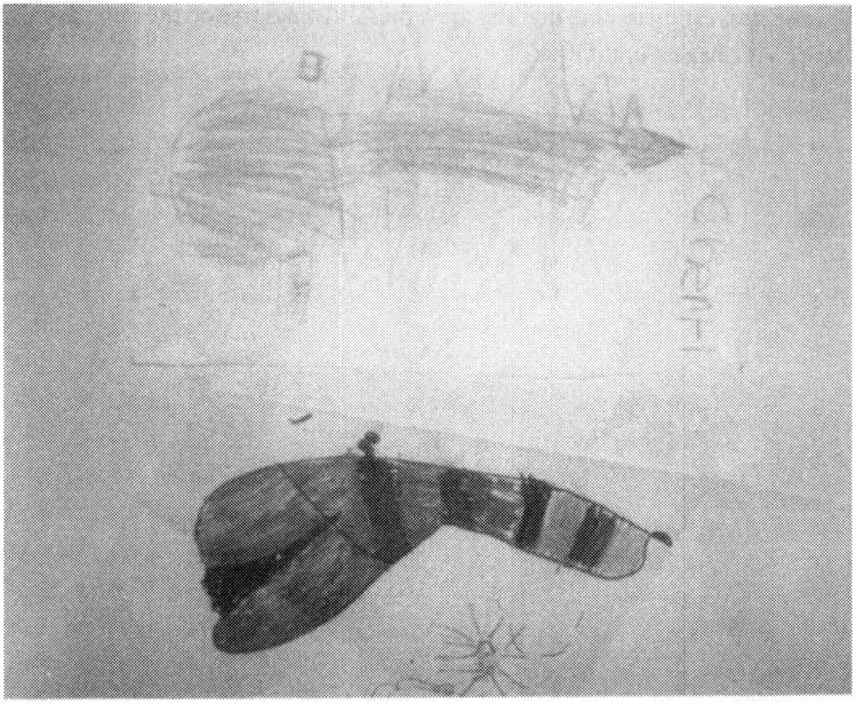

Figure 4.12 Comparison of the 'Heart' with the 'Christmas Tree'

their hands. My final session with Marie was spent playing with toys. At the end of the session, she drew a picture on a chalkboard of her house and crossed out the bathroom window. She also said that her parents' bedroom should be in a 'yukky green' colour. My interpretation was that she was possibly being abused in the bathroom, which is a common place for sexual abuse to occur. I did not, however, attempt to derive any details from her, but continued to relay my concerns to the authorities.

My role in this case was several-fold. One was to establish a trusting relationship with Marie and to attempt to work through some of the difficulties she was having with her mother. While there was no suspicion of sexual abuse at the outset, the child's artwork began revealing images which aroused my suspicion. Her symptoms became worse and she regressed to a much younger developmental level around the same time that her artwork became more sexually explicit. In reviewing her previous artwork, I believe the child had been trying nonverbally to communicate with me about what was happening to her. Another role I played was to offer the mother therapeutic support in order to help her to deal with Marie more effectively. The use of artwork enabled Marie to express her feelings and conflicts in a variety of art media, including painting, drawing and clay sculpture. It also graphically revealed the dynamics between her and her mother. My final and perhaps the most important role was my attempt to protect Marie from further abuse. My relationship with the child was a warm one and she enthusiastically looked forward to coming to see me. Because I moved away, I did not learn the final outcome of this case. I would hope, however, that Marie's positive experience with a therapist would enable her to seek therapy in the future should she need it.

Many times working with sexually abused children is short-lived. It involves not only counselling and art therapy, but also vigilance in protecting them from further abuse. When children made disclosures of sexual abuse to me, it was not unusual for their mothers to stop bringing them for further treatment. I had, however, served as a catalyst for further investigation and ultimate protection of these children. Even though the therapeutic relationship may come to an end, it is important to remember that the therapist has nevertheless played a vital role.

Group work and the use of art in counselling

The use of art with counselling in groups and theoretical considerations were discussed in Chapter 1. Children's groups are especially useful and provide a setting where poor socialisation skills and self-esteem can be improved. Sexually abused children need to know that they are not the only ones who have been abused. They often ask each other about their abuse experiences in an attempt to make sense of what happened to them. It is not unusual for child survivors of sexual abuse to grow into middle age before they meet anyone else who likewise has been abused. Unfortunately many never do, and carry with them the belief that no one could ever understand what they have been through. To meet other survivors who are ordinary people helps them to overcome feelings of stigma and isolation.

Case example: Group of sexually abused girls

This work was carried out in an established treatment programme in California with referrals coming from various sources including the District Attorney's office and Adult and Juvenile Probation departments. The programme offered therapeutic services to sexually abused children, their siblings, their mothers and to their offending fathers or other offenders, including adolescent offenders. The female children in the group ranged from age 7 to 11. The group sessions were held for one and a half hours each and the duration was a total of eight months. The first half-hour of the sessions involved verbal counselling where various issues were explored along with events currently happening in the girls' lives. The second half-hour was spent being involved in artwork and the final portion of the session was spent talking about the artwork and tying together any other issues. Specific therapeutic goals for each age group of children were set by the programme and we were expected to incorporate them into our work. My co-therapist was a clinical social worker who had a considerable amount of counselling experience and was enthusiastic about including art therapy techniques in the group counselling process.

All of the girls in the group had been sexually abused by their fathers. For many, the disclosure of the sexual abuse resulted in dramatic and very upsetting experiences as these children observed their fathers being taken away by police officers and sent to jail. The guilt they experienced was considerable. Their mothers, fortunately, were all in treatment within the same programme, along with their offending fathers. The girls frequently minimised what their fathers had done to them and felt sorry that they had been removed from the home, either in jail or involved in the diversion programme, being required to live in a separate residence. They were allowed no contact whatsoever with their daughters. The girls' relationships with their fathers included a good deal of affection along with the abuse, and it was understandable that they would be so confused. Getting these children to understand that what their fathers had done was *not* acceptable and that sex was appropriate only for consenting adults was sometimes quite difficult. These young girls exhibited symptoms of depression, anxiety, acting-out behaviour, eating disorders, inability to trust others, difficulty in expressing anger, relationship difficulties with their immature mothers and others, and extremely low self-esteem. The format of the group included spending some time having the girls share what they had done during the previous week. Any evidence of their fathers having contacted them was immediately relayed to appropriate staff in the programme for further investigation. If the offenders attempted in any way to contact their daughters against stringent court orders, they were expelled from the programme and sent to prison.

Each week, particular themes would emerge as the girls talked at the initial part of the sessions. These themes were then addressed with artwork in a variety of ways. The girls looked forward to the art process and asked at the beginning of each session whether they would be able to do artwork. At the outset, the goal of all art projects was to establish group cohesiveness and help the girls with their low self-esteem. Art projects were chosen which were non-threatening in subject matter, such as initially drawing or painting whatever they wanted to, group murals building a city together, collages of flowers from seed catalogues suggesting the theme 'If I were a flower, what would I look like?' and a magazine collage on the theme of 'This is Me'. It was interesting to note at the outset that the girls had some difficulty working together on their mural, but as the process continued, they began enjoying themselves more. In one session, paper was pre-cut into large circular shapes (a mandala) and the resultant collages of flowers were indeed lovely. Each girl shared with the group why they chose the flowers they did and much positive feedback was exchanged, further enhancing their self-esteem. Again, I gave them large pieces of pre-cut circular paper for their magazine collages of themselves, and it was interesting to note that in all cases, the girls depicted themselves as much older and more sexualised than they appeared outwardly, having chosen photographs of teenagers or adult women with heavy make-up (Figure 4.13).

The art projects were always met with a great deal of enthusiasm. As the group cohesiveness developed, I carefully listened to the main theme arising out

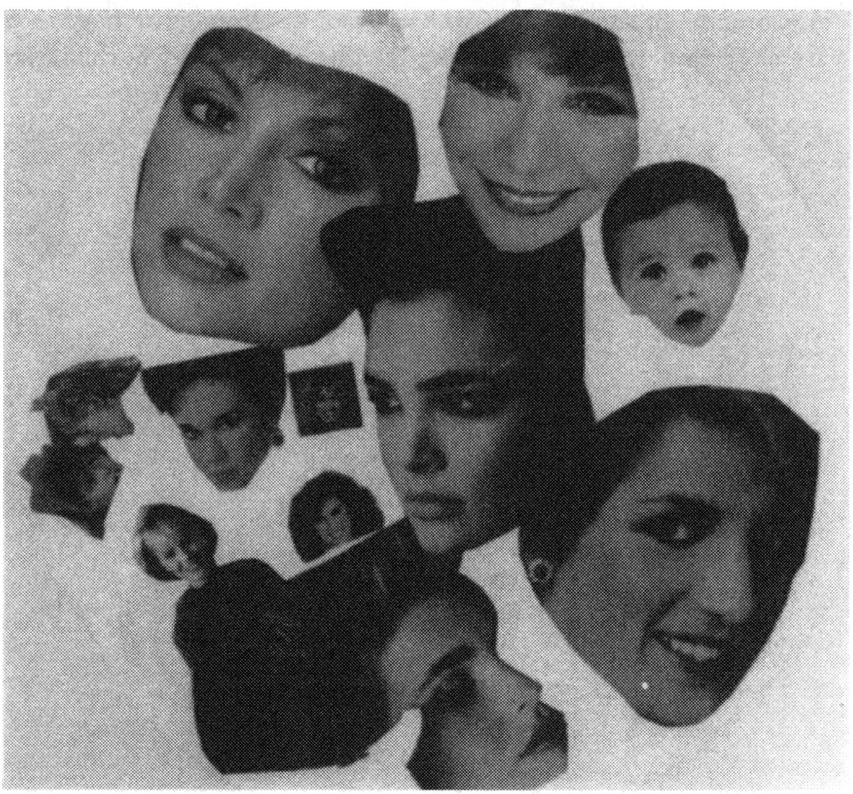

Figure 4.13 'This is Me'

of the counselling portion of the session. Topics began to emerge as the girls were ready to deal with them, such as family relationships, relationships with their mothers, who they told about their abuse, how they felt about having been sexually abused, and ultimately their feelings about the offender. I then asked the girls if they would like to carry the theme into an art project. Each session I brought along an assortment of white and coloured papers together with felt-markers, oil pastels and occasionally tempera paints and brushes.

Family relationships were explored through art materials. The girls were first asked to do a drawing of their families using coloured sugar paper and oil pastels. The drawings were then pinned up on a notice board and the girls stood back at a distance and talked about what they had put in their pictures. In a subsequent session, the girls created collages from cut-out shapes of coloured paper pasted onto a base of coloured paper (Figure 4.14). Each shape was to represent a different family member. A discussion followed about various family members and their relationships with each other. In a following group meeting, we explored the girls' relationships with their mothers. It was interesting to note that some of the girls identified very closely with their mothers. One child asked

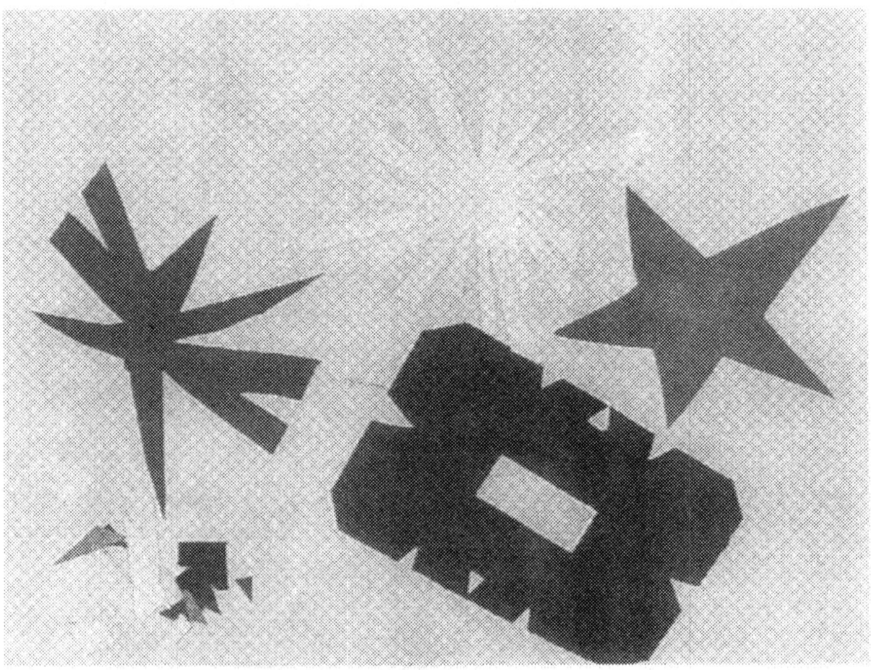

Figure 4.14 'Family Collage'

if she could make her drawing abstractly because otherwise she would draw herself and her mother looking exactly alike. Her abstract drawing, interestingly, resulted in the same phenomenon (Figure 4.15).

After about six months, the girls were able to deal with their feelings of depression and anger that they had been abused. Several sessions were spent creating art

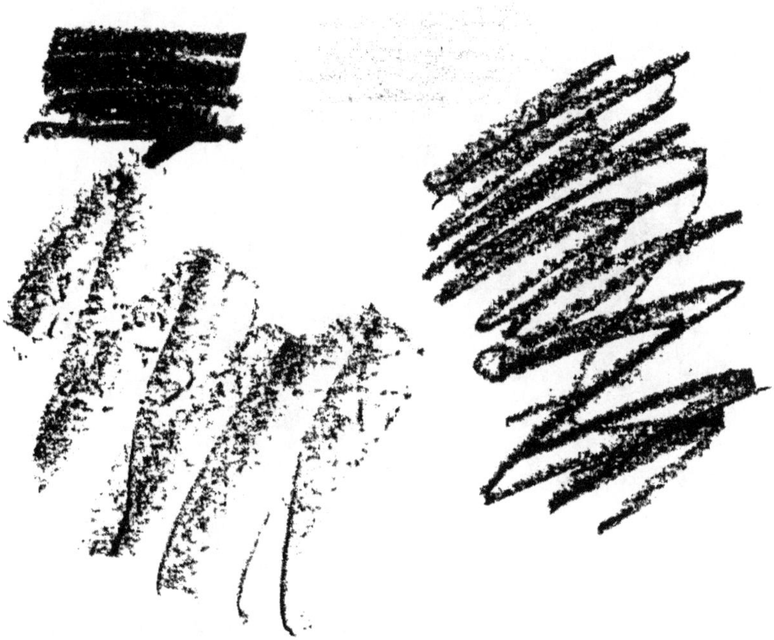

Figure 4.15 'My Mother and Myself'

projects expressing some of these emotions. When asked how they felt about having been sexually abused, one child illustrated how she felt mixed emotions including anger, confusion and guilt (Figure 4.16). The girls gradually began to select black paper spontaneously and used oil pastels to illustrate their feelings. One very gifted child drew a picture of her father, the offender, in jail. She illustrated herself holding a balloon to show her love for her father. She was crying on the steps of the prison and standing in a pool of tears (Figure 4.17). This particular piece of artwork very dramatically demonstrates the intense feelings and confusion that survivors of sexual abuse commonly experience.

When the eight-month period was coming to an end, I was leaving the programme to work elsewhere. It was important to let the girls know at least a month in advance that I would be leaving and to be able to discuss why I was going. The girls

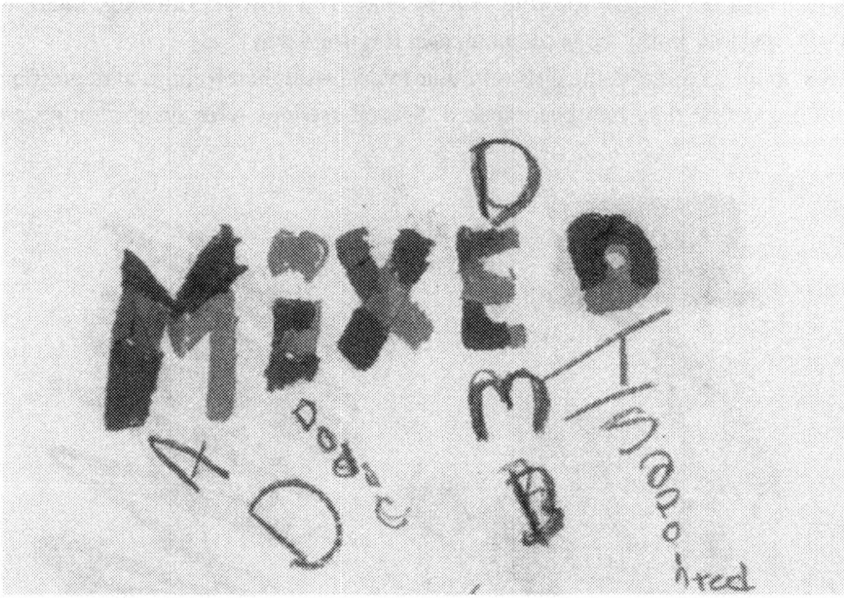

Figure 4.16 'Mixed Feelings'

needed a forum to express their feelings about saying good-bye and to have reinforced by myself that it was in no way their fault that I was leaving. Therapists need to be prepared for children's emotional reactions during the final stages of therapy. One child, for example, came to me and threw her arms around me, telling me that she loved me. Another child who I had no idea had become so attached to me cried for quite a while at the end of our last session; I needed to spend time with her consoling her. Her own mother had abandoned her many times, and for her, it was a reliving of the same painful experience. It was always very difficult to maintain my own emotional distance when this occurred, but I have concluded over the years that there is nothing wrong with letting those with whom we work know that we truly do care about them. This is especially true when working with survivors of sexual abuse, children and adults alike.

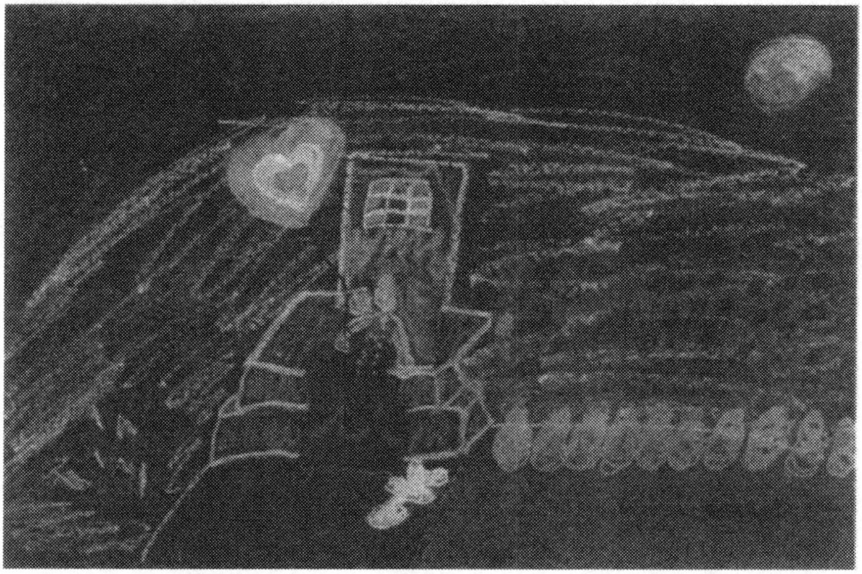

Figure 4.17 'Love and Sadness for My Father'

Summary

This chapter has presented three case examples of working with sexually abused children. The first case illustrated how art was used in working with a 3-year-old child who had been severely sexually abused. The second case demonstrated work with a 5-year-old girl and her mother. The third case was a group of young girls between the ages of 7 and 11 whose fathers had sexually abused them. It demonstrated how the use of a variety of art materials and approaches can be used within a group setting and how enthusiastically these children became involved in the art process to address their many issues as survivors of sexual abuse.

I found in many instances in working with children with considerable psychological problems that when sexual abuse was strongly suspected, the mother often became angry and did not want to bring the child for therapy any longer. I learned, however, that I had to be the catalyst to set in motion the possibility of protecting these children from further abuse. I also discovered that many times these mothers would eventually continue in therapy with another therapist or become involved in treatment programmes which I had recommended. The girls' group, for example, consisted of children whose mothers had worked through their denial and had enrolled their children as well as themselves in a rigorous therapeutic programme. Most mothers of sexually abused children go through a period of shock and denial at the outset. In these cases my consolation has been that if sexually abused children cannot be protected (which tragically is often the case), it is hoped that as adults they will be able to come forward for further treatment. Chapter 5 will focus on problems of mothers of sexually abused children in more detail.

CHAPTER 5

The Use of Art in Counselling Mothers of Sexually Abused Children

The importance of counselling for mothers of survivors of sexual abuse cannot be overemphasised. Unfortunately in many settings their treatment and support are largely neglected. This chapter is based on therapeutic work with mothers of children who were victims of incest or other forms of sexual abuse (Hagood 1991a). It represents my own clinical experience with approximately 130 of these mothers since 1983. Where it was possible to involve the use of art, mothers typically responded enthusiastically, reporting that they were able to gain more insight into their problems through the artwork they had created. My work in California took place in a variety of settings including programmes specialising in the treatment of families of sexually abused children. In Scotland, my work with mothers of sexually abused children has been carried out within the National Health Service or in private practice.

It must be emphasised that there are many variations in the characteristics of mothers of sexually abused children and they should not be pigeon-holed in any way. Earlier literature tended to describe mothers of sexually abused children globally in terms of considerable pathology, which unfortunately fed into the common assumption that these mothers were largely to blame for the abuse. More recent writers, however, suggest otherwise. In a review of the literature, for example, Joyce (1997) concluded that, on average, mothers of sexually abused children have no more serious psychological problems than mothers of nonabused children. Joyce strongly challenges the notion that mothers collude with the sexual abuse of their children. This attitude sadly still persists within many areas of clinical practice, as well as the criminal justice system, as a reason for the occurrence of sexual abuse. The mothers with whom I worked varied in the degree and extent of psychological problems. This chapter addresses these difficulties and attempts to demonstrate how the use of art has facilitated the therapeutic process. A case example illustrating how these mothers participated in the art process is also included.

Mothers of sexually abused children

When incest or any other form of sexual abuse is disclosed and reported to legal authorities, not only the victimised child but also the whole family is thrown into a state of crisis. The mother is no exception. Mothers have reported feelings of shock, numbness, anger, horror, fear of losing their minds and so on, when learning that their husbands, boyfriends or someone outside the immediate family, either a relative or a neighbour, had been sexually interfering with their child. A common reaction for a mother who is able to believe her child is to take the side of the child and begin a long period of blame and anger toward her partner or other abuser. It is extremely rare for the abuser ('perpetrator' or 'offender' in legal terms) to admit to such an accusation. On the other hand, the mother truly may be unable to believe what has happened and sometimes sides with the abuser, accusing the child of lying (Bentovim *et al.* 1988). I have seen conflicted mothers suffering considerable emotional turmoil, being very much in love with their husbands but feeling protective toward their daughters at the same time.

Both child and adult survivors of sexual abuse are reluctant to disclose their sexual abuse to their mothers for fear of hurting them. In the United States, it is estimated that the vast majority of incidents of sexual abuse are never reported. It is fairly safe to assume that this situation occurs in other countries as well. In Scotland and other parts of the United Kingdom it is common for children who are sexually abused to mature and live out their entire adulthood with serious psychological difficulties and never to have the courage to disclose the abuse to family members for fear of what other people think and/or breaking the family apart. I have heard older survivors say that they could not tell their elderly mothers because 'it would kill her'. The pressure on such survivors to keep the secret to themselves is immense.

Goodwin, McCarthy and DiVasto (1981) found in their study that 24 per cent of mothers of sexually abused children were sexually abused as children themselves and it is these mothers who are most likely to exhibit considerable psychopathology. When disclosure is made that their child or children have been sexually abused, they are likely to suffer the symptoms of PTSD with the disclosure triggering their own unresolved trauma (Berliner 1995). The emotional distress of these mothers is considerable and is strongly related to whether or not they receive support from family and friends (Hiebert-Murphy 1998). Recurrent nightmares, inability to sleep, flashbacks, extreme irritability, suicidal ideation and hypervigilance are likely symptoms which may be reactivated when they learn of their child's sexual abuse.

Faller (1988) found that some mothers of sexually abused children are protective but some are not. Some mothers are very nurturing but others are not. Some mothers believed their children when they reported the abuse; sadly, others did not. We are becoming increasingly aware that sometimes a mother sexually abuses her child, more commonly a son. This is usually not disclosed unless he has been in long-term psychotherapy (Lawson 1993). During the 1990s, unfortunately there were increasing reports of men having been abused by their mothers in childhood. Because this often does not come to light until adulthood, these incidents typically are not recorded in public statistics. Krug (1989) argued for the need to become more aware of the incidence of mother–son incest because of its long-term consequences to men. I have worked with a few mothers who were involved in the sexual abuse of their daughters. In these cases these mothers were usually pressured by their partners to involve the child in a *ménage à trois* situation, and because of the mothers' emotional dependency and inability to be assertive, they went along with it. I have seen a few extreme cases where mothers have made their children (both male and female) sexually available to male friends. The damage to these survivors is severe. When a mother is involved in the sexual abuse of her children, she is just as much responsible for the abuse as male offenders. The focus of this chapter, however, is on non-offending mothers. In this chapter any reference to 'offender' is in the male gender, but this is not to imply that women do not also commit sexual offences.

To place responsibility onto a non-offending mother for the sexual abuse of her children is non-productive. Full responsibility *always* lies with the abuser. To blame the non-offending mother takes the heat off the offender, scapegoating and further abusing the mother. In my view, reunification programmes where the goal is to allow the offender to return home after he has received a considerable amount of treatment should not make mothers responsible for monitoring his behaviour. If he is still not to be trusted, he should not be back at home. I have seen mothers in treatment programmes psychologically abused with this approach, being made to feel excessively responsible for their partner's recovery.

In my clinical experience, the many non-offending mothers with whom I worked ran the entire gamut, from highly motivated women to those with little or no incentive to obtain therapy for themselves, much less their children. Fortunately, however, most of the mothers I have seen were quite serious about gaining help in order to enhance their parental roles and to learn better ways of protecting their children from further abuse. For the most part, they also welcomed the opportunity to obtain therapy for themselves in order to gain insight into their own difficulties. In some instances, older mothers learned about the abuse later in life when their daughter (or son) was well into adulthood and finally disclosed the abuse. In this situation the psychological impact was usually severe and these mothers had even more difficulty in coping with the revelation, reacting with considerable guilt. Sexual abuse of female children is often perpetrated by a brother or other relative such as an uncle, cousin or grandfather. The mother is in serious conflict, particularly if she has a close relationship with her offending son or other relative. She may have a particularly difficult time believing the disclosure and when she does, she is likely to blame herself.

Sadly, I have dealt with a few mothers who were poorly motivated, highly manipulative and in a state of extreme denial. Lying and conning sometimes occurred in individual sessions, which was discovered only upon consultation with other involved professionals. In these cases, it was not unusual to learn that the mother had been telling her social worker one thing and myself something entirely different. Anger toward me was often openly expressed whenever limits were set or further disclosures were made by the child of sexual abuse by other family members. Attempts were sometimes made to scapegoat me by alleging that I was 'making up' such disclosures. Needless to say, working with this type of mother can be both challenging and extremely frustrating. In instances when I had to report the new disclosure of abuse and the mother became extremely angry, she typically felt she could no longer trust me. In circumstances where I could no longer work with her therapeutically, I referred her elsewhere. My role in reporting such disclosures to the authorities was legally and morally mandated; bringing about the crisis was necessary not only to protect the child, but also to create an opportunity for the mother to become engaged in the therapeutic process elsewhere.

My more recent experience with Scottish mothers of sexually abused children has indicated that they have been, for the most part, less willing to come forward for help. Self-help groups, however, are gradually becoming more available to offer support specifically for these mothers. To date, few opportunities exist in the United Kingdom for these mothers to receive psychological treatment specifically for their own issues as mothers of sexually abused children. Little focus is given to these women unless they are survivors of sexual abuse themselves and come into the health service system because of their own symptoms. Published work specifically focused on the use of art with such mothers is only now beginning to be developed in the United Kingdom (Murphy, in press).

Mothers of sexually abused children fall into a broad range of occupational, cultural and socio-economic backgrounds. Among the mothers with whom I worked, some were professional women with important positions. At the other end of the spectrum were blue-collar workers or unemployed working-class women. Ethnic backgrounds of women in California included Caucasians, Blacks and Hispanics. In Scotland, all women have been Caucasian, but strongly influenced by the Scottish culture, which stigmatises seeking therapy much more than in California, where the highest rate of disclosure of sexual abuse in the United States occurs. Such stigmatisation makes it difficult for these mothers to come forward for help. I have found that no matter which ethnic or cultural group these women belonged to, the psychological pain and the reactions to their children being abused were the same.

Therapeutic goals

Facilitating self-awareness, improving self-esteem, encouraging personal growth and behavioural changes and developing the mother's protective abilities are primary therapeutic goals. Helping a non-offending mother to learn how she unknowingly and inadvertently has played into the drama can be very helpful. To look back at possible signs and clues that her child was being abused and to help her to understand why she did not connect these cues with sexual abuse is reassuring.

Whether or not sexually abused themselves, most of the women with whom I have worked have come from severely dysfunctional families. Symptoms of extremely low self-esteem, poor self-identity and a general lack of assertiveness are common. The child's victimisation frequently brings up issues previously unaddressed or repressed by the mother in cases where she too was sexually abused as a child.

Living with a sex offender entails many difficult problems as these men frequently are emotionally, physically and sometimes sexually abusive to their partners as well. Conning and manipulation are tactics that sex offenders commonly use, not only with their victims but also in their relationships in general. These women frequently experienced feelings of guilt, intense anger, helplessness and hopelessness. Some have poor parenting skills because of their own childhood history. In instances where they were unable to provide their children with adequate supervision and protection, it was usually because they did not receive it themselves from their own mothers. Sometimes they became emotionally or physically abusive to their children because of the abuse they received from their partner or their inability to cope with the extraordinary stresses they were experiencing. Poor assertiveness skills and inability to set appropriate limits with their children were also common problems. Encouraging these mothers to attend parenting classes and work on their parenting skills is frequently an essential part of treatment.

Considerable anger toward their daughters for being 'the other woman' are often strong, but these women typically have a great deal of difficulty admitting such feelings. Resolution of these feelings is very important in order to improve their relationships with their daughters. Learning about role reversal and how they have turned to their children inappropriately as confidants for support is another issue they may need help with. In most instances where they have turned to their children it was because they had no other supportive friends or relatives. Encouraging them to develop healthy peer relationships with other adults outside their own dysfunctional family systems is another important therapeutic strategy.

A commonly used defence mechanism among these mothers is that of denial, according to Sgroi (1982). 'Denial' is a term originating from psychoanalysis and defined as an unconscious defence mechanism in which painful perceptions are denied. Often the mother will truly have considerable difficulty believing the child's disclosure and may attempt to get the child to retract her story in an effort to make the problem disappear (Faller 1988). Much of this inability to perceive the reality of the abuse is genuine and not malicious. It is not difficult to understand why denial can be so strong, since the mother may have her life turned upside down if the allegations are true and her husband or boyfriend is ordered out of the home. With no other means of support, she may have to return to the workforce. If she has no marketable skills, she may become a part of the government benefit system or have to turn to her parents for support. Because such a situation is so threatening to her survival, she truly *cannot* take in what has happened. She will need much reassurance to overcome the guilt she is likely to experience when she ultimately does come out of denial, emphasising that the offender was totally to blame for the abuse. Assisting the mother to understand that she did not consciously wake up in the morning and decide that she wanted her daughter to be sexually abused gives her more self-acceptance so that she does not need to hold on to her denial as strongly.

One of the key advantages to group work is that when these mothers hear that they are not alone, they are able to come out of denial more quickly.

Mothers who are unable to be nurturing and protective need to be treated with compassion as well. When unprotective mothers have been sexually abused themselves and have not dealt with their feelings about what happened to them, they are sometimes unable to be angry with the abuser and turn the anger in on themselves. This passivity may be transmitted to an inability to believe or to protect their own children, or in some instances to blame the children in the same way they blame themselves. Many survivors of sexual abuse have problems blaming the offender rather than themselves. Sadly, some mothers who are unable to protect their children may refuse to leave their offending partners because they are so needy and emotionally dependent on them and the child may need to be placed outside the home.

Some mothers who were also victims of sexual abuse may have developed a borderline personality organisation, making their therapeutic treatment very difficult (Mark 1980). The link between borderline personality disorder and a history of sexual abuse has been well established, as well as a reliance on self-harming behaviours to cope with emotional pain. If a mother has a history of sexual abuse, it is important to assess further for such self-harming behaviours such as self-cutting, head-banging, eating disorders, drug/alcohol abuse, suicide attempts and so on. Appropriate referrals for more specialised treatment, such as Dialectic Behaviour Therapy (Linehan 1993), may also be in order.

Intense fear of intimacy and possible abandonment may make it difficult for some of these mothers to remain in relationship to the therapist, particularly in one-on-one therapy (Austin 1980). Anger at the therapist for not being able to supply an endless source of emotional support or for setting limits and boundaries is common, and the therapist may be seen as a 'bad' mother. A high incidence of missed appointments and other forms of resistance can also create negative counter-transference issues for the therapist, who may in turn begin to feel abused; there is a risk of the therapeutic relationship breaking down. Treatment of these women in group therapy often minimises this problem. Mothers with borderline features frequently use the defence mechanism of 'splitting' where they choose one mental health professional to be the 'good mother/father' and the other to be the 'bad mother/father' (Mark 1980). They will sometimes attempt to turn two professionals against each other. Unless professionals are aware of this common phenomenon, a good deal of misunderstanding can develop between team members as the split is enacted on a broader basis within the treatment system. When therapists within the same setting find themselves polarising over a particular client, they need to look at how the women's dynamics may be having a 'ripple effect' on the therapeutic system.

It is also important to screen for domestic violence because many women who are being physically assaulted by their partners are unlikely to disclose it unless asked. Children who grow up in a family where there is domestic violence are more likely to be sexually abused within that family. Likewise, children in these families may be subjected to severe physical abuse themselves, and the emotional abuse and resultant PTSD experienced by children who observe their mothers being beaten is considerable (Perry 1997). The therapist must be constantly vigilant to notice any further abuses, sexual or physical, which may be going on within the family, and to see that they are appropriately reported to legal authorities. If a mother is suffering from physical assault, she may need the additional services of a battered women's shelter. She should be properly coached on how to find a place of safety if the violence starts again. She also needs to understand the dynamics of wife-battering (Campbell 1993; Jones and Schechter 1992; Martin 1977) and to realise that the violence perpetrated on her is *never* her fault.

Chemical dependency may complicate the picture as mothers with drug- and alcohol-related problems need special consideration for referral to appropriate treatment and recovery programmes. Occasionally a mother may be dependent on the abusing father for her supply of drugs or alcohol, which only adds to treatment difficulties. In these cases, her ability to protect her children may be minimal or non-existent. Confronting her directly with her addiction often jeopardises the possibility of her attendance in therapy, and she may refuse to bring her children for more therapy. The subject of addiction needs to be handled very delicately. Some American programmes insist on random drug tests with the reports coming back to the treatment agency as a criterion for the mother staying in the programme. If a mother has an alcohol problem she may be required to bring proof of attendance at regular Alcoholics Anonymous meetings. If a mother wants an opportunity to retain custody of her child, she must cooperate. In private practice settings this kind of monitoring is much more difficult.

Family dynamics

Many of the women with whom I have worked have had difficult marital relationships. These women tended to be over-nurturers toward their childlike and often passive husbands and carried the bulk of the responsibility for the family.

They also exhibited many 'co-dependent' behaviours similar to those found in alcoholic marriages. Co-dependency is a word derived from American chemical dependency treatment programmes in the late 1970s. Beattie (1987) defines a co-dependent person as 'one who has let another person's behaviour affect him or her, and who is obsessed with controlling that person's behaviour' (p.31). The link between alcohol abuse and sexual abuse has been well established and these women may have learned the role of co-dependency in order to survive. These behaviours often consist of over-nurturing and rescuing their irresponsible partners, inadvertently enabling them to remain so.

Earlier writers, such as Stern and Meyer (1980), observed three types of marital relationships in mothers of sexually abused children: 'dependent-domineering', where there is an inadequate man and a stronger domineering woman; 'possessive-passive', where the father controls the marital relationship and family, and the mother tends to be downtrodden and passive; and 'dependent-dependent' (or 'incestrogenic'), where one or both of the parents have been sexually abused by their parents or other family members as children. In this third case, these adults cling to each other and cannot meet each other's needs or those of their children. They instead look to their children for love and parenting. Mothers and daughters frequently reverse their roles. The phenomenon of the 'parentified child' is seen where the child controls the relationship and the mother behaves in a childlike and dependent manner, leaning excessively on her daughter for emotional support (Machotka, Pittman and Kalman 1967). Guilt feelings also tend to make the mother more susceptible to manipulation by the child. The sexually abused child eventually feels so responsible for his or her mother's feelings that the abuse may not be disclosed for fear of hurting her. In instances where mothers have not been emotionally available to their children, there is likely to be a good deal of fear on the part of the child that he or she will not be believed.

Sexually abused children usually sense that if the secret is told, the family may break up and this usually adds to their burden of guilt. The offender sometimes threatens physical harm to the child or other family members if the secret is broken. Threats that may be as severe as murdering the child or someone else, or killing a favourite pet, are common. In addition, the abuser may convince the child victim that he or she likes it and is completely to blame. Other common threats are that no one will believe the child's story or that the abuser will go to prison and it will be the child's fault. Some stories I have heard from adult survivors regarding threats they received from their abusers were even more bizarre and horrifying. It is little wonder that these children have so much difficulty disclosing their abuse to their mothers.

Improving the mother–daughter bond is an important therapeutic goal espoused by Giarretto (1982), founder of the Parents United movement in the United States. The mother's feelings toward her daughter may have been negative over a long period of time, perhaps inadvertently making the child more vulnerable to the approaches of the abuser. Many of these mothers have also had poor relationships with their own mothers. Brooks (1983) hypothesised that mothers of incest victims may unconsciously project hostility toward their own mothers onto their daughters. This difficulty in the relationship between mother and daughter may create a weakening of the maternal bond and makes it easier for the daughter to turn to her father or another male father-figure to meet her emotional needs. She thus may become more vulnerable to the possibility of sexual abuse. Herman and Hirschman (1980) noted that the most striking feature they observed in incestuous families was an estrangement between mother and daughter prior to the occurrence of overt incest. Faller (1988), on the other hand, found in her research that a good number of mothers were indeed very nurturing and protective of their daughters. Nevertheless, overcoming such deep estrangement when it does exist is clearly a necessary goal for treatment. Regardless of relationship difficulties between the mother and daughter, again, the offender is *always* to blame.

While many of the family dynamics reviewed here are common to dysfunctional families in general, it is essential to realise that adding a sex offender to the family with his own individual pathological ways of functioning, such as lying, conning and abusive behaviours (see Chapters 7 and 8), compounds family problems several-fold. Earlier programmes strongly relied on family systems theory without emphasising the impact on a family system of a sex offender's own pre-existing pathology and propensity for sexual abuse. It was believed that strengthening the bond between the mother and child would lessen the likelihood of further abuse, still placing responsibility for the abuse onto the mother. It was the common view at that time in the field of child sexual abuse that many offenders were 'regressed' offenders, not paedophiles, and that because their emotional and sexual needs were not met by their partners, they 'regressed' and turned to their children, again insinuating that if the mother had been more responsive, the abuse would not have occurred (see Chapter 8 for further discussion). The evidence since then has demonstrated that many adult sex offenders began their abuse in adolescence or even earlier (Cunningham and MacFarlane 1991). Research into sex offenders has revealed many more complex problems associated with offender treatment than a family systems approach alone could address. The major insight achieved in the past few years was that many sex offenders were offending well before they became involved with their partners; blaming their offences on their 'dysfunctional family' is clearly inappropriate.

I have found it particularly useful to encourage these mothers to take a look at how they became involved with their offending partner at the outset. There were several common situations expressed by many of these women. Many expressed their sense of loneliness when they met their partner and his ability to 'charm' them and tell them what they needed to hear. His apparent 'love' for their children also was endearing. Low self-esteem and desperation to find a partner made them particularly vulnerable to such deception and manipulation. It is important that these mothers learn to become more independent and to meet their emotional needs in healthier ways. Lone mothers are particularly vulnerable to sex offenders who sometimes specifically target divorced or separated women with children. Advertisements, for example, on the Internet from men looking for someone with children is an ever-increasing problem at the present time. Sadly, some of these men may be sex offenders. A balance is needed, however, to avoid feeding into these women's paranoia about all men, assuming that they are all abusive, which is not the case. Helping them to become more psychologically healthy and to realise that they deserve to be treated well needs to be a main focus of therapy.

While it is good to help these women look at their relationship patterns, it is also extremely important not to perpetuate the myth that abused women *always* pick the same kind of partner. Such an assumption again tends to shift the blame for abuse onto the mother. It is believed by some professionals of psychoanalytic persuasion that women who suffered from father–daughter incest themselves 'unconsciously' select a partner like their fathers. This view seriously ignores the tremendous ability of offenders to con and manipulate vulnerable women. Research indicates that many women in domestically violent relationships had *no* previous abusive experiences either in their family of origin or in previous relationships with other partners (Jones and Schechter 1992). It is also the case that many women who become involved with sex offenders have no history of sexual abuse themselves.

Use of art in counselling mothers of sexually abused children

Art therapists have increasingly learned the value of using art in group work with mothers of sexually abused children (Hagood 1991a; Shields 1991). Any therapeutic issue can be addressed pictorially by the use of art materials. Many mothers of sexually abused children, for example, have considerable difficulty in expressing their emotions. Identifying their feelings can be facilitated in a variety of ways. It is possible, for example, to create collages with a variety of coloured papers which will help them to experience their feelings more easily. Cutting or tearing various coloured symbolic shapes with coloured sugar paper and pasting them onto a larger sheet of paper is one example. Another is the use of tissue paper which can be layered in various ways, mixing the colours for a wider variety of hues. Coloured crêpe paper can be moulded to make three-dimensional bas-relief creations. The less realistic the artwork, the more likely it is to elicit feelings. Magazine collage can be used effectively as well. Selecting pictures of various facial expressions commonly reveals what these women are feeling. Helping them to learn that it is healthy to experience the full gamut of feelings from anger, fear and sadness to hope, joy and happiness is essential.

Problem-solving can be done with drawings. Self-esteem can be enhanced by the creation of art products. Directly exploring issues such as feelings about their abused daughters, feelings about the offender, their relationships with their own mothers, their hopes for the future and so on can have a greater impact through the use of collage, drawings, paintings and sculptures. A sense of their own identity is often lacking and using magazine collages can help them to explore areas of possible employment, hobbies and social outlets. Creating artwork can help them to see themselves as useful women with their own unique qualities and to begin to form an identity of their own other than the stigma of being the mother of a sexually abused child.

Group work is useful in helping them to share how the sexual abuse of their child or children has affected them. As has been discussed, they are likely to experience strong and mixed feelings of anger, guilt, sadness, a sense of betrayal, inability to trust and jealousy. Helping them to learn that all these feelings are human and normal under the circumstances is important in order to help them to stop judging themselves so harshly for experiencing such negative emotions. Using artwork where they can actually *see* each other's thoughts, feelings and problems helps them to become more easily engaged in the therapeutic process. Expressing empathy and support for others in the group also aids in the healing process. Exploring issues around sexuality and feelings of shame and inadequacy need to be addressed and worked through.

Looking at relationship patterns with their current or previous partners is valuable using role-playing in groups. Much insight may be gained when two people pair off and do drawings together with one mother role-playing herself and the other role-playing the partner. Subsequently reversing roles and creating another drawing together helps them to see how they interact with their partners, as well as how their partners feel. The impact of 'seeing' the situation in the artwork is likely to be far stronger and more effective than just talking about it.

Exploring relationships with their own parents and learning about characteristics of dysfunctional families helps them to understand how they got to where they are at the moment, and may result in their feeling less self-critical. Creating family genograms with coloured collages can be useful in understanding their own family patterns and relationships (Bowen 1978; Lerner 1989; Lieberman 1979; Satir 1972). Cutting out shapes of coloured paper representing family members and pasting them onto a larger sheet of paper or sculpting family members with clay are two additional ways to incorporate artwork. Many of these women have unhealthy relationships with their own mothers, who often interfere in their lives and treat them as children. Doing drawings of themselves with their mothers, how they feel about them, and how they would like their relationship to be, is also a useful technique.

Individual work

Individual therapy with mothers of children who have been sexually assaulted provides an opportunity for the mother to receive more personalised attention. It allows her more focused therapy which is less available in a group setting. It provides a safe place to develop a trusting relationship with the therapist and to express feelings on a deeper level. A longer period of time may be spent processing artwork and exploring it more deeply than can be spent in group art therapy. The mother can be allowed to move from one piece of art to another, staying with her problem until it is better resolved. When working in a group, she is much more limited because time must be spent processing other group members' artwork.

Working with some mothers in individual therapy, however, may be extremely difficult unless the mother is highly motivated. She may need to deal with her own history of victimisation. When the mother is referred for individual treatment only and is not concurrently involved in a group, her motivation can be low without the additional reinforcement of group members. Unfortunately, once the crisis intervention stage (immediately after the abuse is disclosed) has passed and life becomes more routine, it may be more difficult to engage the mother in continuing long-term therapy for either herself or her child. Where there is reason to believe that the mother may not be truthful, it may be essential for the therapist, with appropriate consent, to consult on a regular basis with the social worker assigned through the local child protection agency to monitor the case. In some instances, sadly, there may be no social worker involved. A major therapeutic issue for such a mother may also be to help her to work through her own feelings of being victimised by the system.

On the brighter side, mothers who are beginning to come out of denial may be more therapeutically accessible. They are often happy to have the attention that individual therapy provides. It becomes an opportunity for them to explore their relationship patterns, to learn more about their family of origin, and to work through their feelings about their daughter's molestation (as well as their own, if such is the case). Individual sessions provide an opportunity for the mother to take an in-depth look at her situation. Art therapy techniques may be used addressing most of the issues discussed above.

Group work

A group setting provides a place for these mothers to learn to trust one another as well as the therapists involved. In my experience, the ideal situation for mothers of sexually abused children is to be in both individual and group treatment with individual and group therapists available to each other for regular consultation. If the mother is receiving therapy from both sources within a well-structured treatment programme, this is much more easily orchestrated. The mother needs peer support and feedback and to realise that she is not alone in her situation. As stated earlier, she is much less likely to remain in a state of denial after hearing stories from other women who are experiencing the same difficulties with group work providing such a forum. When she hears other mothers in the same situation, she is better able to come to terms with what has happened and learns to give support and consolation to others in the group (Hildebrand and Forbes 1987; Shields 1991). Incorporating artwork into whatever issues emerge during the group process is a highly effective way for these mothers not only to *see* their own problems, but also to observe what is going on with other group members at the same time.

Case example: Groupwork with mothers of sexually abused children

This case example describes an ongoing art therapy group consisting of women who were mothers of victims of sexual abuse (Hagood 1991a). The group was attended on a weekly basis by between five and twelve women within an agency that specialised in the treatment of sexually abused children and their families.

Group members had previously been involved in verbal counselling approaches. The group leaders consisted of myself and two other counsellors, who were keen to learn ways to incorporate the use of art materials into the group counselling process. Art therapy techniques were initiated and integrated into the usual therapeutic issues and served as a catalyst for group interaction. The artwork frequently uncovered feelings and problems that had been previously withheld on a verbal level and also served as a source of increasing self-awareness.

The women in this particular group were from a variety of career backgrounds. Occupational groups represented were executive secretaries, administrators, teachers, electronic assembly workers, food service workers and unemployed homemakers living on public benefits. The vast differences in their backgrounds, however, did not seem to interfere with their ability to become cohesive and very supportive to each other. Most women were well groomed and had pleasant personalities. Happy chattering was heard among the group members. Several women were considerably overweight; it usually transpired that they had been sexually abused themselves and used the excess weight as a defence against unwanted sexual advances. Denial of actual feelings was demonstrated during art therapy sessions where drawings were frequently made depicting extreme happiness. In reality, the circumstances these women experienced were such that it would have been virtually impossible to experience the joy shown in the artwork.

Feelings of anger and jealousy frequently are harboured by mothers toward daughters who have been incestually involved with their fathers (Bentovim *et al.* 1988), but such feelings were seldom openly expressed in this group. Angry feelings were often symbolically represented in artwork portraying their relationship with their daughters, but verbally denied. It is important to the therapeutic process for these women to acknowledge and express these feelings in an atmosphere of acceptance in order for them to develop healthier, more authentic relationships with their daughters.

The women in the group exhibited in their artwork a view of themselves as having little control over their lives. This perception not only was due to their own sense of learned helplessness, but also was reality based. The constant intrusion of professionals from within the legal and mental health systems, such as district attorneys, probation officers, investigative police officers, social workers, child protection workers, detectives, parole officers and welfare workers, gave these women an extreme sense of helplessness and reinforced their feelings of being victimised. In addition, they were expected to be involved in a treatment programme where staff members and counsellors also had an integral role in managing their lives. These factors, along with housing difficulties and work-related problems, in fact did create an actual ongoing situation contributing to their sense of helplessness. It was necessary to encourage these women to discuss such problems with each other outside of the group to prevent the entire group time from being taken up with complaining and little actual therapy taking place.

Once these women realised the serious consequences of the sexual abuse to their daughters' mental health, considerable guilt was expressed over not having consciously realised that the incest was going on. In some instances, clues had actually been given by the daughter, such as preoccupation with cleanliness, layering of clothing, indirect attempts to disclose the abuse verbally to their mother, failing in schoolwork, nightmares and so on. Unfortunately, because of the horror of the possibility of incest, some mothers could not see these rather obvious symptoms. Much support was required for these women to be able to forgive themselves for their denial mechanisms unconsciously at work. Help was also needed in uncovering ways they might unknowingly have colluded with the incest, such as being absent from home a great deal, leaving their children with their father alone, being unavailable emotionally, missing clues given by their daughters and so on. It was important to stress that the purpose of understanding the part these mothers played in the family scenario was not to blame and accuse them, but rather to help them to gain insight. It is also essential to reinforce to the mother that her partner had possibly committed sexual offences well before he had become involved with her, obviously without her knowledge.

Techniques using art in counselling

Whenever it was determined that it would be more therapeutic to let the women take their artwork home or to share it with their individual therapists, they were encouraged to do so. It was always pointed out that the artwork was primarily theirs, and they were given the choice of what to do with it. This was therapeutic in itself because it taught the women to feel entitled to ask for what they wanted – an issue they constantly needed to work on. They were encouraged to keep their art projects in an appropriate place at home as a reinforcer of the issues they had explored in the group.

A good number of these women require improved socialisation skills because they have been isolated from relationships outside of the immediate family. This situation again reflected a common characteristic of closed dysfunctional family systems (Minuchin 1974). In such families there is typically little interaction with people in the community except for relatives and therefore no means of learning healthier ways of functioning. After the sexual abuse is disclosed, they may become even more isolated out of fear of their friends or neighbours finding out about the abuse. Hence, the family pathology becomes reinforced and is believed to be 'normal'. It was not unusual to see the amazement on their faces when these women discovered that not everyone lived as they had. The group setting provided an opportunity to improve on peer relationships as well as to explore problems specific to being mothers of victims of sexual abuse. Receiving support, nurturing and feedback from other mothers as well as realising that their problems were shared provided benefits that individual therapy alone could not have afforded (Hildebrand and Forbes 1987). As other group members told their stories, it was not unusual to see memories return about incidents leading up to the child's abuse, enabling mothers to make more sense out of what happened. Often the mother's memories of their own sexual victimisation as a child began to surface. The unconscious defence mechanism of repression of one's own past abuse became more difficult as stories were disclosed in the group. It is important to state, however, that some mothers have not been sexually abused; no pressure should be placed on them to recall such abuse.

Group members were encouraged to paint or draw a particular theme already being addressed verbally. In so doing, all mothers were drawn into the process and it was not unusual to see group members who previously had not shared their issues on a verbal basis suddenly become more involved as they were asked to say something about their artwork. The option not to share was always available: this was important with these women because it afforded them an opportunity to assert themselves and set personal boundaries. It was common, however, for all group members to participate once others began sharing their artwork. The more outgoing group members frequently expressed how happy they were to hear from the quieter ones and the door was opened for more self-disclosure in sessions to come.

When these women became involved in expressing themselves through art, they usually moved into a playful phase. At the beginning of most sessions when the art materials were presented, there was an initial phase of chattering and laughing. Comments such as 'I feel like a child again' were heard. After having been through so much trauma, these women found such playing to be very healing. Defences began to come down and group cohesiveness further developed. Friendships began to evolve as group members experienced the art process together week after week.

As each mother explained her art creation, feelings often came to the surface. It was not unusual to see these women begin to cry when they took a second look at their artwork. Not only were pent-up feelings released, but also other group members were able to provide a good deal of encouragement and emotional support.

MAGAZINE COLLAGE: 'THIS IS ME'

Group members were provided with a variety of magazines, scissors, glue sticks and large sheets of newsprint. They were requested to create individual collages depicting themselves using the theme 'This is Me' (Dalley 1984). The therapeutic goal of this session was to help them develop a sense of identity. It was important to begin focusing on the identity of these women as individuals to help them get beyond the stigma and guilt of being 'mothers of victims of sexual abuse'. This was not intended to lull them back into denial about their role in the drama of sexual abuse, but rather to help them rebuild their shattered self-images. The pictures were subsequently shared and feedback from members of the group was encouraged. Insight was gained as to how the women viewed themselves versus how others saw them. The women's reactions to the feedback they received was very positive, as shown by their smiles and laughter.

DIALOGUE PAINTING

Watercolour paints, an assortment of paintbrushes and art paper were provided. Members were asked to pair off and to communicate with their partner graphically without the use of words. The therapeutic goal of this session was to improve socialisation skills and to learn to feel more comfortable with each other. It was interesting to notice two particular women in the group who were sisters and had an excessively close and dependent relationship. They always sat together clinging to each other and were fearful to relate with anyone else in the group. They each were asked to choose someone else as a partner in order to begin learning to relate to other women. As a result, they felt freer to interact with other group members in subsequent sessions and no longer sat together. The women shared their feelings about working with others and group cohesiveness continued to develop.

INDIVIDUAL DRAWING: 'AS I SEE MYSELF TODAY'

The women were asked to make a drawing as a statement of how they viewed themselves at that time. The media used were oil pastels on newsprint. Emphasis was placed on the importance of seeing themselves with their own individual identity and reducing the tendency to stigmatise themselves as mothers of sexually abused children. Much support and positive comments were expressed, enhancing their self-esteem.

GROUP MANDALA MURAL: 'MERRY CHRISTMAS'

Group murals are an effective form of using art in counselling focusing on the dynamics of group members' interactions with each other (Liebmann 1986; Waller 1993). At the end of the last session before Christmas, the women were provided with a large round of cartridge paper 5 feet (1.5 metres) in diameter and oil pastels. They were instructed to make a group Christmas ornament (or mandala). In Jungian terms, the mandala is a symbol of the self or wholeness. As a group process, it depicts the 'self' of the group and again reinforces group cohesiveness (Slegelis 1987). The women were able to make an easy transition into a playful state. The activity also served as a 'reward' for their hard work in therapy during the previous sessions. They enthusiastically decided to hang the colourful mural in the reception area of the counselling centre and it continued to be a source of improved self-esteem, with other clients and staff members making positive comments about it.

FEELINGS ABOUT THE OFFENDER

The women in the group often expressed their anger at their partner who had sexually abused their child or children. In one session they were encouraged to create drawings using large felt-markers to illustrate such feelings. One woman graphically depicted her husband, an alcoholic military officer whom she named 'Major Shmuk', shooting three apples out of a tree (Figure 5.1). Each apple represented herself and her two teenage daughters, who had been so severely abused that they still experienced constant night terrors. In a subsequent drawing, the woman drew a picture of shoving her husband in the sea to a shark (Figure 5.2). This particular mother had a great deal of difficulty expressing the anger she felt, turning it in on herself, and was severely depressed. Being involved in this art project enabled her to share with the group feelings she had been suppressing for a very long time, as well as gain a good deal of support from the other women. Another woman in the group illustrated the love she felt toward her husband and the dilemma she faced because she had to return home to tell her daughter that her husband had been sent to prison for six years (Figure 5.3).

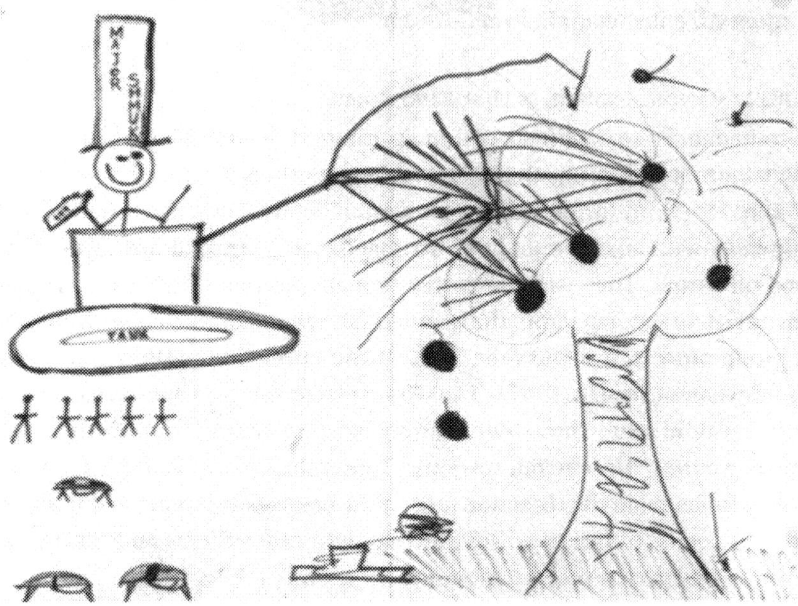

Figure 5.1 'Major Shmuk'

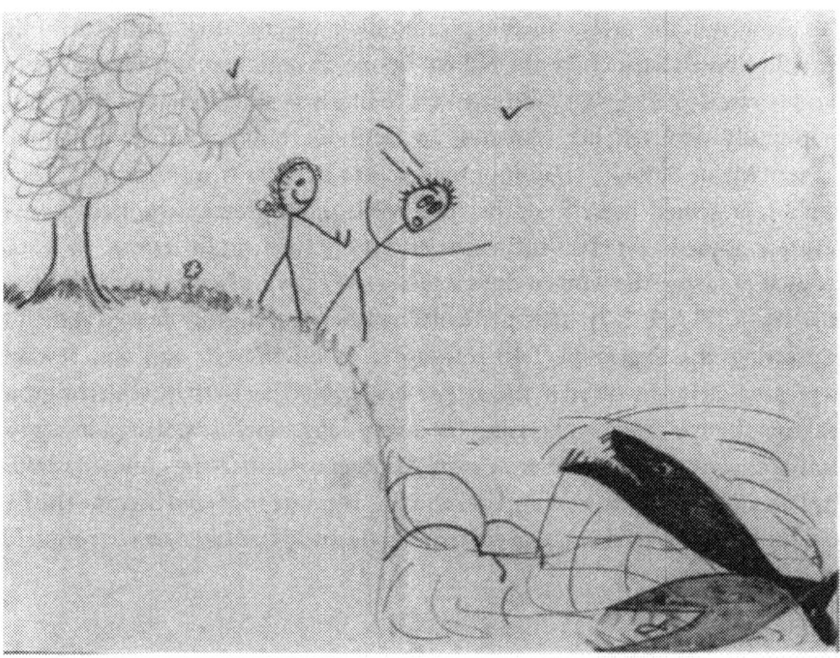

Figure 5.2 'Throw Him to the Sharks!'

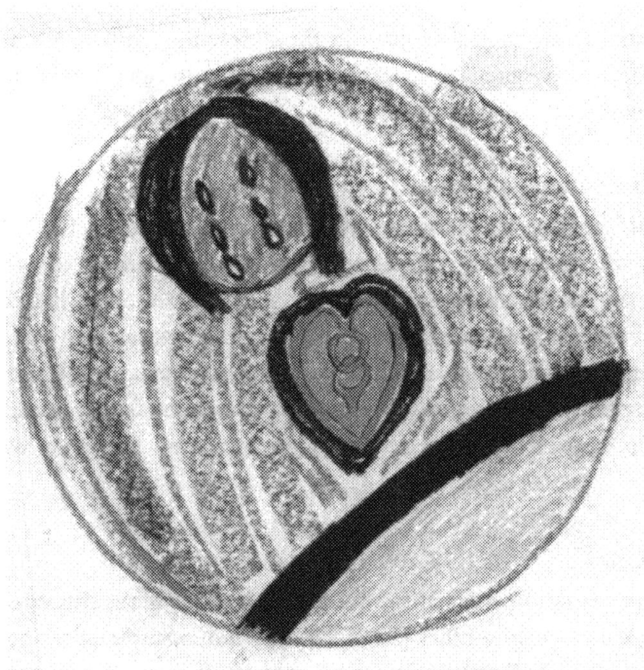

Figure 5.3 'Dilemma'

VISUAL IMAGERY FANTASY DRAWING

The group participated in guided visual imagery (Leuner 1969) in which they were guided to fantasise taking a trip to the beach all alone and writing their name over and over in the sand as the waves rolled in and washed it away. Several new members had been incorporated into the group during this session. They were experiencing considerable anxiety, and the older members expressed feelings of being somewhat invaded. Mothers of victims of sexual abuse are accustomed to being in closed family systems and typically have a difficult time letting new members into their already established circles. Such closed systems serve to reinforce pathological ways of relating. It was important for these women to experience accepting new members in a non-threatening way as well as for the new ones to feel included.

The seashore theme was carried over into the drawing as members were asked to write their name and to create a piece of art around it in whatever way they chose. They were provided with oil pastels and assorted coloured sugar paper from which they selected whatever colour they wanted. As members shared their artwork, cohesiveness once again began to take place very effectively and the new members were more easily integrated into the group. Issues around sexual abuse appeared even in these drawings and as the similarities between the new women and the older members became more apparent, a feeling of mutuality began to evolve.

KINETIC-FAMILY-DRAWINGS (KFD)

During this session, the women were asked to make a KFD depicting themselves with their family in the process of doing something together (Burns and Kaufman 1970). Various colours of sugar paper and oil pastels were provided. Family issues were addressed and the drawings provided clues for further assessment and served as a catalyst for verbal interaction. Once again the drawings depicted a good deal of happiness within the family, which actually was not the case. The desire to deny and minimise the pain was clearly portrayed.

TRIANGULATION

A didactic presentation was made to the group explaining the theory of triangulation in dysfunctional families (Bowen 1978). An example of triangulation is the occurrence of one family member going to another member to express frustration toward a third family member instead of going directly to the person with whom there is a problem. It was explained that it was much healthier to go directly to that person to resolve problems. The women were then asked to draw all of the triangles in their family that they could think of and illustrate these family members with faces or symbols of their choice. The drawings were then shared and the women began to realise how much triangulation was going on within their families.

GENOGRAM COLLAGE

The genogram, an effective tool used in family therapy, was adapted to an art therapy exercise (Lieberman 1979). The group was instructed to create a genogram with coloured sugar paper. They were to select whatever colour they wanted as a base for their artwork and then to cut out or tear other variously coloured pieces as symbols for family members. They were asked to portray their grandparents' generation, their parents' generation, their own generation and their current family as best they could. Similarities between the generations were compared and the women learned how much family behaviour had been passed down from one generation to the next, and how the cycle of intergenerational abuse could continue if the family did not participate in treatment.

Even if family members were not willing to go into treatment, the women were encouraged to be the 'prime mover' for change in their family patterns.

CO-DEPENDENCY ROLE-PLAY

Members were asked to pair off and to draw together with coloured crayons on one large sheet of drawing paper. They were instructed to play the roles of over-nurturer and dependent spouse as they jointly drew a picture of their mutual choosing. The object of this session was to help the women to get in touch with feelings they tended to promote in their childlike and dependent husbands. One partner played the role of controlling and directing the other, being critical, doing the work for the other, and feeling angry and impatient. The member playing the opposite role began to experience feelings of helplessness, guilt and low self-esteem. Then they were asked to reverse roles with each other on the reverse side of the art paper. The group was asked to share the artwork and feelings experienced during the exercise. Most women had not been aware of how their partners might feel when they exhibited such behaviour and seemed surprised to experience these feelings for themselves. Helping these women to understand their co-dependent behaviours was an integral part of improving their marital relationships (Beattie 1987).

MY MOTHER/MY DAUGHTER

Members were asked to draw their relationship with their mothers and remembered feelings during childhood using felt-tip markers on the left side of their art paper. On the right side of the drawing paper using felt-tip markers, they were instructed to draw their present relationships with their daughters and resultant feelings. Interestingly, when the mothers in the group were asked to compare their relationships with their daughters to their relationships with their own mothers, once again denial seemed to occur. Relationships with daughters were usually described as being positive and much better than were their relationships with their mothers. One of the women in the mothers' group illustrated feelings toward her own mother on the left-hand side and feelings toward her daughter on the right (Figure 5.4). She described her feelings toward her daughter as being more positive, but symbols of anger were seen with sharp angles and jagged lines looking much like barbed wire. Here the value of using artwork was clearly illustrated because what the mother said verbally and what she depicted (probably on an unconscious level) were clearly different. It appeared that this mother was in denial about her true feelings toward her daughter. It seemed easier for these mothers to depict negative feelings toward their mothers and to be able to verbalise these feelings openly. These women discussed their determination to make their relationships with their daughters better than the ones they had experienced with their own mothers. Because of such motivation, such improvement was quite likely to occur as these women proceeded through therapy.

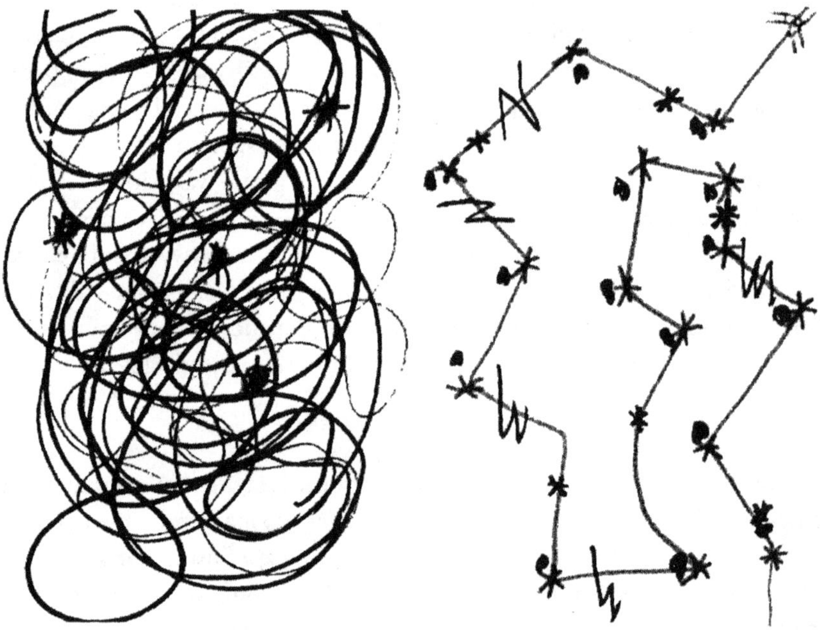

Figure 5.4 'My Mother/My Daughter'

INDIVIDUAL MANDALAS

The purpose of making individual mandalas was to teach the women how to create their own personal art journal. They were instructed to do this by daily drawing a mandala and free associating with lists of words or writing poetry. This exercise was based on Jung's theory that such a mandala revealed the psychic state of the person at the time it was drawn (Slegelis 1987; Jung 1973). Using a dinner plate as a guide, the women drew a circular outline. They were instructed to start in the centre of the circle and to create spontaneously whatever images came to mind (Kellogg 1978). One woman began talking about her anger about her daughter having been sexually abused. While she was working on her drawing, she began creating bright red flames emerging from the circumference of her mandala (Figure 5.5). She expressed amazement at what she had drawn and said she really had not been aware of what she was doing.

LOST IN A STORM

This session again used visual imagery (Leuner 1969) representing each mother alone and lost at sea in a terrible storm, an analogy of the dilemma in which they had found themselves as mothers of sexually abused children. They were then asked to illustrate with felt-markers what it was like to be in the storm (Figure 5.6). Next they were asked to portray how they escaped the storm. Feelings of sadness, anger, loneliness and fear were openly expressed among the women.

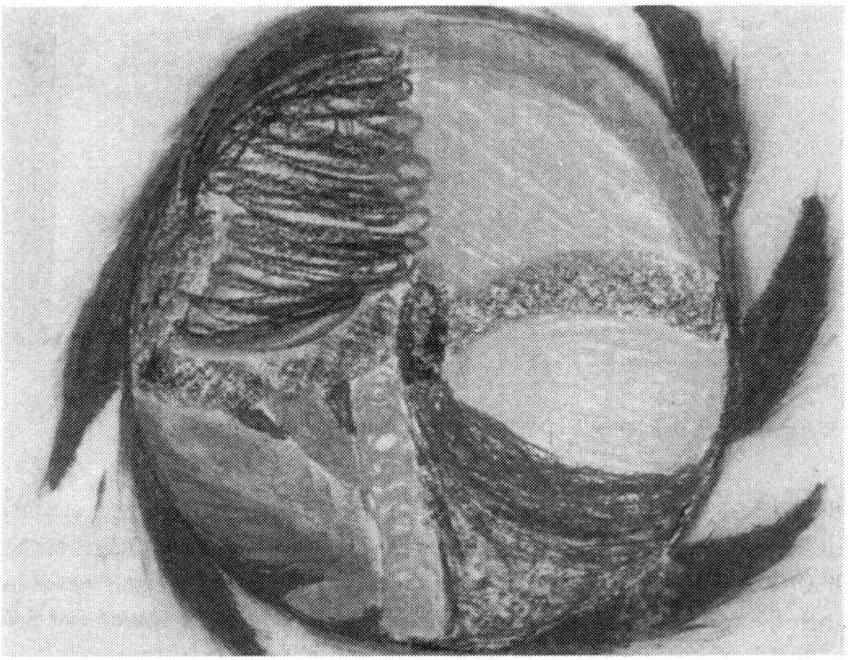

Figure 5.5 'Mandala in Flames'

The second phase of the drawing session, however, moved them into feelings of empowerment and hope.

LIFE MANDALA

During the last session of this group series, mothers were asked to create a 'Life Mandala'. Visual imagery was again used to encourage them to reminisce through their lives from birth to age 5, from age 6 to age 13, from age 14 to age 20, and so on in five to seven year increments. They were then instructed to create a mandala with layers of colour and design representing each span of

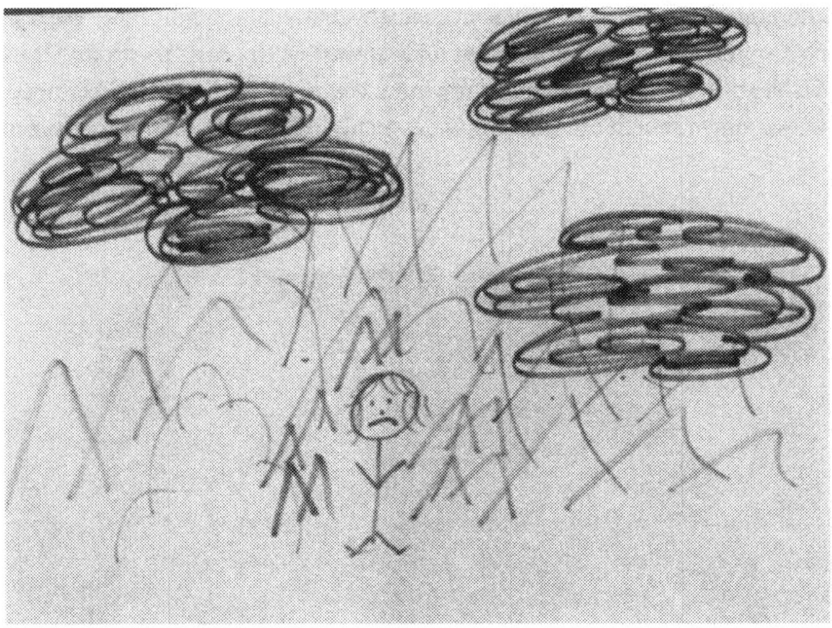

Figure 5.6 'Lost in a Storm'

their lives, working from the centre outward. Each mandala was uniquely different as various colours and patterns were used to depict these stages of their life. The purpose of the project was to integrate memories and feelings about their lives in an abstract manner. Periods of their lives were shared and brief comparisons were made of the similarities and differences of the evolution of each woman's life.

Summary

This chapter reviewed the many dilemmas faced by mothers of sexually abused children and complex therapeutic issues needing to be addressed during their treatment. It demonstrated some ways that incorporating art materials into the counselling process may be used in working with these mothers. An understanding of specific issues relative to mothers of sexually abused children is the primary basis for therapeutic intervention. I would argue that knowing basic counselling or art therapy theory and skills is simply not enough.

It has been demonstrated that a variety of art materials may be used creatively to help these mothers to visualise their problems in a more concrete way and amplify verbal approaches in dealing with them. Individual art with counselling affords these mothers a one-on-one experience with the therapist and allows more time for deeper psychotherapy to take place. In group art therapy several mothers can be drawn into the therapeutic process, with encouragement and feedback from other women who have been through similar experiences. Insight is gradually gained as artwork provides a visual experience and becomes a catalyst for group process. Problems in individual therapy can also be brought into the group and more easily resolved with the support of others. In both therapeutic situations, the use of art enhances verbal counselling by encouraging expression of deep feelings and providing additional insight.

The psychological well-being of the mother of a sexually abused child is essential not only for her own benefit, but to facilitate the treatment of her child as well. The mother is deeply traumatised along with her child and the achievement of her mental health paves the way for her child's recovery. The attainment of therapeutic goals benefits both mother and child and may indeed help to stop the vicious repetitive cycle of child sexual abuse for generations to come.

CHAPTER 6

The Use of Art in Counselling Adult Survivors of Sexual Abuse

This chapter will discuss various aspects of therapeutic work with adult survivors of sexual abuse, including the use of art. A review of the literature on art therapy with adult survivors will be presented, along with developmental issues, problems likely to be encountered, and possible uses of art media. Examples will be given illustrating how artwork was incorporated into the counselling process.

During the early years of working in the area of child sexual abuse, most of my time was spent with children and their mothers, many of whom had also been sexually abused. Since 1996, however, my work has focused on adult survivors of sexual abuse. As awareness of the extent of sexual abuse has increased within the National Health Service, referrals by general practitioners (GPs) to the clinical psychology departments where I have worked have increasingly consisted of adults with a history of sexual abuse. Many referrals have initially been made to psychologists for anxiety and depression, but further assessment has revealed that many of these patients have a history of sexual abuse. Since 1996 40–70 per cent of my caseload has consisted of adult survivors. Since 1999 I have worked in an occupational health department serving NHS employees, as well as privately for employee assistance programmes serving major computer companies. Many of the clients I have seen in these settings are also adult survivors of child sexual abuse and are having considerable difficulty coping at work. Such a history often makes them more vulnerable to workplace stress. They may become easy targets for bullying and harassment because of their inability to be assertive and their extremely low self-esteem.

Like the United States and other parts of the world, perpetrators of sexual abuse have included fathers, stepfathers, mothers' boyfriends, grandfathers, brothers, brothers-in-law, cousins or extra-familial sexual abusers. Male survivors with whom I have worked have been abused by various relatives and in some instances by women. Regardless of who the perpetrator was or whether the survivor is male or female, the damage to self-esteem and resulting psychological problems have been considerable.

Because of the culture in Scotland, the psychological energy expended in keeping the secret of sexual abuse is massive. The 'secret', of course, is what creates a fertile ground in which sexual abuse thrives. Obtaining convictions of sexual offenders is difficult and sentences are usually short. Little, if any, treatment is provided to sex offenders and waiting lists for the few established programmes are one year long or simply closed. Scottish society in general is still in denial about the frequent occurrence of child sexual abuse. Churches have not seriously acknowledged either its frequency or the serious psychological damage it causes. It is not a subject easily discussed in 'polite society'.

In some families several siblings were sexually abused, but no one has dared to speak to anyone else about it. Some women well past middle age are only now plucking up the courage to tell their GPs, psychiatrists, counsellors and psychologists what happened. Entire villages collude to keep the secret even though inhabitants are often aware of what is going on. Employees are fearful to go to their employee assistance programmes or occupational health departments for counselling because of the stigma and fear of colleagues finding out that they were so abused. In tight-knit villages where gossip is rampant, possible persecution for disclosure is severe. Fear of retribution from the offender is strong and serves to keep the survivor from reporting the abuse to police authorities. My personal experience with Scottish police is that some are still reluctant to believe allegations, listening to other family members who were unaware of the abuse or in denial, rather than to the victim.

The Scottish scene has been extremely different from my work in California, where the culture is much more open. While I was still in California police were quick to investigate, solid systems were in place for such an investigation, and the protection of the child was paramount. People openly discussed their experiences of sexual abuse among themselves or publicly on television. Many American books have been written, some by well-known celebrities, about their sad experiences of sexual abuse as children. To meet people in California, or other parts of the United States, who openly discuss the fact that they were sexually abused is not unusual. The development of so many therapeutic programmes has created a culture where people more easily reach out to each other for support and the stigma of obtaining counselling or psychotherapy is considerably reduced. This is much less so in the United Kingdom, and especially in Scotland.

Many mental health workers are still fearful to deal with the issue of sexual abuse, having had very little training. They frequently find it extremely difficult to listen to disclosures and if they are survivors of sexual abuse themselves, they are often unable to cope at all in such a situation. The impact of being unable to listen to an adult who has waited for years to find some way to unload what happened can be devastating and such a situation feeds into their well-entrenched feelings of victimisation. Such survivors can spend years being recycled through the NHS for treatment of depression and anxiety, never dealing with issues of their abuse. Superficial symptom-reduction approaches are frequently used without ever dealing with the trauma itself.

The stories I have heard included aspects of sexual abuse ranging all the way from subtle, affectionate grooming to severe rape of very young children. While I consider myself to be somewhat desensitised to stories of sexual abuse, some of the stories I have heard were still overwhelmingly horrendous. One survivor, for example, was beaten on the bottom of her feet during sex from the age of 7. Another was repeatedly threatened to be drowned in the bathtub at age 10 and then abused. Yet another was threatened with being stabbed by a syringe (the offending brother was diabetic). I still, from time to time, hear a story even more appalling than previous accounts and remain horrified that such crimes have been perpetrated onto so many helpless children. It is little wonder that these children grow up without being able to tell anyone about their abuse.

It is one thing to read journal articles or books on the subject of sexual abuse, but it is entirely different to have someone sitting in front of you struggling to be heard. The relief expressed when survivors are believed and supported is considerable and a huge burden is lifted. It is not unusual to see their symptoms of depression begin to disappear shortly after the disclosure, provided it has been done in a totally supportive and accepting environment. Some survivors, however, are very fearful to talk about their abuse and must wait for months to establish enough trust in a therapist to be able to disclose what has happened. They fear that they will no longer be liked if someone knows what happened and again, much reassurance is in order. They are usually very surprised in group therapy to find that other survivors in the group are just ordinary people and that they are likely to know many others who have been sexually abused, but who have never let anyone know about it. They tend to believe that they are alone in their experiences. Immense relief is experienced when they have an opportunity to listen to others with similar stories.

Psychological effects of child sexual abuse

The effects of child sexual abuse are manifested by psychological symptomology listed in numerous publications. These symptoms frequently carry over into adulthood if the child has not received proper therapeutic intervention and been removed from the abuser. The symptoms, however, can become more entrenched and part of the overall coping style of survivors. New coping mechanisms have to be learned. Old ones which served their purpose before now tend to get in the way of living a healthy and productive life and need to be given up.

Post-traumatic stress disorder involving flashbacks, nightmares, hyper-vigilance, paranoia, difficulty in concentrating and remembering, and high anxiety levels are commonly observed with these survivors. The term 'survivor' has been adopted because it emphasises the strengths of the person and his or her ability to overcome victimisation. As discussed in the Introduction, alcohol and/or drug addiction, dissociative disorders, suicide attempts and re-victimisation in an adult relationship are commonly seen with adult survivors. Chronic entrenched depression is a common symptom of those who have been sexually abused and some survivors cannot remember ever *not* being depressed. Shifting long-term depression is a major therapeutic goal, and also may be very time-consuming. Research into children's brain development is now revealing that growing up with severe abuse influences vulnerability to psychiatric orders in adulthood, including schizophrenia (Perry 1996; Read 1998). Sleeping disorders, headaches, stomach problems, anger management problems, relationship problems, dizziness, passing out, sexual problems, fear of others, excessive washing, feelings of inferiority, guilt and unreality, out-of-body experiences and eating disorders are additional symptoms frequently experienced by survivors (Ainscough and Toon 1993; Briere 1992; Finney 1990; Gil 1988). Problems with severe low self-esteem and lack of assertiveness also tend to set survivors up to be victimised in other situations.

Guilt and shame, panic disorders, phobias, somatisation and hysteria, interpersonal difficulties and social withdrawal are commonly found in survivors of sexual abuse. In addition, cognitive-perceptual symptoms including hallucinations and learning disabilities may be seen in some adult survivors. Some were unable to concentrate during their early educational years and were labelled 'stupid', which became a self-fulfilling prophecy. My colleagues report that a high percentage of adults with learning disabilities seen by psychologists in the NHS were also sexually abused as children.

In the current climate in Scotland, gaining access to long-term therapy is increasingly difficult, with the NHS, employee assistance programmes and health insurance companies offering only brief or solution-focused therapy. Anyone who has worked extensively with survivors of sexual abuse knows that in some instances, at least two to three years of therapy will be required. Those receiving short-term treatment may gain relief from some of their symptoms, but often will not be able to come to terms with what has happened to them in such a short period of time. Many are likely to reappear in the mental health system again at a later time.

Adult survivors in psychiatric hospitals are sometimes perceived negatively and accused of being 'manipulative' and 'attention seeking' without understanding that such behaviours were necessary in order to survive the horrific circumstances these people experienced as children. They are no longer effective and must be 'unlearned' if the adult survivor is to be able to manage his or her life effectively. Disclosure of sexual abuse is sometimes seen as 'attention seeking' and may be ignored.

Dysfunctional family dynamics are nearly always present in families where sexual abuse has occurred, particularly in instances of intra-familial incest. Severe family problems exist, particularly isolation from the environment. Such families discourage growth and change which would normally enable children to establish outside contacts and to leave home eventually. These people rarely have relationships outside of their immediate family and relatives, and may remain childlike and dependent. Behaviour problems are further exacerbated by families where there is likely to be greater family conflict and lower family cohesion (Freidrich *et al.* 1988). Such family dysfunction is seen in adult survivors who have gone on to recreate these dynamics in their present relationships, including domestic violence. It is important, however, to state that some women who have come from more healthy family backgrounds with no previous experience of physical or sexual abuse can inadvertently become involved with abusive men. It is unfair to tell women that they have 'unconsciously' selected these men and lead them to believe that it is somehow their fault (Jones and Schechter 1992).

Sibling incest, related to dysfunctional family dynamics, is estimated to occur five times as often as father–daughter incest (Conn-Caffaro and Caffaro 1993). Little has been written on the subject of sibling incest to date, but in my experience, those survivors of such abuse with whom I have worked suffered the same symptoms, or in some instances worse symptoms, than survivors of other types of sexual abuse. Some writers claim that when siblings consent to such sexual interaction, it is not abusive and harmless (Canavan, Meyer and Higgs 1992; De Jong 1989; Russell 1986). This view leads to an underestimation of the damage that can be done to survivors of such abuse. Relationship difficulties, developmental effects limiting the sibling's ability to form meaningful relationships within his or her peer group, and dysfunctional family dynamics are also evident with survivors of sibling incest. Sibling incest is often considered to be insignificant compared to father–daughter incest, or other types of sexual abuse, but the damage can still be considerable and the effects of this type of sexual abuse should not be minimised. Sexual abuse by other younger family members, such as cousins, likewise can take a serious toll on those who are victimised, especially when there is an age difference of four to five years. Where coercion, threats and other forms of abuse of power have taken place, the damage can be just as great.

False Memory Syndrome

False allegations of sexual abuse occur only in a minority of cases. In cases where false allegations do occur, it is mostly by adolescents who are caught up in custody battles between their parents, and in some instances are influenced by the parent seeking custody. False Memory Syndrome (FMS) (Loftus 1993) can, however, occur when therapists or others tell someone that they definitely have been sexually abused even though they cannot remember it. The power of suggestion to a vulnerable client can be very strong. It has been common practice among some therapists whenever someone had a cluster of symptoms commonly found in survivors of sexual abuse to assume that they had been so abused and to tell them so. I recall in my early days of working in treatment programmes in California that as trainees we were told that we must have been sexually abused or we would not be working in this area. I remember spending many painful hours trying to recall whether I had been so abused, but never came up with anything. I would argue that such an approach with a patient is emotionally abusive. There continues to be considerable debate over whether FMS can truly occur, but until the matter becomes more clearly resolved, I believe it is advisable to err on the side of caution.

When I have new clients who tell me that they have been sexually abused, but cannot remember it, I investigate why they believe they have been abused and whether or not a previous therapist has put the idea in their head. One survivor with whom I worked had been told by a previous therapist that she had been sexually abused, but had absolutely no recollection of it. She was determined to uncover her memories, but without success. Using art therapy did not elicit any memories, nor did her going to a hypnotherapist for six months. Her father, who she believed was the abuser, was elderly and she had grown to hate him because of the suggestion by her therapist that he had abused her. She desperately wanted to know whether he had sexually abused her, because if he had not, she wanted to make amends with him before he died. To have such claims put forward to a vulnerable client with no direct recollections can in my view be dangerous. If they were abused, sometimes they need to leave those memories deeply in the unconscious to protect their sanity. Defence mechanisms serve a very useful purpose and should be respected. On the other hand, if this woman was not abused, she has been placed in a terrible situation compounding the psychological problems she already had. If a survivor does not remember such a history it can be for at least two reasons: either it never occurred at all, or if it did occur, the person may need to keep it at an unconscious level in order to cope. To break down the natural psychological defences before the patient is ready or feels safe to do so is psychologically abusive, and in some instances can cause a psychotic breakdown. Symptoms of sexual abuse also appear in many people who have suffered other types of abuse (e.g. emotional and/or physical abuse). It does *not* mean that because someone has similar symptoms that they actually have been sexually abused. If someone is told something often enough, they are likely to come to believe it, especially when told by an 'authority' figure such as a therapist or doctor.

False allegations of sexual abuse can create horrendous problems for those so accused as well as for family members and others involved. Lawsuits are rife in the United States where therapists have led their patients to believe they were sexually abused. Defending solicitors in Scotland already are well aware of the False Memory Syndrome and allege that survivors of sexual abuse who have made allegations against their abusers have been told about their abuse by their therapist. If the alleged offender is not charged, it is likely that the survivor will face more abuse from him after the trial is over. It is essential to adopt a therapeutic style which is cautious regarding 'leading' ideas and questions, much the same as working with sexually abused children. If adult survivors are functioning reasonably well, it may be best not to try to dig 'it' up. Some clients are afraid they have been sexually abused if they cannot remember parts of their childhood. I would argue that it is fairly normal to have forgotten many parts of one's childhood.

Multiple Personality Disorder

In the same way that therapists must beware of participating in FMS, caution is equally necessary when working with Multiple Personality Disorder (MPD). Therapeutic programmes in the United States specialising in child sexual abuse have been in existence since the 1970s. There have been increasing claims of the occurrence of MPD (now called Dissociative Identity Disorder or DID) in those who have been sexually abused (Putnam 1993). Even though such awareness also existed in the nineteenth century and was known to Pierre Janet and other clinicians (Carson and Butcher 1992), it is only now that it is being increasingly linked to the trauma of sexual abuse. This disorder is a more serious version of dissociation which can develop with more clear-cut symptoms in adulthood and until recently was believed to be rare. Ross *et al.* (1989) argued that 79.2 per cent of 236 cases diagnosed as MPD had a history specifically of sexual abuse in childhood. Likewise, Putnam *et al.* (1986) reported childhood abuse of a sexual nature in 83 per cent of the MPD cases in their study. Treatment approaches in working with MPD advocated by Putnam (1989) are primarily psychoanalytic and involve having the patient relive earlier experiences in order to be able to give up such 'compartmentalisation' of their personality structure. Such treatment is extremely painful and time-consuming. The famous psychiatric case history of Truddi Chase, who had 95 personalities, but ultimately chose not to integrate them, became an American best-seller (T. Chase 1987).

There is considerable controversy on both sides of the Atlantic about the possibility that, similar to FMS, MPD is actually being created by therapists. Awareness of MPD is gradually increasing in the United Kingdom, but such symptoms are still likely to be diagnosed as schizophrenia or psychosis in some form. The treatment of MPD is not taken seriously in Britain to date, because of concerns about the iatrogenic effects of the therapist on the patient abound. I find it interesting that in the many cases of adult survivors with whom I have worked, I have never encountered this disorder myself. I recall a visit to California where my American colleagues were excitedly reporting that they had finally found a case of MPD because a patient had used the term 'we' instead of 'I'. Using 'we' for 'I' is a normal colloquialism in many Scottish villages and a reflection of the culture, not a disorder. My British colleagues also claim they have never seen a case of MPD. I personally remain sceptical and concerned that therapists may again be doing their patients a disservice. Where true cases of MPD do exist, appropriate treatment is obviously desirable. Needless to say, much continued research needs to be carried out, and a great deal of caution exercised by those of us working with survivors of sexual abuse lest we find ourselves on the 'bandwagon' of finding MPD cases and become guilty of creating the condition ourselves.

Disclosure of sexual abuse

When someone wants to disclose sexual abuse, my approach is to tell them that I do not require them to go into every detail of their abuse. I am there to listen and to support them if they want to disclose such detail, but will not insist that they talk about anything they do not want to. They have been forced too long to do things against their will, and to use coercive measures in therapy is not appropriate and somewhat abusive. If undisclosed abuse is suspected as the root of other problems, pressuring a survivor to talk about it before he or she is ready may break down much needed psychological defences and could in some instances cause a psychotic breakdown. I have seen workers in psychiatric hospital wards using so-called 'disclosure therapy' where patients were required to talk repeatedly about all of the details of their abuse. Only when they began to develop psychotic symptoms was this type of abusive therapy stopped. It is absolutely essential to create a safe and trusting environment for survivors to begin the healing process. Using behavioural techniques such as implosive therapy with survivors of sexual abuse is dangerous in my experience. If a client's needed defences are broken down and they are hospitalised, further stigma is added and such an experience contributes to their entrenched sense of victimisation. In some instances in Scotland, family members or acquaintances in small villages may use the fact that they were psychiatrically hospitalised for further emotional abuse because of the stigmatisation of those suffering from mental illness.

When survivors feel ready to talk about what has happened, it is equally important to be available to hear the sordid details without overreacting, being disgusted or judgemental in any way. There are considerable variations of such abuse which are extremely repulsive to listen to. It is useful to have had training to desensitise oneself to such disclosures, but such training is difficult to obtain. Those with considerable experience working with survivors of sexual abuse do become desensitised to a certain extent and are more easily able to listen. Unfortunately, some solve the problem by telling the patient or client *not* to talk about it, or to talk to someone else. This simply reinforces the fears they have always had about telling anyone and feeds into their feelings of rejection. To be helpful, workers need to remain calm and believe and support the person. If they have been sexually abused themselves and their own unresolved abuse issues are triggered, they may need to seek personal therapy. It may be advisable for a period of time for them not to work with abuse survivors.

Disclosure of sexual abuse is important, but it is only a beginning. Talking about it in itself will not solve all the person's problems and talking incessantly about the abuse can reinforce feelings of victimisation. In my experience just talking about the abuse will not 'cure' someone. It is important to look at what is going on in the survivor's life *now* and how current problems may relate to what happened before. Standard treatment approaches are still required for depression, anxiety, eating disorders and so on; these problems rarely disappear just because a disclosure has been made.

Sexual abuse can sometimes be enjoyable if it begins with gradual grooming by the offender and becomes linked with affection and rewards. It is not always experienced as negative. Guilt about enjoying some aspects of it is common and a survivor often concludes that she is a 'slut' if there was some enjoyment, further damaging her self-esteem. Sexual feelings *are* pleasurable and if mixed with other forms of abuse create confusion regarding sexuality and sexual identity. Pain, sexual feelings and love may become linked and lay the groundwork for considerable problems in adult relationships.

The ability to trust may be severely damaged. Fears of abandonment and rejection are common because of many threats in childhood. In addition to the ones mentioned earlier, examples are: 'Cooperate or I'll kill your kitten', 'I'll abuse your sister', 'I'll go to jail if you tell and it will be all your fault', 'I'll kill you, hit you, stab you', 'It will hurt Mum if she finds out', 'She'll never believe you' or 'They'll take you away from the family' (which more often than not *does* occur upon disclosure). In the famous case of MPD, Truddi Chase was threatened to be thrown into a pit of snakes if she refused to comply with her father's demands (T. Chase 1987). Bribery is frequently used with gifts, money, special outings, sweets and so on. Alcohol and/or drugs may make the victim less likely to resist, and can lay the groundwork for substance abuse later on.

Treatment issues

One of the major treatment strategies in working with adult survivors is to focus on their strengths and help them to overcome a 'victim mentality', which is a carryover from a history of abuse that tends to continue to affect the way they perceive events. Their heightened sense of helplessness is easily triggered and they sometimes unwittingly set themselves up for more abuse in their present life experiences. Those with an entrenched pattern of passive behaviour and inability to be assertive feel helpless a good deal of time and they either perceive themselves as victims, or become victims, in many situations.

It is also useful to help survivors to get in touch with their anger over the abuse, particularly when they are very depressed and turning their anger inward. While this may be useful in order to shift the depression, it is also important to avoid encouraging them to become stuck at that stage. Continued catharsis and repeated expression of anger can become self-reinforcing and addictive. I have seen many adult survivors of sexual abuse involved in long-term therapeutic programmes be continually encouraged to express their anger. As a result, they developed problems moving beyond that stage and continuously acted out this anger onto others in their life, inviting retaliation and more abuse. It may be useful to get repressed anger out at the early stages of treatment, but survivors eventually need to move beyond the anger for their own physical and mental well-being. To be in a state of constant anger not only is physically unhealthy, but also invites more abuse, rejection and victimisation. Survivors need to gain insight on how they may set themselves up for such abuse. 'Getting-back' at parents with confrontations which consist of extreme emotional abuse toward the parents is a repeat of abuse dynamics and not productive. Therapeutic work with abuse survivors must include helping them to deal with their own abusive behaviour as well. I have observed group therapy situations where group members have 'confronted' each other allegedly in the name of openness and honest expression of feelings. Such confrontation, used as catharsis, sometimes consisted of verbal and emotional abuse, and in my view does *not* belong in any strategy to move toward healthy and nonabusive relationships.

Perhaps one of the most difficult aspects of therapeutic work with adult survivors is to get them truly to believe that the abuse was not their fault. They may have been told repeatedly by the offender that no one would believe them and that it was their fault. Current sexual relationships are frequently damaged because of flashbacks, guilt and shame. Partners may also develop psychological problems such as chronic anger and depression when they learn of the abuse. Working these feelings through with sensitivity with both the survivor and the partner can be helpful (Ainscough and Toon 1993; Briere 1992; Finney 1990; Gil 1992).

Use of art in counselling adult survivors of sexual abuse: Background and history

One of the earliest case studies involving a female adult survivor of sexual abuse using the art therapy process was written by Margaret Naumburg (1953), who was one of the pioneers of art therapy in the United States, with extensive training in both Freudian and Jungian analysis. The case study involves long-term therapy (34 months) of working with a 20-year-old woman who was a victim of paternal incest. Naumburg engaged this woman in a series of artwork beginning with many small crayon drawings which led later to the development of a larger and more complex series of drawings and paintings. Naumburg often made use of the 'Scribble Drawing' (Cane 1951) where she requested that the patient make a scribble on a blank sheet of paper and look for images within the scribble (much like 'cloud reading'). The image was then developed into a final piece of artwork. Naumburg believed that unconscious material surfaced using this method and the patient was able to integrate it with consciousness, a primary goal of psychoanalytic treatment.

Naumburg's patient created a total of 450 images during three years of art therapy. Naumburg observed how the patient's artwork was reflective of her stages of therapy and that the images enabled her to talk about her issues. Naumburg also observed how being involved in the art process enabled the patient to increasingly remember what had happened to her. Naumburg presented this young woman's art productions at three psychiatric meetings, the American Psychiatric Association in 1949 in Montreal, Canada, and in Cincinnati, Ohio, in 1951, and another exhibit at the International Congress of Psychiatry in Paris in 1950.

Publications on using art in the therapeutic process with adult survivors of sexual abuse have appeared increasingly in recent years. Some have focused on the content of art expression and symbolism associated with sexual abuse (Spring 1985, 1993; Ticen 1990). Other writers, however, have described a variety of approaches and theoretical models elaborating on the effectiveness of using art media in helping survivors work through their feelings, overcome symptoms, and come to terms with what had happened to them. Yates and Pawley (1987), for example, followed Naumburg's approach in using art therapy to help an incest survivor explore and resolve her trauma. They argued strongly in favour of allowing the client to lead the direction of treatment. Serrano (1989) reported on combining art and other expressive therapies in the treatment of adult survivors of sexual abuse. She utilised art and movement in treating a group of female incest survivors using clay and drawings to confront the reality of their distorted body images and to bypass their use of intellectualisation. Peacock (1991) used a single-subject design to demonstrate the positive effects of the use of art therapy with a survivor of sexual abuse using Kelly's Personal Construct Theory (Kelly 1955). Nez (1991) used art therapy with a survivor of sexual abuse working with the Jungian concept of archetypes. Levens (1994) demonstrated how she used guided fantasy in art therapy with survivors of sexual abuse and noted the omission of images about their mothers and the high need of survivors to have control over their lives. Guided fantasy is a psychodynamic technique derived from Jung's use of 'Active Imagination'. Levens also noted the link between sexual abuse and eating disorders. Simonds (1992) observed the link between sexual abuse and a negative body-image and described how she used art to help a survivor of sexual abuse resolve her conflicting feelings. Jacobson (1994) utilised art therapy in working with a survivor of sexual abuse and found it to be especially effective in helping her to recover memories of the abuse.

Group work utilising art therapy has been discussed in a small research project comparing group verbal therapy with group art therapy in the treatment of female incest survivors (C. A. Waller 1992). While the numbers were too small to generalise to other groups, the trend was favourable on the side of the benefits of art therapy. Waller found that drawings used facilitated cohesion, catharsis and insight. She used a structured series of art therapy interventions and contrary to advocates of non-directive therapy, found positive benefits in a more directive approach. Anderson (1995) described group work with adults survivors of incest using clay. Her approach was theme-oriented and she concluded that her use of a time-limited art therapy approach using clay was effective with feedback from participants' individual therapists six months later being predominantly positive. Brooke (1995) outlined a brief-therapy model for using art therapy with sexual abuse survivors. She concluded that incorporating art in the group process was particularly useful in improving self-esteem. It also provided a forum for the expression of emotions in a safe environment and helped the survivors to learn to trust in others.

Capacchione (1991) wrote a book on expressing the 'inner child' using a variety of art techniques. Her work was inspired by that of Carl Jung (Jung and Kerenyi 1969), Alice Miller (1984) and W. Hugh Missildine (1963). The metaphor (or archetype) of the 'inner child' has been used successfully by many psychotherapists working with survivors of abuse. The client is encouraged to get in touch with his or her 'inner child', nurturing and embracing it, and giving it the care and protection that it did not receive in real life. Many survivors with whom I have worked, both male and female, have told me how they have naturally and spontaneously used this metaphor in their healing process without it even being suggested to them. Artwork provides an effective avenue for working with this metaphor by encouraging a survivor to do paintings or drawings on how they can nurture and protect their 'inner child' and create a happier ending.

It is clear that the use of art in the therapeutic process has been explored from a variety of theoretical models and found to be useful by the proponents of those models. While I have referred to some basic counselling and art therapy models in Chapter 1 which I found the most useful, I would encourage exploration of these other models as well. One of the beauties of incorporating artwork into counselling and psychotherapy is its adaptability to so many theoretical approaches.

Developmental issues

Developmental maturity is frequently affected by child abuse, whether it is physical, sexual or emotional. It is proposed by Trikett and Putnam (1993), for example, that problems in both psychological and biological processes of development occur as a long-term result of sexual abuse. It is common in working with adult survivors to observe that they tend to be developmentally immature as well. It is clear that awareness of the effects of child sexual abuse on psychopathology and problems relative to behaviour, development and relationships continue to emerge on an ever-increasing basis.

Adult artwork in general usually reflects a much earlier stage of development due to lack of training. According to Edwards (1979), the majority of adults in the western world do not progress in art skills much beyond the level of development they reached at age 9 or 10. The development of drawing skills halts at an early age for most people, and as a result most adults draw like children, no matter what levels of psychological development they may have attained in other areas of life. This is especially important to bear in mind when working with adult survivors of sexual abuse to avoid jumping to conclusions that there is something wrong with them because they draw like children. It is also important to make them aware that this is a normal phenomenon, because their very low self-esteem may make it difficult to engage in the art process.

Earlier psychoanalytic theory tended to focus on human development up until entry into adulthood, believing that such development stopped at that time. We are now much more aware that we continue to progress through various developmental stages and life transitions as adults (Dworetzky 1984; Erikson 1950). An awareness of these issues is important in working with adult survivors of sexual abuse and may compound presenting psychological problems and influence appropriate therapeutic interventions. Someone in their twenties and thirties, for example, may be primarily concerned with issues of creating a family or launching a career. A female survivor in her late forties will possibly be facing an 'empty nest', the menopause and caring for elderly parents. A woman in her sixties may be grieving her career ending at retirement and struggling to re-establish herself as a member of the 'Third Age'. She is also likely to be dealing with the bereavement of one or both of her parents. Unresolved issues related to a history of sexual abuse may make such transitions much more difficult. Men in their fifties who are made redundant will be facing feelings of hopelessness and helplessness exaggerated by their previous history of abuse. Increasing health problems in older age and continued grieving of friends as they die also may impact considerably on one's psychological well-being. While survivors go through the same stages of development as nonabused adults, the way they handle each stage is likely to be affected by their history of abuse, and the problems normally encountered at each transition may be considerably exaggerated.

Characteristics of artwork in adult survivors of sexual abuse

A considerable amount of effort has been made to study systematically the differences in artwork between sexually abused children and other groups (Hagood 1999). This appears not to be the case with adult survivors. Anecdotal case studies have been published illustrating common themes and symbols, along with various theoretical approaches involving artwork. Rigorous scientific comparisons of adult survivors' artwork with that created by adults who were not abused, however, have not been made, to my knowledge. Because adult survivors of sexual abuse experience so many psychological problems in addition to having been sexually abused, their artwork is likely to vary considerably depending on what those problems are.

Spring (1985) noted in her group work with several adult survivors of incest that *wedges* and *eyes* appeared repeatedly in their drawings. Levens (1994) used guided fantasy in her group work with adult survivors of sexual abuse. She noted that following discussions about mothers, there was a noticeable absence of images of mothers in their drawings. She speculated that this was perhaps due to the survivors' angry feelings towards their non-protective mothers.

In my own clinical experience, themes of hopelessness, depression and despair have been common, reflecting the survivor's inner state in a graphic way. One characteristic, however, that I have repeatedly observed is that of male phalluses created either realistically or in some sort of abstract form and incorporated into paintings or drawings (see case study later in this chapter). This phenomenon is frequently observed in children's artwork as well and is discussed in Chapter 9. These 'phalluses' are often out of the conscious awareness of the survivor who has painted, drawn or sculpted them. Interpreting such images to the survivor needs to be approached with a good deal of caution because it can break down defences which are still needed.

To search for 'indicators' of artwork in the paintings and drawings of adult survivors of sexual abuse may be interesting, but I have increasingly come to believe that the major purpose in using artwork should be to facilitate their recovery. The continued search, however, for such characteristics in children's artwork to detect the possibility of sexual abuse and thereby offer protection from further abuse is still well worth pursuing, even though such a search has been difficult and inconclusive to date (Hagood 1999).

It is important for counsellors and therapists to have had some art training in order to appreciate fully the various ways media can be used and how they may impact on one's feelings. Training enables the therapist to teach the client how to use various art materials. Many art therapists have the advantage of having a first degree in fine art and such a background is strongly encouraged by both the British Association of Art Therapists and the American Art Therapy Association. I have a strong background in fine art, which has enabled me to explore a wide variety of media and their impact on emotions. Because of this I was able to develop a better understanding of mixing paints, colour theory, composition, working with watercolour, wedging, handling and firing clay, and so on. Counsellors and other therapists with no such background are strongly encouraged to become involved in some sort of art training and experience themselves.

My focus on working with adult survivors has increased in the past few years. My use of artwork has been considerably restricted due to the nature of working on a clinical psychology team. As such, I have been able to incorporate the use of art on a somewhat limited basis, even though I have worked with a considerable number of survivors. There have been severe limitations on space in which to make art, time-management problems, and travelling to several clinics each week has made using artwork difficult. In instances where artwork was used, the survivors usually made it at home and brought it to the clinic to discuss.

Many adults have been the object of ridicule by family members and/or school teachers when they were engaged in artwork as children and have developed a lack of self-confidence in being involved in the art process. Women in group work frequently are very worried that their artwork will be judged negatively by others. Beginning with media which is non-threatening is especially important. In my experience, once group cohesiveness begins to develop, the fear to express oneself in a variety of art media diminishes. Involvement with a variety of art materials creates a playful environment which in itself is healing.

Art media

Most art media discussed in Chapters 2 and 3 can be readily adapted to working with adult survivors. More imaginative combinations of art media can be used with adults than with children who have various developmental limitations, depending on their age (Liebmann 1986; Rhyne 1984). I have encouraged adult survivors to use a variety of media to resolve their feelings about having been sexually abused. The combinations of various media can become very exciting and the therapist has the opportunity to become very creative in deciding which media might be appropriate for various therapeutic issues, as well as enlisting the ideas of those with whom they are working.

Media requiring more control, such as pens, pencils and felt-markers, are often preferred at the outset of treatment by survivors who are fearful of their feelings. The use of words alone in magazine collage or in ink drawings is common and tends not to elicit emotions as strongly. Gradually moving such a person, when the time is right, to using looser art media and more abstract expression is more likely to allow feelings to surface. Encouraging the use of abstract shapes, symbols, patterns or designs are ways to enable one to break away from using only realistic artwork. If the survivor resists using any type of media offered, that resistance needs to be fully respected at all times. Using clay and/or fingerpaints is likely to elicit more emotional expression and is regressive as well. Regression is not necessarily a bad thing. It is common to see group members begin to play and giggle as young children during the art process. Such 'regression' is very therapeutic, because most of them never had a chance to play as children. Regression, however, where needed defences are broken down too quickly, can become a problem. Sensitivity regarding where each survivor is in their therapeutic process is essential.

Watercolour provides little control, but still can be effectively used with assistance on how to work with it. When working on problem-solving issues, more controlled media to illustrate problems and possible solutions can be very useful. One area where I would use extreme caution is that of mask-making, especially those made of plaster or clay and placed directly over the face. Asking a survivor to lie still while gauze and plaster are slowly layered on the face can elicit feelings of panic and helplessness, and for that reason, I would *not* recommend using this type of medium with anyone who has been sexually abused.

Collages

Magazine collage is both cost-effective and easy to use. A variety of magazines can be easily collected by both the therapist and survivors. One problem, however, is that it is quite time-consuming and for this reason, I frequently ask clients to create a collage at home and bring it into the next session. Collages using a variety of coloured paper such as tissue paper, crêpe paper and sugar paper are especially effective for emotional expression. Tearing the paper and leaving it with ragged edges may elicit feelings more than shapes which are cut precisely with scissors. Crêpe paper can be stretched, twisted and moulded into three-dimensional artwork. Pieces of coloured tissue paper can be pasted overlapping each other, a process which offers an opportunity for colour-mixing. Sugar paper and cartridge paper provide stable backgrounds for any type of collage work. Other media such as oil pastels and coloured markers can also be mixed in with collages to create various mixed-media effects.

In addition to non-directive work with collage, many themes can be addressed in working with survivors of sexual abuse. Possible themes for magazine collage are 'Who Am I?' for addressing identity issues, 'If I Could Do Anything in the World with My Life, What Would It Be?' for goal-setting, and 'This is My Family' for greater insight into family dynamics. Problem-solving can be aided by the use of insight gained during the use of magazine collage. Other relevant topics may be explored as they arise in the therapeutic process, whether it is in individual sessions or in group work. Collage is less threatening to those who have little confidence in their artistic abilities.

Common themes emerging in collages of those who have been sexually abused are images of self-hatred and facial expressions of pain and agony. Splitting the 'bad self' from the 'good self' is also common, illustrating the borderline tendency for black and white thinking and little integration of themselves. They may view themselves and others as either all good or all bad, which is a carryover from their early developmental stages which were not worked through during childhood (see Chapter 2).

Collages often include pictures of infants or small children, reflecting survivors' basic need for nurturing. In some instances such pictures have to do with the age the sexual abuse began. Themes of loneliness, guilt, searching for love and the desire to feel happy and safe are also commonly depicted. Confused feelings, fear, depression, anxiety, feelings of hopelessness, eating problems, body-image problems, problems with alcohol, lack of confidence and problems with relationships are also likely to emerge spontaneously in collages, or any other type of art media. On the positive side, hopes and aspirations such as finding love, travelling, going to university and so on may also be included.

The use of magazine collage or any other pictures which are selected are highly revealing due to the process of projection. Projection, according to psychodynamic theory, is an unconscious process whereby one selects images which may have an unconscious meaning. An interesting illustration of how this process works is the selection of Christmas cards or cards thanking me for my help which have been sent to me by patients. It has been fascinating to see how often they had selected cards unconsciously depicting the dilemma they faced as child victims. One Christmas card, for example, showed a small teddy bear looking through a lace-curtained window holding a candle. This woman had repeatedly told me how her grandfather sexually abused her from the age of 3 while she was waving out the window (with lace curtains) to her mother, who was leaving the house. Another Christmas card given to me illustrated two children playing on a quilted bed. The abuser had been an older brother and the abuse began when the female survivor was only 6 years old. She had recurrent nightmares of the quilt on the bed and was very confused because she also loved the brother who had abused her brutally for a number of years. The Christmas card graphically illustrated her affection for her brother along with the guilt; it seems that it was selected without any conscious awareness of its meaning. A 'thank you' card sent to me by another female survivor depicted a tattered teddy bear on crutches with patches sewn all over it. The woman was unable to attend for further sessions because of financial limitations, and unconsciously illustrated how she was feeling in the card. Fortunately, she was able to resume therapy at a later time.

Drawings

Felt-markers are an easily transportable medium and can be used to help survivors portray specific incidents. One young survivor, for example, did a series of drawings depicting her court hearing where she had to face her abuser. The expression on the offender's face while she testified haunted her for a long time with flashbacks and nightmares. She was able to depict the courtroom scene with large felt-markers including herself and the abuser. She continued with additional drawings expressing her anger at him and her desire to move on with her life. She reported that after doing the series of drawings, she no longer had flashbacks of the offender's face. Line drawings are also very useful for problem-solving.

Felt-markers provide a high degree of control, which tends to get in the way of expressing emotions. On the other hand, for those who need such control, various ways of handling the medium can be useful in addition to simple line drawings. One adult survivor with a good deal of artistic talent drew a carefully sketched drawing of herself as a faceless woman searching for her identity

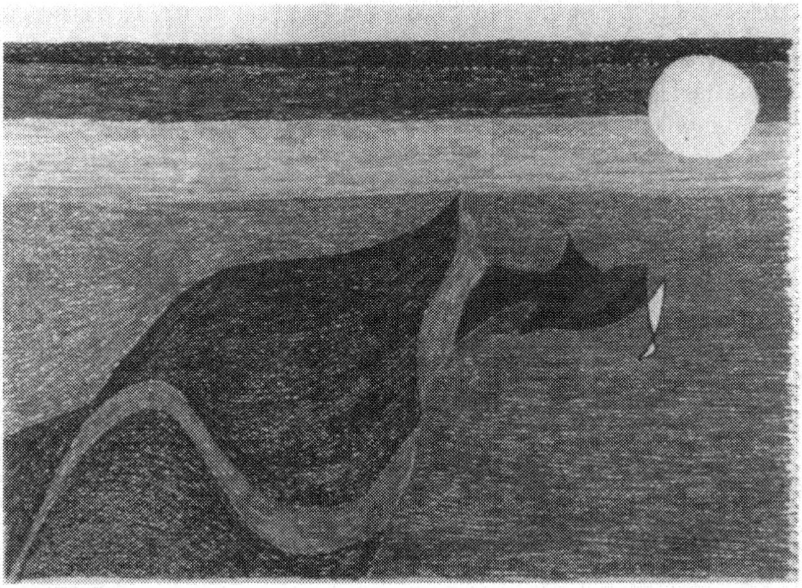

Figure 6.1 'Faceless'

(Figure 6.1). The way she used the markers created the effect of a painting. Felt-markers are particularly useful for problem-solving where the presenting problem is drawn and then additional drawings are made with possible solutions.

Clay sculptures

A female survivor with whom I worked on an individual basis spontaneously created a series of fifteen clay sculptures over several weeks while she worked through her feelings about her relationship with her father, her feelings of sadness and finding her own identity separate from her father. She did not recall any details of actual sexual abuse, but reported that she had slept in the same bed with her father until she was 18 years old. She reported that her father was childlike and very emotionally dependent on her. She had spent a good deal of her childhood nurturing and supporting him. She demonstrated a considerable amount of artistic ability, and the sculptures indeed were lovely. Because she so easily engaged in the clay work, I worked with her non-directively. She created the sculptures at home and we reflected on them together during her sessions. My approach with her was that of Betensky's (1995) phenomenological viewing and accounting (discussed in Chapter 1). She would distance herself from the sculptures and relate to me how she had felt during the process and what each art piece meant to her. I then fed back to her my observations, which often increased her insight. Creating and talking about each sculpture helped her to work through her feelings of guilt and confusion. Her own identity as a sexual woman in her own right became stronger. Her original symptoms of suicidal ideation and bulimia disappeared completely by the time she had completed the series, and she embarked on a new relationship which has been much healthier.

Pastels

Oil pastels provide rich colours and are easily mixed and blended to create a variety of colours and effects. They contain much less wax than ordinary crayons. Several examples of the use of oil pastels are discussed in Chapter 5 with mothers of sexually abused children, many of whom were also survivors of sexual abuse themselves. Chalk pastels on coloured sketching paper offer an opportunity to create subtle and interesting effects. One female survivor used this method to depict herself being cornered by a monster, feeling helpless, small and trapped (Figure 6.2). She created other drawings with the same medium clearly illustrating how victimised she felt by her abuser (Figure 6.3).

Mandalas

Jung discovered that psychiatric patients with whom he worked were likely to spontaneously create paintings and drawings in a circular shape. He went on to develop a rather elaborate theory on the use of the 'mandala' in psychotherapy.

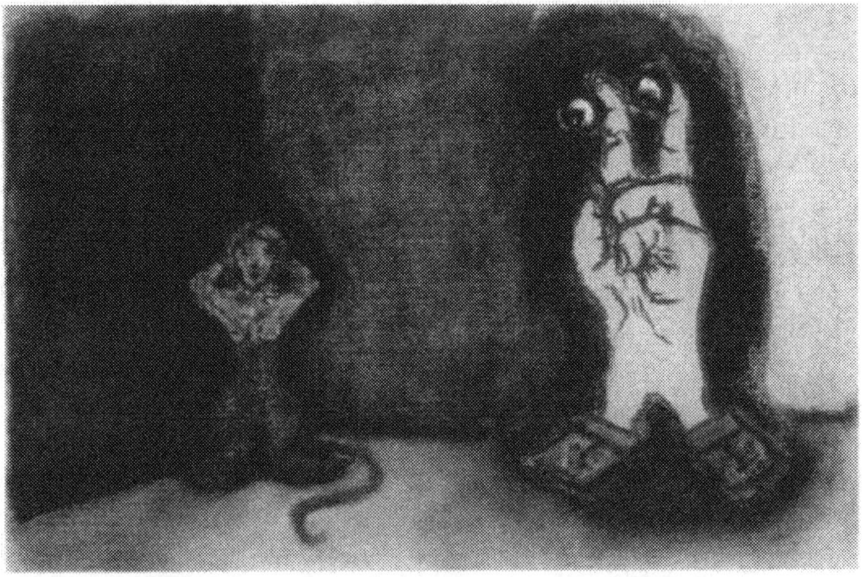

Figure 6.2 'The Monster'

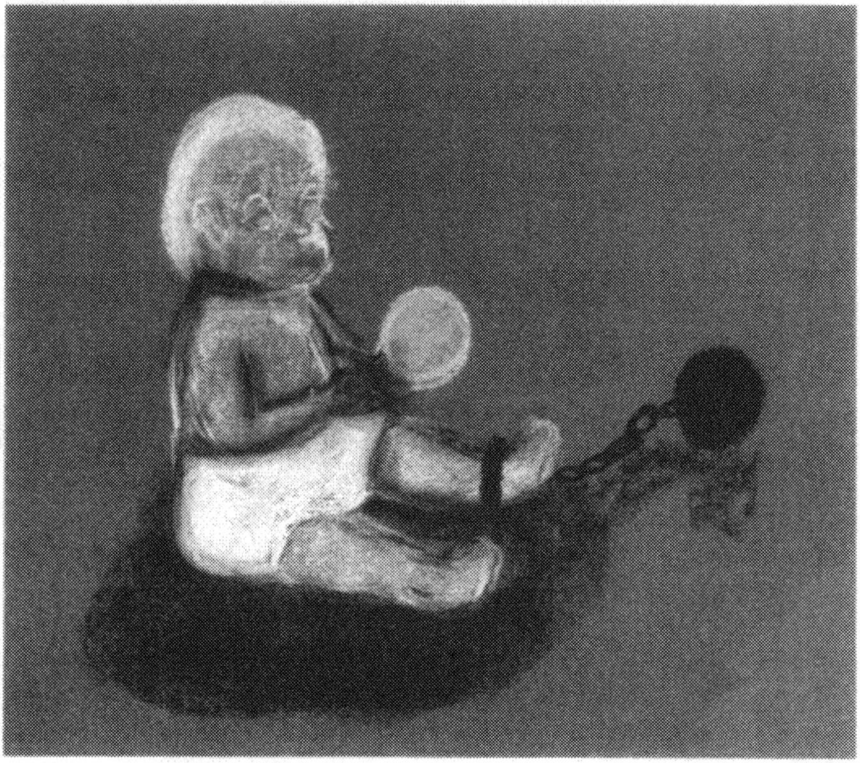

Figure 6.3 'Trapped'

When his patients came to a point in their therapy where they began describing their dreams, but had difficulty doing so, he asked them to paint them (Jung 1933). Many of these paintings were circular in shape, forming a mandala. He collected a large number of mandalas and classified them into several common categories (Jung 1973; Slegelis1987). Jung sketched his own mandalas on a daily basis for thirteen years before developing his theory on the use of the mandala in psychotherapy. He believed that they were a 'snapshot of the psyche' at any particular moment in time and that creating artwork within a circle had a calming and healing effect. He found the mandala to be a useful tool in helping to integrate polarities within the unconscious, and those which his patients created clearly depicted opposite themes such as night and day, winter and spring, and so on. As the person progressed through therapy, themes became much more integrated.

Joan Kellogg (1978) has done extensive work with mandalas, using them with severely disturbed patients, and has developed a mandala assessment system. She typically had patients draw a circular boundary with a dinner plate and instructed them to start in the middle and spontaneously draw whatever came to mind. She reported that this process helped to calm very disturbed patients. A small study I carried out (Slegelis 1987) found that artwork within a circular outline appeared to encourage more positive and hopeful themes while drawings within a square outline encouraged more angular, perseverative and less creative drawings. Further research into the effects of various art media and shapes of paper chosen is needed.

Group murals

Group work can be very effective with adult survivors of sexual abuse (Ainscough and Toon 1993; Ney and Peters 1995). Murals are effective ways of developing group cohesiveness. Timing their use in a group is important, because to introduce murals too soon may be threatening to group members until they know each other better. Starting with non-threatening themes such as 'Build a City', 'Make a Christmas Ornament' (discussed in Chapter 5), making a large mandala together spontaneously (Ireland and Brekke 1980; Richmond 1977) or some other non-threatening theme mutually decided on by group members is usually a good idea at the earlier stages (Liebmann 1986). Once group cohesiveness is more established and members begin to trust each other more, other themes more specific to sexual abuse may be introduced, or spontaneous group murals can be created (Waller 1993) and be experienced as less threatening at a later stage.

Group murals can be created with large sheets of paper cut into circles, squares or long rectangles and can be either spontaneously made by group members or created along a particular theme. They can be painted, drawn or used with collage with group members surrounding the mural paper, or the paper can be hung along a wall. Murals are excellent for identifying difficulties that survivors typically have in relating to each other. Boundary issues are common when some group members paint or draw into someone else's space with little regard for the other person's personal boundary. This can create feelings of invasion and animosity in others. The opposite boundary problem can occur when some group members make their part of the mural totally separate from everyone else, again most likely representing their desire to protect themselves or fear of joining in because of severely low self-esteem. Talking about various aspects of group murals and feelings evoked can be very revealing, enabling members to learn more about themselves and each other.

One woman with whom I worked was involved in a group mural using batique in an occupational therapy session with other patients while in a psychiatric hospital. She made herself nearly invisible among the figures of the others in the group, a behaviour very common with both adults and children who have been sexually abused. The desire to be 'invisible' can evolve from a very young age in order to protect oneself from being noticed and abused again.

Recurrent nightmares

Images are extremely powerful in evoking emotions and insight. Respect for this power and the importance of appropriate timing in any feedback to the survivor cannot be overemphasised. I have seen abstract paintings of phallic shapes, blood and gore, distorted bleeding faces and themes of helplessness and terror created by adult survivors as illustrations of their nightmares. One man drew a recurrent dream of faces laughing at him. The distorted faces were all cut up and bleeding. He had been sexually abused by several men when he was a young boy and the faces represented the abusers.

One woman with whom I worked made a painting in a circular shape (a mandala) with a gun on one side and a huge anatomically correct male phallus on the other surrounded with blood. When I asked her to tell me about it, she had not been consciously aware of what she had created; as she began describing it and realised what it was, she became hysterical. Because she had a history of psychosis, I discouraged her from delving into her nightmares with artwork for the time being. The power of artwork to uncover defended material very rapidly needs to be respected at *all* times. Uncovering too much too soon can create a considerable amount of psychological distress and a possible psychotic episode.

Case example: Female survivor of sexual abuse

Sandy, a very attractive 36-year-old woman, was referred to me by her GP for depression. At the outset of treatment she appeared very well groomed and took considerable pride in her appearance. She had been the victim of a recent rape attempt by her brother-in-law, who had broken into her apartment. She managed to escape from him and to report the incident to the police. He was released on bail and she was fearful to go anywhere because he was very angry and had a history of violence. Her mental state began rapidly deteriorating shortly after her first session with me. The rape attempt had also triggered her memories of her earlier sexual abuse, and each time she came for a session, she appeared more distraught and anxious. She had stopped sleeping, and I became very concerned that she was headed for a psychotic episode. She was assessed at the local private psychiatric hospital and voluntarily admitted herself, where she was an in-patient for two weeks. I visited her regularly while she was in hospital to keep the therapeutic relationship strong and offer her ongoing support.

From when Sandy was only 4 years old, she had been severely sexually abused for a number of years. Because she was so pretty, she had been regularly photographed for child pornography material, in addition to being sexually abused by several men, and constantly threatened to be drowned in the toilet if she did not cooperate. When she later disclosed the abuse to her family, they had nothing more to do with her; she had lost contact with them for a considerable number of years.

Sandy's self-esteem was extremely low, even though she had held a responsible secretarial job for a number of years and had seemed to be able to cope very well. She told me that she was interested in art and I began encouraging her to become involved in the art process. At the outset she began sketching and drawing various scenes in nature and found that this process was therapeutic in itself. It helped to raise her self-esteem, because she felt proud of her artwork. I asked her to make a magazine collage of how she saw herself and she created a scene of herself as a very little girl feeling lost and alone. I began using the 'inner child' metaphor with her and encouraged her to continue to protect and love this small child within who had been so abused and abandoned. She hung the collage up at home to remind herself of her need for self-nurturing. She created another collage depicting what she wanted to accomplish in her life, but had little faith in her ability to do so. I encouraged her to hang it up as well to help her to visualise what she wanted and to inspire her to work toward attaining her dreams.

As therapy progressed, Sandy began exhibiting considerable mood-swings, coming to one session very depressed and the following in a manic state. I had her further assessed by her psychiatrist for the possibility of bipolar disorder, but he did not concur with me. Nevertheless, I attempted to learn what was triggering her mood changes, and experimented with integrating a combination of behavioural therapy and Jung's concept of the mandala. She agreed to make a series of mandalas using a dinner plate to outline each circle. Starting in the centre of the circle, she allowed whatever images spontaneously came to mind to unfold in the drawing. I asked her to make a note of how she was feeling at the time of each drawing and to note what possible events might have triggered her changes in mood. This process enabled Sandy to realise that on days when she stayed home alone she was more likely to feel depressed. She began building more structure into her days and became more involved in social activities.

It was interesting to note how the images in Sandy's mandalas often reflected whether she was feeling happy or depressed, alternately depicting flowers and then dark and gloomy themes. In the process of creating the mandalas, phallic shapes began to appear (see book cover). At the same time, she began talking about persistent nightmares about a 'black blob' (Figure 6.4); it seemed to me that there might be a connection between her nightmares and the phallic images she was making in her artwork. When she spoke of the recurrent nightmare, however, she began perspiring profusely and became very panicky, not wanting to talk about it any further. It was obvious that whatever the dream represented, it was far too threatening for her to deal with at that time. While I saw the 'black blob' in her artwork, it was interesting to observe that she did not appear to connect consciously with what she had drawn. Because of her reaction to her nightmare, I did not make any attempt to interpret what I saw and fully respected her need to be defended in this area.

I continued to work with Sandy on parenting issues with her teenage son and problems with her boyfriend, who treated her very badly. Her extremely low self-esteem needed constant reassurance and I kept emphasising her right to be treated with love and respect. We explored her relationship with her family who had abandoned her and she continued to use artwork on her own which helped her to relax and to feel better about herself. I was very aware of her fear of being abandoned, which is common to most survivors of sexual abuse, and careful to inform her if I needed to change an appointment or to go

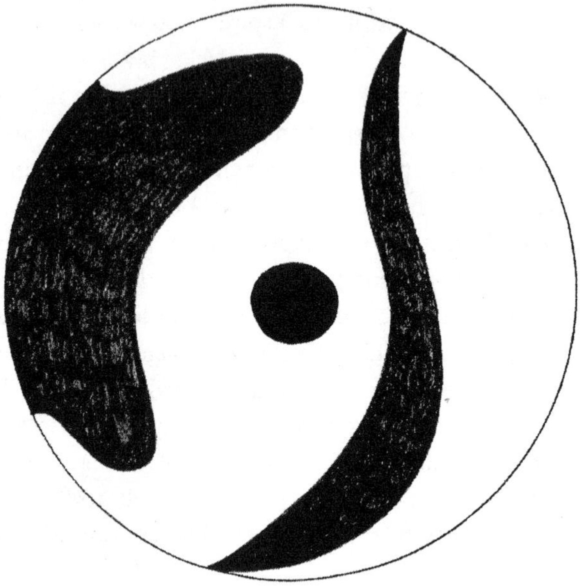

Figure 6.4 'The Black Blob'

on holiday. I constantly reassured her that I was there for her. There were many issues to deal with in addition to the sexual abuse. She was never able to discuss her sexual abuse in any detail, and I fully respected her decision.

When I began writing this book, I wrote to Sandy to ask for permission to use her artwork. She replied stating that her life was very happy and successful and commented on her use of art in the counselling process as follows:

> When I look back at the different therapists I've had and their styles, I believe that doing the artwork really did help me get in touch with my innermost feelings and to get them out. I feel honoured that you still want to use my artwork in the book. I don't care who knows that it's my story. It makes me feel like I'm doing a little bit to help my fellow survivors. Bottom line is that I survived!!

NOTE: One of Sandy's manadalas is on the cover of this book.

Summary

This chapter has examined various aspects of using art in working with adult survivors of sexual abuse. Therapeutic issues and symptoms common to survivors were discussed and a brief review of the literature on art therapy with adult survivors has been presented. The influence of developmental issues on treatment approaches and characteristics of artwork with this population were also briefly explored. Various art media have been discussed along with ideas for incorporating them into the therapeutic process.

It is important to remember that in spite of the serious problems that adult survivors bring to the therapy session, they can and often do go on to experience happier and healthier lives. Some may make only marginal improvements, depending on the severity of the abuse and their motivation to better themselves. All survivors with whom I have worked have stated that having someone with whom to share their story was extremely helpful. I share their sense of helplessness that there are not more therapeutic programmes available in the United Kingdom (and other parts of the world). Survivors with entrenched problems such as eating disorders or other addictions have had a good deal of difficulty giving them up. The lack of programmes such as Overeaters Anonymous and clinics specialising in eating disorders also makes it difficult for these survivors to get the intensive support they need. American survivors are much more fortunate in this area.

Involving survivors in the art process in itself tends to improve self-esteem. Encouraging art-making for its own sake can be highly therapeutic. The power of the image to uncover memories and unconscious material is always to be respected. Defences and boundaries of survivors are special areas to pay attention to. They have consistently had their boundaries violated and need a considerable amount of support from their therapists. Image-making is a very powerful tool in helping the survivor to express emotions. The art process tends to uncover buried memories and to open up more issues to resolve. Proper timing is essential so that the survivor does not become overwhelmed. Artwork enables survivors to have greater insight into their problems and to come up with solutions. It is useful to help them to establish goals and dreams visually for their lives as they eventually feel more empowered.

Even though most therapists may not work directly with sex offenders, I believe that a greater understanding of the reasons for sex offending will enhance work with adult survivors. Survivors of sexual abuse frequently have a great deal of difficulty understanding how someone could sexually abuse a child. Many were abused by adolescent sex offenders such as brothers or cousins, as well as adult offenders. I have found it especially useful to explain to them why offenders perpetrate such crimes in order to help them to overcome their extreme sense of guilt. Chapters 7 and 8 will focus on using art with counselling adolescent and adult sex offenders.

CHAPTER 7

The Use of Art in Counselling Adolescent Sex Offenders

This chapter will focus on therapeutic issues, treatment goals and the use of art with counselling adolescent sex offenders. While the major focus of this book has been on survivors of sexual abuse, many adolescent offenders have been victims of either sexual abuse or physical and emotional abuse. One of the most common questions I have heard from survivors of sexual abuse is how anyone could do such a horrendous thing. I believe it is particularly useful in working with older children and adults with a history of sexual abuse to understand issues relative to offenders. Helping survivors to understand why sex offenders behave the way they do helps them to stop blaming themselves so much. Understanding offenders, however, *never* excuses or condones what they have done, but simply serves as a useful explanation. This chapter will explore the various problems and therapeutic issues relative to working with adolescent sex offenders, along with the incorporation of art with the counselling process. A case example of the use of art with counselling adolescent offenders is included in Chapter 8.

Background

My work with adolescent sex offenders began after having a considerable amount of experience with sexually abused children and their mothers (Hagood 1991b, 1994b). I wanted to understand better the perspective of those who could commit such offences. I believed that such insight would better enable me to work with both child and adult survivors of sexual abuse. The work I did with these young offenders has indeed resulted in a greater insight in helping survivors to make sense of the abuse they suffered. It was carried out in a California treatment programme which specifically focused on working with families where sexual abuse had occurred. I worked only with male adolescent and adult offenders, but this is not to imply that young girls and women do not commit sexual offences. We are now sadly aware that a considerable number of female children and adults sexually abuse other boys and girls (Cunningham and MacFarlane 1991; Johnson 1989). For purposes of this chapter, however, I will refer to adolescent offenders as 'boys'.

Many child and adult survivors with whom I have worked were sexually abused by their adolescent brothers, cousins or child-minders. While the dynamics may be different from father–daughter incest, or sexual abuse by adult offenders, the toll that such abuse takes on its victims is considerable. Sibling sexual abuse is perhaps the most common, and in my clinical experience, the damage to adult survivors whose brothers have abused them is equally as severe as other forms of sexual abuse, and in some instances more so. Other writers such as Finkelhor (1980), Loredo (1982) and Pierce and Pierce (1987) have substantiated the severity of the effects of brother–sister incest. In some instances the offender may even be younger than his sister. Other investigations have revealed that sexual abuse by children starts much younger than adolescence. Cantwell (1988) found that sexual abuse was occurring between children much younger than 10. Mental health workers have become increasingly aware of sexually abusive behaviour in many environments such as nursery schools, primary schools and residential homes. Treatment programmes and approaches have been developed to address this issue (Cunningham and MacFarlane 1991). (Review Chapter 3 for further discussion.) Identifying the age of onset for young offenders abusing is important because the younger the child, the more entrenched the behaviour will be by adolescence.

After my move to the United Kingdom, I presented several workshops on the use of art in counselling with adolescent sex offenders. Various organisations throughout the United Kingdom, such as Barnardo's, the Royal Scottish Society for the Prevention of Cruelty to Children (RSSPCC) and social work departments, were in the early stages of developing treatment methods with these young offenders. I soon discovered that British professionals already working in this area were on the same wavelength as myself and reported similar observations regarding the behaviour and dynamics of adolescent sex offending. Data now emerging from research into child sexual abuse in Britain generally reflect trends similar to the findings in the United States, Canada Australia and other English-speaking countries. There remains, however, a paucity of resources for therapeutic work for young sex offenders in most of the United Kingdom and especially in Scotland (National Children's Home 1990).

Many writers have pointed out that a large percentage of child sexual abuse begins with the offender being under 18 years of age. Thomas (1981) found that in 56 per cent of the reported cases of child sexual abuse, the abuser was younger than 18. Groth, Longo and McFadin (1982) found that nearly half of a sample of 137 adult rapists and child molesters committed their first sex offences between the ages of 8 and 18 years, with the average age being 16. At a child sexual abuse conference in Glasgow, Judith Becker (1988) presented results from a study carried out by the National Institute of Mental Health in Washington, DC. The conclusions were that 60 per cent of adult sex offenders had an onset of interest in deviant behaviour in adolescence. Becker (1988) reported that another large study of 216 adolescent offenders sponsored by the United States Department of Criminal Justice showed similar results with the onset of most adolescent sexually abusive behaviour occurring between the ages of 13 and 15.

The implications for British art therapists in developing methods of working with adolescent sex offenders, as well as others affected by sexual abuse, seem obvious (Hagood 1992b). Adolescent sex offenders on both sides of the Atlantic, in my experience, report feelings of powerlessness, low self-esteem, shame, guilt, fear, embarrassment and anger. These feelings often translate themselves into serious behaviour problems, depression, vulnerability to drug and alcohol dependence and susceptibility to suicide, not to mention the possible recycling of the abuse onto others. These appear to be human issues regardless of culture. With heavy prison sentences and little possibility of therapeutic intervention, the helplessness, denial and rage of a British adolescent sex offender might be even more intense than that of a young American sex offender who has opportunity for a considerable amount of therapeutic help.

In the United States, for example, groups for adolescent sex offenders have been developed in most large cities since the early 1980s. In states such as California, treatment programmes have been partially funded with criminal restitution funds actually paid by criminal offenders as part of their sentence. This created resources to provide counselling and psychotherapy for victims of sexual abuse and their families. In the United Kingdom, however, the Criminal Injuries Programme awards financial lump sums for victims of child sexual abuse, but funds are not specifically earmarked for therapeutic work. Help for children and adults who were victims of sexual abuse is available on the National Health Service, but waiting lists for counselling or psychology input are usually very long. Therapeutic work with adolescent sex offenders is often left to social workers or forensic psychologists in state hospitals.

The American adolescent sex offenders with whom I worked prior to my move to Scotland were distressed when they learned that a British boy in such a situation could get little or no help at all. While there are cultural differences between the United States and Britain in dealing with the trauma of child sexual abuse, it is my belief that the similarities far outweigh the differences. Sexually abused children, which most of these adolescent offenders are, feel victimised regardless of nationality.

Importance of cognitive-behavioural treatment approaches

Because so much art therapy is carried out using a psychodynamic framework, it is essential to point out that these approaches alone are usually not sufficient in treating young sex offenders. Psychodynamic approaches may be effective in helping with resolution of feelings regarding their own history of abuse, or in gaining insight, but there are cognitive, behavioural and addictive components to sexual offending which must be addressed directly and firmly in order to help young offenders learn to control their sexually abusive behaviour and the thinking patterns and situations which render them most vulnerable (Ward *et al.* 1997). In the United States, for example, many children who were initially treated with primarily psychoanalytic approaches later reappeared in the system as the next crop of sex offenders (Ryan 1988). They were often helped to work through their feelings related to their own abuse with art therapy (Stember 1980), but addressing cognitive-behavioural aspects were not usually included in treatment. At that time, however, American mental health professionals were not aware of the phenomenon of sexual offending behaviour in young children, and hence it was not sufficiently addressed. Work has been increasingly developed in the treatment of these 'abuse-reactive' children (Cunningham and MacFarlane 1991). (For further discussion, see Chapter 3.)

Sex offenders, young and old, commonly use cognitive distortions to justify their abusive behaviour. These cognitions also enable them to minimise guilt and the effect of the abuse on their victims. They rationalise their abusive behaviour to justify what they are doing. Sadly, in many instances, they come to believe their own lies, which is one reason why they can be so convincing and so easily able to deceive others. The behaviours of young offenders also need to be dealt with, focusing on how they affect others, as well as how they set themselves up to get into trouble a great deal of the time. Addictive aspects to sex offending need to be understood and dealt with. It is also now believed that low success rates in treatment of paedophiles may be partially attributed to the fact that only recently have American therapists begun to treat paedophilia as an addiction (Nelson 1992). It is believed that the reward of an orgasm and subsequent release of tension is one of the reinforcers. While techniques drawn from psychodynamic theory are valuable, it increasingly appears that addressing the addictive component of sexual molestation must be incorporated into treatment approaches (Chissick 1993). There is, of course, no guarantee that these approaches will totally prevent future offending. There is much debate on the treatability of sex offenders altogether, with some programmes claiming an extremely low rate of recidivism and others remaining sceptical about the possibility of long-term success in rehabilitation. I would argue, however, that we need continually to develop ways to try to stop the cycle of child sexual abuse.

In most British forensic settings, the cognitive-behavioural aspects of treatment are now being carried out by social workers and forensic psychologists, with art therapists still working primarily in a psychodynamic way (Liebmann 1994). I would argue, however, that a cognitive-behavioural approach can be adapted to the use of artwork. Counselling and art approaches focusing on cognitive and behavioural aspects of these boys' difficulties can be effectively used to assist in awareness of reality-based situations and behaviours which lead these boys into molesting behaviour. Understanding the cycle of how the sexual offending behaviour is set up can be made clearer by having the boys paint or draw the situations which reinforce each other and lead to sex offending. The use of art can help them to find ways to alter their lifestyle so that they are not so.

Problem-solving is especially effective using art (Liebmann 1990, 1994). Art can provide a means for young sex offenders to illustrate various situations and to create healthier solutions. Family art techniques (discussed later in this chapter) are valuable in helping these boys with their difficult relationships with family members (Landgarten 1987; Linesch 1992). Regardless of theoretical approach, it is essential to be familiar with issues which are directly relevant to working with adolescent sex offenders. Methods integrating counselling theories, knowledge of these issues and the use of art materials can be developed in a creative way. Art and counselling approaches must be adapted which will enable adolescent sex offenders not only to gain insight and resolve their feelings, but also to learn to improve their self-esteem and sense of powerlessness, correct their irrational thinking, address the addictive cycle of abuse, and, it is hoped, find better ways to manage their behaviour.

Key therapeutic issues in working with adolescent sex offenders

Several writers have discussed various issues and characteristics pertinent to adolescent sex offenders (Agee 1979; Becker 1988; Becker *et al.* 1986; Breer 1987; Fehrenback *et al.* 1986; Groth 1977; Groth *et al.* 1981; Groth and Loredo 1981; Knopp 1982). This section lists many of the typical problems which need to be addressed when working with young sex offenders. Art materials can be creatively selected and used in a variety of ways, depending on the therapeutic goal at the time. Chapters 2 and 3 have discussed the use of appropriate art materials and special problems in working with them and are applicable to working with adolescent sex offenders.

Poor self-esteem, loneliness and isolation

Feeling lonely and isolated are common triggers to sexually abusive behaviour. Because these boys suffer from very low self-esteem, they tend to avoid social situations, particularly with peers. Katz (1990) studied a large number of adolescent child abusers and found that social skill deficits and social isolation were major risk factors that may predispose some adolescents to commit sexual crimes against children. These young people are prone to developing a lonely lifestyle for a variety of reasons. There may be a strong fear of relationships with other boys because of their belief that a male victim of sexual abuse is homosexual. Because of this fear, it may be very difficult to engage these boys in appropriate peer relationships.

Dealing with the issue of sex-identity confusion is extremely difficult to do in a group situation. It may be advantageous to address these issues in individual therapy. Sometimes just making a comment about how many young people who were sexually abused feel confused is enough to let them know that they are not alone; this can be reassuring. Requesting any artwork on this topic is likely to arouse a great deal of anxiety and to stimulate acting-out behaviour. If a young offender is clear that his orientation is homosexual, he may have considerable difficulty in coming to terms with it, especially in cultural environments where strong prohibitions to homosexuality exist. Helping him to accept himself and to find ways of healthy living within a gay framework is difficult, but useful. Fear of 'coming out' is very strong, with the likelihood of further rejection by family and friends.

Adolescent sex offenders frequently experience a fear of relationships with girls because of extremely low self-esteem. In many instances, relationships with girls involve abusive behaviour and power issues. This may be due to a variety of reasons, ranging from having an abusive father as a role model to a high need for power and control because of his own victimisation. He may be able to relate to girls only through sex and develop a promiscuous lifestyle. His concept of love is often distorted since he has not had appropriate role models with his own parents and has not grown up in a home environment where healthy love and affection was expressed. Exploring what constitutes healthy relationships, regardless of sexual orientation, is an important therapeutic goal. Engaging these young people in art projects depicting relationships with others helps them to see their situation more clearly and graphically. They can be helped to understand that being with others is an important way to improve self-esteem, as long as they are not involved with people who are abusive. Artwork can also be used to help them envision a more positive future (Larose 1987). Using drawings or paintings to depict how they would like their life to be is another useful technique.

Ignorance of accurate sexual information

These boys have a multitude of misconceptions about sex and love, including inaccurate information on birth control. A lack of understanding about sexually transmitted diseases, safe sex and personal responsibility for himself and others is not unusual. A good deal of sexual knowledge is likely to have been learned erroneously from other children and involves crude 'street' language. Frank and open discussions about sex with accurate information are important during treatment. Issues such as birth control and personal responsibility in sexual relationships are also important to address. A greater understanding of human sexual anatomy and reproduction is useful. Exploring values and feelings surrounding sexual issues are likewise important. These boys may initially feel uncomfortable with a female therapist, but (in my experience) usually end up respecting her and learn much from hearing her perspective about relationships with females. Using artwork to illustrate relationship issues would provide a visual forum for exploring these issues more fully.

Poor relationships with parents

Power struggles and oppositional behaviour are common with these boys. They need to learn constructive ways to deal with their parents (or other authority figures). They need to learn that rebellion is not a choice, but a *reaction* against authority. It is often helpful to point out to them that this is the case and help them to consider ways they can stop reacting and actually make more constructive choices. They frequently do not know how to get what they want in appropriate ways and assertiveness skills are important. As long as they are dependent minors, they must learn to live within the situations in which they find themselves, whether it be living at home, in residential homes or foster care. They need to learn to negotiate with respect for others and this is more likely when they learn to have respect for themselves. They also need insight into how they set themselves up for more punishment and abuse. Artwork can be used to clarify these issues. One example might be to ask them to draw a picture of their situation, talk about their feelings, and then to create another drawing depicting how they could have handled it better.

Dealing with abandonment by parents (emotional or physical) is obviously very difficult for these boys. These boys are frequently abandoned by their parents in various ways and given many false promises which may not materialise. Having a trusting and predictable relationship with counsellors is a must. Therapists who miss appointments or group meetings create more feelings of abandonment and resultant anger, depression and feelings of being a 'victim'. Because of extreme fear of abandonment, appropriate processing of feelings around termination issues or endings is also essential. Again, the creative use of art materials in illustrating and processing feelings around these issues can be very effective.

Family dynamics of adolescent sex offenders

Family dynamics of adolescent sex offenders are commonly very dysfunctional. Landgarten (1987) gives excellent examples of ways that art therapy can be integrated with family therapy. Using artwork may help a young offender to visualise more clearly his relationship with other family members and better understand what is happening. Many times, unfortunately, the families of these boys do not want any help and cannot see that they have anything to do with the problem. To help a boy on his own can be very difficult, but a greater understanding of his family can be useful.

Family portraits can be drawn increasing understanding of the family situation. Kinetic-Family-Drawings (KFDs) showing a family doing something together can be used (Burns and Kaufman 1970). In families where sexual abuse has occurred, however, such an approach may elicit extremely graphic sexual material, and should be used with caution in a group situation. The KFD can be used as an effective tool to get a young offender to discuss what is going on at home. Its use, however, as an assessment tool is highly questionable because it has not been rigorously validated empirically and is highly subjective in its interpretation (Gersten 1978). As demonstrated in Chapter 4, collage projects may use coloured sugar paper, tissue paper or crêpe paper for cut-out symbols representing different family members. Magazine collage can be similarly used with the selection of photographs. It is uncanny how often pictures are selected closely resembling various family members.

Adolescent offenders frequently experience poor contact with their fathers, who are emotionally distant or physically absent. In instances where the father actually was the abuser, the situation is made worse. The boy's identity with his father during his early years of development is often lacking if the father has been absent. Unfortunately, many fathers of these boys are emotionally, physically or in some cases sexually abusive. This provides the scenario where the boy can identify with his father and learn abusive behaviour patterns. On the other hand, where there is no abuse from the father, there is a need to encourage the father, if available, to spend special time with the boy. It may be difficult for the father, who may resist, but it is important to engage him if at all possible. The father may have had a poor relationship with his own father; he is simply repeating the pattern and may not know how to relate to his son. Encouraging and supporting a nonoffending father are important. If the father will not become more involved, the boy might be encouraged to be involved with positive male role models, such as other relatives, or activities with good male role models. It is important, however, to be careful about who they are. Paedophiles often volunteer for programmes which involve young adolescent boys, such as after-school programmes, Boys Brigade (Boy Scouts) and so on.

In order to develop a stronger sense of responsibility, it is essential that these boys understand how their abuse of another child has affected the rest of their family. Parents frequently feel guilty when their sons have committed such an offence and incessantly blame themselves. They may be overprotective and in denial about what their son has done, which unfortunately enables the boy to minimise his offence and to take little responsibility for his behaviour. Legal repercussions have obvious emotional and financial consequences on these families. These boys need to understand not only how their victim felt, but also how family members have been victimised as well. In some instances, parents may be so embarrassed that they abandon their son altogether.

Numbing of feelings

Children who have been repeatedly abused learn to hide their feelings, or to repress them altogether. They may learn that if they do not show their feelings, they may be less likely to be further abused. These are usually attempts to cover extreme psychological pain experienced within. Bullying behaviour toward others may occur in an attempt to frighten others because the boy is scared. If a counsellor feels afraid of a young sex offender, he or she can assume that fear is at the heart of the boy's external intimidating behaviour. The more powerful and controlling the behaviour, the more helpless and scared the young person probably feels.

Sexually abusing other children

The incidence of children sexually abusing other children was discussed earlier in this chapter and in Chapter 3. Attempting to abuse other children sexually is usually a re-enactment of the young offender's own victimisation and is a power issue ('get back'). I have heard these boys actually say that they wanted someone else to hurt as much as they had. Such abusive behaviour also provides temporary relief of negative feelings and can become self-reinforcing and addictive. Porter (1986) speculated that if the young offender is narcissistic, he will probably abuse a child of the same sex. If the driving force behind his offending behaviour is the need to feel powerful and omnipotent, he will probably abuse a girl, or a boy who is much younger.

More has been written in recent years about methods to stop children from abusing others and these techniques can be appropriately introduced into a group setting (Cunningham and MacFarlane 1991). Predominantly cognitive-behavioural approaches are advocated, and drawings can be made to illustrate the situation more clearly. Artwork again might be used to demonstrate ways in which they become vulnerable to abusing other children. Directly asking them to do artwork about how it feels to be lonely and not like oneself might be appropriate once a good level of trust has been established with the therapist and/or group members. Themes of loneliness and low self-esteem frequently spontaneously emerge regardless of the theme of the art project. Non-directive art therapy is also likely to elicit these themes as well.

Delinquent behaviour and substance abuse

Adolescent sex offenders are vulnerable to problems with drugs and alcohol, are often truant from school, incorrigible at home, have problems with stealing, getting in fights, and so on. These are all ways of acting out feelings of anger, helplessness, need for attention and attempts to attain some sense of power, even though the behaviour is extremely self-defeating. The use of alcohol and/or drugs is also a way to escape painful feelings. Artwork can be used to address these issues and provides a format for further exploration. One example might be to have them draw a picture about how it feels to get into trouble and compare it with how it feels to receive positive attention. Addressing feelings of depression leading to substance abuse can be achieved through the use of a variety of art media and simply asking them to paint or draw how they felt before using. The use of abstract shapes tends to elicit emotions more than line drawings. Another method might be to illustrate situations that have actually happened and how they might find more constructive ways to have their needs met, or to manage their anger.

Cognitive-behavioural anger management techniques are useful, such as relaxation and learning to walk away and cool down. It is important to help them to see that they can make choices as to how angry they become by learning how their thinking feeds into anger. Techniques such as distraction and thought-stopping, commonly used in the treatment of anger management, are additional tools to give to these young offenders. A major problem, however, with these approaches is where there is a lack of motivation to apply them. Constant encouragement and reinforcement is usually necessary. Drawing cartoons or line drawings might be an additional way to helping them to identify the chain of thoughts or events leading up to extreme anger and/or violence (Liebmann 1990).

Little or no empathy for the victim

Empathy is usually formed in the early years of development and some children who are abused do not develop it. If it is not experienced from parents or others, it is not likely to be incorporated into the child's character. Helping these boys to learn empathy is a major goal of treatment. There is often a serious lacking of guilt or remorse. Artwork around the theme of empathy can be encouraged to enable them to translate how they felt when they were abused to the realisation that their victims felt similarly.

Involvement with baby-sitting

It has been found that a high percentage of sexual abuse occurs during baby-sitting, with most abusers being boys (Snets and Cebula 1987). These young people are frequently involved in child-care activities to earn money and to avoid peer relationships. This is the age where they should be developing their own identity separate from their parents, and healthy participation in social activities with other adolescents is an important developmental need. Baby-sitting can provide a fertile ground for sexually abusing younger children. Boys who have sexually abused another child should never be allowed to baby-sit. It is valuable for parents to understand that allowing their teenagers to baby-sit or letting their younger children be cared for by teenagers is sometimes risky. With increasing availability of sexual themes in films and television, and easy access to pornography on the Internet, teenagers are now much more sexually informed than in past generations, where baby-sitting was a common occurrence. Dysfunctional families often discourage their adolescent children from having friends outside their family circle. Some fundamentalist religions encourage young people to socialise only within their families or relatives, or only with members of the same religion. This creates a very closed system where dysfunctional behaviour reinforces itself and can provide a breeding ground for sexual abuse. This is not, of course, to imply that everyone from dysfunctional families or fundamentalist religions may be involved in sexual abuse.

Prior history of physical, sexual or emotional abuse

It is commonly believed that young boys who sexually abuse others have been sexually abused themselves. Research, however, has surprisingly indicated that a history of physical abuse with no previous sexual abuse is also frequently the case. Wolf (1989) reported that adolescent sex offenders very often have been sexually abused or severely physically and emotionally abused, all of which contribute to their sense of powerlessness and helplessness. The literature reports varying statistics as to what types of abuse these boys have experienced, but it is clear that many who sexually abuse were not sexually abused themselves.

Use of unconscious defence mechanisms

These boys commonly use at least three defence mechanisms which need to be addressed regularly. The first is that of denial and/or minimisation of the offence. A view of being a victim in the world is maintained by these boys who have little or no inner locus of control. They typically fail to see how they have set themselves up for many problems they incur, with most events perceived to be the result of what someone else or the 'system' has done to them. This perception is very real to them and it takes slow and supportive work to get them to see differently. Accusing them of being irresponsible, for example, serves only to lock them into their defences.

The second defence mechanism seen regularly is that of projection, where everyone else is blamed for what the boy has done instead of being able to take responsibility for his own behaviour. Parents, the system, probation officers, school teachers and police are all seen as the problem – not what these young offenders have done. There is often a high degree of mistrust of others and paranoia. The world is 'out to get' them and this view needs to be challenged constantly. The third common defence is splitting, where the boy sees everything as being either all black or all white. Dichotomous thinking is common and people are seen as being all good or all bad. Adolescent sex offenders sometimes develop characteristics commonly seen in borderline, narcissistic and antisocial personality disorders, which are largely due to problems in early development and frequently require very intensive long-term therapy.

High anxiety levels

These adolescents often carry grudges and worry obsessively. Anxiety is normal to a certain extent in adolescents, but that experienced by young offenders is frequently more excessive. The use of anxiety management techniques can be applied to assist treatment, such as relaxation techniques, cognitive restructuring and so on. These boys usually experience lowered inhibitions and poor impulse control, which makes them more susceptible to suicidal behaviour if they are severely depressed. These boys are at high risk for suicide and should be assessed periodically if other symptoms of depression are occurring. They are also highly susceptible to alcohol and drug abuse in order to self-medicate for depression.

Behavioural strategies to stop sex offending

At the outset of treatment, whether individually or in a group, firm criteria need to be established to create boundaries and limitations on what behaviour is acceptable and what is not. Some therapists advocate the use of the term 'offender behaviour', which is any behaviour which impinges on the rights of others, or hurts others. Young offenders need to be confronted when they are using 'offender behaviour' because it has become such a norm for them that they are frequently unable to determine the difference. It is hoped that the feelings underlying such behaviour can be explored and resolved.

These are several suggested ways to establish limits. A contract with the boy that he will *not* sexually abuse another child again needs to be made, both verbally and in writing. He needs to be told firmly that any future offences will have to be reported. He needs to understand clearly the consequences of any further offences and what the law says about further sentencing in young offenders units, longer probation periods or, if old enough, what prison sentences he is likely to face. He needs to understand clearly what realities he will face within the criminal justice system. He also needs a sense of empowerment over how to manage his own behaviour. A structure as to what he can do if he feels tempted needs to be put in place. Examples might be contacting the therapist and/or someone else who is in on the contract. He must agree not to be alone with any younger child – *ever*! He also needs to identify someone immediately available to talk to when he is feeling isolated.

Young offenders need to learn self-protection strategies from sexual abuse from other boys or adults (especially necessary if living in foster homes or residential homes). This involves who he should tell and how he can avoid getting into such a situation. These boys are often easy targets for further sexual abuse. Their loneliness and low self-esteem set them up to be vulnerable to advances from other sex offenders. Helping them to develop self-respect and a deep sense of entitlement *not* to be treated badly is a key goal in therapy. They are less likely to want to hurt others if they are no longer being abused themselves.

Behavioural problems during therapeutic sessions

These boys are likely to have several behavioural problems which will be disruptive to group work if not managed positively. They typically suffer from poor attention span with possible Attention Deficit and Hyperactivity Disorder (ADHD: commonly diagnosed in the United States and increasingly being diagnosed in the United Kingdom) usually due to a high level of anxiety. Disruptive behaviour is likely to erupt when discussing issues relative to sexual abuse. Hyperactivity and distracting behaviour are also used to deflect from having to deal with painful and embarrassing issues. He may change the subject frequently in order to avoid dealing with painful feelings. He may attempt to shock the therapist or even be actively verbally or physically abusive. The most common reason I have observed in working with troubled adolescents is that they are afraid to form a relationship with me or anyone else because they fear further abandonment. It is easier to alienate the therapist and get him or her to give up on the boy than to risk such an attachment.

One young sex offender with whom I worked threw art materials at me. Another threatened to vomit all over the room. Another drew pictures of cannabis and cigarette packs all over a group mural in an effort to shock and alienate me. In the case where art materials were thrown at me, I clearly and firmly told the boy that I did not like being treated in such a way and expected it not to happen again. Fortunately, this approach was effective in future sessions. In the instance where the boy threatened to throw up, I asked him in a very nonchalant way to please do it in the sink, which quickly diffused the situation and he was not rewarded with the shocked reaction he was looking for. I 'joined' the boy who drew cigarettes and cannabis leaves by asking him if he was having a 'nicotine fit'. Such a response not only diffused the situation, but also added an element of humour to which the boy responded warmly and actually enhanced our therapeutic relationship in the months to come.

Unfortunately the nature of many therapeutic settings is that workers do change placements or jobs on a regular basis, and it is likely that the boys will be abandoned again. Ending therapy in a constructive and reassuring way over time is absolutely essential with these troubled young people. I have been asked: 'Are you going to leave us like everyone else has?' I was able to promise to be there until the end of the year, but I ultimately had to move to another placement. At least explaining those boundaries to him was reassuring.

Seductive behaviour toward the therapist is common, and needs to be contained appropriately. One young boy flirted openly with me and insisted on helping me hand out the art supplies and clean up afterwards. His artwork was blatantly sexually seductive and shocking. It was essential not to react emotionally to his behaviour but calmly to set firm boundaries as to what was acceptable and unacceptable behaviour without rejecting him.

When carrying out group work, it is not unusual for these boys to become physically violent toward each other. They may hit each other, throw things at each other, pull chairs out from under each other, or other inappropriate 'offender behaviours'. It needs to be emphasised that this type of behaviour is *totally* inappropriate and will not be tolerated in the group. Feedback from other group members about how it makes them feel is especially useful because they are peers and not perceived as an authority figure, as therapists usually are. No put-downs are allowed in the group and are identified again as 'offender behaviour'. Insults hurt others and are a form of bullying. Discussions and accompanying drawings can ensue exploring how it feels to be insulted versus how it feels to be praised.

Art exercises, such as making greeting cards for each other, might be implemented to help them experience the difference between compliments and put-downs at a deeper level. A remarkable change in attitude toward each other is likely to ensue when positive feedback has been exchanged. These boys will usually have a great deal of difficulty saying anything positive to others as well as believing anything positive about themselves. There is typically a fear and reluctance to express any feelings. This can be for a variety of reasons, but most commonly because they may have been abused emotionally and/or physically for showing their feelings in the past. Boys in particular are taught that any demonstration of feelings means they are weak. When tears are shed, it is very embarrassing for them, and they need much support. I have observed situations where one boy may be crying while other group members are being disruptive in order to avoid dealing with their own feelings and are totally unable to console the person who is upset. This situation requires very sensitive management, but provides a fertile opportunity for exploring feelings.

These boys may regularly be truant from school and likewise miss therapy sessions if given the opportunity. Their reasons for non-attendance are often not true and it is frequently necessary to check out their stories. If it is discovered that the excuses are not true, therapeutic issues around lying and deceit, which are also 'offender behaviours', need to be addressed. If a therapist is conned, it is important to realise that these boys are 'experts' at it, and it is not necessarily the fault of the therapist. Many times they have been lying for so long they have difficulty keeping fact from fiction, and come to believe their own lies. As experience is gained, however, in working with these boys, it may become easier to detect lies when they occur. It is important to listen to one's gut reaction if there is suspicion that the truth is not being told. It is helpful to explore the situation further when the boy's words do not add up with his emotional response. Saying something directly like 'I'm having a hard time believing what you are saying' may trigger an emotional overreaction and further elaboration of the lie. It can then be processed with the rest of the group by asking the other boys how they feel when someone has lied to them. If done in a supportive manner, the boy may be able to admit that he lied and needs a great deal of praise for his honesty and acknowledgement of how difficult it was for him. Feedback from group memebers will be more readily heard than will that of the therapist.

Having a network of other professionals to consult with from time to time may be essential, as long as confidentiality is carefully maintained. Informed consent needs to be given to the boy at the outset of treatment and he needs to understand that other professionals may be consulted on his behalf. Professionals do need to be careful not to misuse information, but to work together on behalf of the therapeutic progress of the young offender. Such consultation not only helps therapeutic intervention, but also may prevent other workers from being conned as well. This situation has the potential of being fraught with problems and needs to be handled extremely carefully in order to avoid destroying the boy's trust. These boys often feel angry at counsellors when they can manipulate them, and need firm limit-setting and confrontation when it occurs.

The turmoil of normal adolescence will be exaggerated in these boys. Teenage years are usually difficult for most young people. Problems of self-esteem, school pressures, relationship and dating problems, breaking away from parents in order to establish their own identity, fears about being able to get a job or go to university, hormonal changes and how to handle them, along with many other issues are difficult for teenagers. With boys who have been abused and have become sexual abusers, these problems will be exaggerated considerably.

Use of art in counselling adolescent sex offenders

Art therapists are becoming more knowledgeable about treatment issues involved in working with adolescent sex offenders (Aulich 1994; Gerber 1994; Hagood 1991b, 1994b). The use of art in counselling is effective for a variety of reasons. It is an enjoyable activity and adolescent offenders usually respond well to it. In my experience, they enthusiastically looked forward to art-making. The art process held their attention to a greater extent than just talking. Young people with severe behavioural problems usually become drawn into the art process and somehow are able to concentrate at a deeper level with a cessation of acting-out behaviour. Poor attention span is common with these boys, and artwork appears to help focus on issues as they emerge and to enable group members to see problems visually. It encourages sharing and feedback and often pulls everyone into the group process. In my experience, art therapy in groups enables others to realise that they are not alone in their situation, problems and feelings.

Putting a stop to sexual offending behaviour is *top priority.* Helping these boys to gain a sense of control and management of their sexually abusive behaviour is foremost. A deeper exploration of this issue and treatment approaches is discussed in Chapter 3 in the discussion on abuse-reactive children. Adapting artwork to help these boys identify areas where they are vulnerable to offending is very useful. Asking them to draw themselves when they are feeling lonely and vulnerable, to draw what they are thinking and feeling about themselves and to problem-solve what they will do when they feel tempted to offend are helpful interventions. Cognitive restructuring can be amplified with the use of the visual image created in artwork whereby a young offender can visualise his situation more clearly, share it with the counsellor and other group members, realise he is not alone, and be empowered not to abuse anymore. These concepts will need to be reinforced over a long period of time and short-term treatment is not advised.

Artwork helps the young people to focus on the issues at hand by seeing the problem concretely in a drawing and to be better able to come up with solutions. It also assists in identifying cognitive distortions leading to sexual abuse. In group work, the use of art encourages sharing from other group members who can *see* what one is thinking or feeling instead of only hearing words. Group members are invited to comment on each other's artwork and to relate it to their own problems. Involving art materials tends to attract everyone into the group process. Boys who initially resist joining in tend to participate later on in the session if they are not pressured. They do not want to be left out and notice that others are enjoying themselves. Artwork also enables others to realise that they are not alone in their problems or feelings and helps them to reduce their sense of isolation. It is not uncommon to be asked at the outset of each session if they would be allowed to do artwork, because they looked forward to the experience.

In most instances the completion of a piece of art to show to others instils a sense of pride, contributing to higher self-esteem. Kramer (1971, 1975, 1979), one of the founders of American art therapy, began her work in a home for delinquent boys. She frequently had them exhibit their artwork, including many colourful paintings, in a central location within the facility because they felt so much pride in what they had done. More directive artwork, however, done in a therapeutic group may deal specifically with confidential issues and would not be appropriate for such a display. More appropriate art projects can be created specially for such a purpose.

Art therapists and cousellors typically have training and experience in a variety of theories and techniques. A good deal of art therapy training is based on psychoanalytic theory. American literature on art therapy with adolescents is psychoanalytic in approach as well (Linesch 1988). British art therapists working with offenders largely focus on the same approach (Liebmann 1994). Art materials are used to enable young offenders to express their feelings and to become more aware of unconscious material. This approach may be highly beneficial as far as expression of emotions is concerned. Most young offenders have learned to suppress their feelings from a very early age; enabling them to get in touch with their emotions is highly therapeutic. Common feelings of emotional pain, confusion, guilt and suicidal ideation need to be expressed. Self-harming behaviour is common and is usually a way used to avoid painful feelings, along with drug and alcohol abuse.

Because artwork accesses feelings better than words, it is not unusual to see adolescent offenders break down and cry with the impact of looking at what they have created. They need much support when this happens because it is especially embarrassing to cry in front of their male peers. Cultural values in many countries against male expression of feelings are very strong and to cry is considered unmanly. These boys struggle with their fragile male identity anyway, and need much support and validation. Encouraging other boys in the group to be supportive to each other is important and should help them to develop empathy.

The use of art also helps the therapist to be more aware of defence mechanisms such as denial and minimisation which are heavily relied on by these boys. Denial is more difficult to maintain when artwork is used. Someone can insist that they are happy, but the artwork may reveal otherwise. A boy can argue that a particular relationship is very good, but a drawing of the relationship in many instances proves otherwise. Exploring the reality of the situation and enabling the boy to express his feelings are very useful.

Involving art media in the counselling process influences the development of group cohesiveness. These boys isolate themselves and tend to avoid group situations in their everyday life. Because of the openness of the content of the drawings, self-disclosure becomes easier when participants see others creating similar images. These boys begin to realise that they are not totally alone because others in the group feel similarly and have very similar problems.

Paintings and drawings can help to retrieve childhood memories and to gain insight into the present situation. Creating artwork around a childhood memory usually elicits more memories and can be very powerful. Because of the ability of artwork to evoke strong emotions, such an approach should be used cautiously. Repressed memories can surface too quickly and create further psychological regression and even psychotic reactions if the boy is susceptible to such. Knowing the psychological history of these boys is important. Care must also be taken not to allow an increasing awareness of these boys' own childhood abuse and trauma to become an excuse for offending against others. Such awareness, however, is an essential part of helping them to develop empathy for their victims. Development of empathy is always one of the key components of working with sex offenders, whatever their age.

Using art materials to illustrate situations where they find themselves worrying, what they worry about, who they would talk to if they are feeling suicidal, and so on can be very helpful. Using cartooning methods in identifying various situations and how they set themselves up for their difficulties is also a useful art therapy technique (Liebmann 1990; Rhyne 1984). Helping these boys to become more aware of their repressed feelings and to express them with a variety of art media is especially useful. Gerber (1994) illustrated a variety of ways to incorporate art therapy into the treatment of juvenile sex offenders within a cognitive-behavioural model.

Summary

At first glance, young sex offenders may appear as ordinary young people. They may come from a variety of situations, some from foster homes, some from poor neighbourhoods and some from well-to-do families. Sexual abuse crosses all socio-economic and cultural strata. I have found it useful to view these young boys as positively as possible. Within each of them lie many gifts and strengths to build on. That they have a vulnerability to abuse others sexually, however, is not to be ignored. They see themselves as lonely, unlikeable and much worse as a 'sex offender' hated by society. They typically have no vision of a happy and healthy life ahead of them. Immediate gratification which consistently gets them into trouble sadly is often the case. I believe that to build on young sex offenders' talents and ultimate usefulness to the world is just as much a part of counselling and psychotherapy as to focus only on extinguishing bad behaviour. In eliminating offensive behaviours, new and healthy behaviours, thoughts, feelings and aspirations need to take their place. These boys are entitled to a fruitful life as much as ordinary adolescents. To have a vision of making something successful out of their lives gives them a sense of empowerment and, it is hoped, making them less likely to abuse others.

A 17-year-old American adolescent sex offender with whom I worked clearly summarised the need of young sex offenders to be treated well. He was very upset when he learned that most young offenders in the United Kingdom were unlikely to receive therapy. He wrote the following words when he learned that I was moving to Scotland and asked me to bring them along with me:

> Perpetrators are people too, so treat them like so. Remind them from time to time that they are in good hands. Try to encourage them to continue counseling, long-term counseling. In order to talk to them, you must be kind, or they won't open up.

Evidence is increasingly demonstrating that most sex offending begins in adolescence, or even earlier (Becker 1988; Becker *et al.* 1986). The need for treatment is crucial at this level to prevent the establishment of an entrenched pattern of molesting as these adolescents grow into adulthood. There is still much to learn about how effective these approaches are with younger offenders, who may not be able to respond because they are not developmentally mature enough. Outcome studies in any area of counselling or psychotherapy are sparse, and the need for such research has clearly been established. Methods in working with adolescent sex offenders are no exception. A general lack of outcome studies in the effectiveness of therapeutic work with adolescent sex offenders sometimes leaves us with the dilemma of not knowing whether working with this population is worthwhile (Keller *et al.* 1989). As research in art therapy is expanding, there is ample opportunity to demonstrate its effectiveness in the therapeutic process with adolescent sex offenders. It is my belief that we must start somewhere in developing methods of working with these young boys in the hope that the cycle of child molestation might someday be reduced.

As discussed in Chapter 1, there are various ways that artwork may be incorporated into counselling. A variety of counselling theories can be used, adding visual approaches to amplify what is usually said in words only. Chapter 3 reviewed special problems in using art with young survivors of sexual abuse and Chapter 4 presented illustrations of how artwork was used with sexually abused children. Many of these problems occur in working with adolescent sex offenders as well, and the methods of using artwork with sexually abused children are also applicable to working with adolescent sex offenders. My main approach in working with adolescent sex offenders was simply to take whatever themes emerged during the group process and ask them to create artwork to illustrate them. Issues were depicted graphically which validated much of the literature written by clinicians with considerable experience in this area. It is one thing to read about therapeutic issues of young sex offenders and another to see these boys spontaneously reveal them in the way they create artwork. The impact of visual images on the young offenders was much greater than only talking. These images also have an impact on the therapist who can see what is going on at a visual level, providing greater insight and understanding.

This chapter has discussed the many problems and therapeutic issues which need to be addressed in working with adolescent offenders along with suggestions for ways to incorporate art materials in the counselling process. Because there is considerable overlapping in issues with adolescent sex offenders and adult sex offenders, case examples of group work both with adolescent offenders and adult sex offenders will be presented in Chapter 8. A discussion of problems of adult sex offenders will also be presented.

CHAPTER 8

The Use of Art in Group Work with Adolescent and Adult Sex Offenders

This chapter will present a brief discussion of basic characteristics of adult sex offenders and difficulties likely to be encountered when working with them. Two case examples of using art with counselling will be presented, one working with a group of adolescent sex offenders, and the other representing work with adult sex offenders. Many of the issues discussed in Chapter 7 on working with adolescent sex offenders are also relevant to working with adult offenders. Greater insight into the problems of adolescent sex offenders should lend itself to a better understanding of adult offenders who have taken on a lifetime of severely entrenched and damaging behaviour. This chapter illustrates how the use of art materials can amplify therapeutic work with both adolescent and adult sex offenders. Again, because my work was exclusively with male sex offenders, I will refer to offenders in the male gender. This is not to overlook the fact that women may sexually abuse children as well (Finkelhor, Williams and Burns 1988). Some of the offenders with whom I worked had been sexually abused by women when they were very young.

As I wrote in Chapter 7, my decision to work with sex offenders, both adolescent and adult, was because I believed it was important to my therapeutic work with child and adult survivors to understand more about abusers. Because of my experience with sex offenders, I have been better able to help survivors of sexual abuse understand why the abuse occurred and more clearly why it was *not* their fault. As discussed in Chapter 6, a major treatment objective in working with survivors, both children and adults, is to get them fully to incorporate the fact that nothing they did or did not do had anything to do with their abuse. It is *always* the offender's fault. In working with offenders, a constant reminder had to be made that no matter how justified they felt to abuse children, they had no right to do so and as part of their treatment they had to learn to accept fully that it was their fault and that they were totally responsible.

Working with adult sex offenders

Working with adult sex offenders requires very directive work (Becker 1988; Ryan 1988). Many counsellors and art therapists strongly believe that a non-directive approach is the only way to work. I would strongly challenge this view when working with sex offenders, both adolescent and adult. There are times when non-directive approaches are useful to establish a warm and authentic relationship and to enable expression of feelings. To rely on them exclusively, however, is likely to allow the sex offender to continue in the denial and minimisation of what he has done. These men are used to deceiving and lying, and a major danger in using person-centred non-directive therapy alone is in being too gullible. Challenging their cognitive distortions is an extremely important part of therapeutic work with adult sex offenders (Becker 1988; Marshall *et al.* 1991; Ward *et al.* 1997). These men have deceived themselves by rationalising every aspect of their abusive behaviour and it is extremely important to confront these thinking patterns consistently. Being too supportive and accepting without challenging thoughts and behaviours serves to collude with the offender in his maintenance of denial and minimisation. By confrontation, however, I do not mean being abusive as a therapist. I have observed some highly confrontational therapy groups in drug rehabilitation programmes in California where the verbal abuse carried out by therapists allegedly to 'break down defences' was appalling! Sex offenders, regardless of what horrendous acts they have committed, are still human beings who deserve to be treated humanely. They have experienced enough abuse and need positive role models for nonabusive behaviour. Otherwise they are likely to become more resistant to treatment and continue to experience the same abuse they experienced as children, which set them up to become abusers themselves. Such treatment not only provides poor modelling, but also feeds into their already low self-esteem and feelings of helplessness, which are known triggers for sexual abuse.

Characteristics of adult sex offenders

The characteristics of adult sex offenders overlap considerably with those of adolescent sex offenders. There are also variations between sex offenders, but generally speaking the following characteristics along with those discussed in working with adolescent offenders were observed in my work with them, and are well substantiated by other writers (Bolton and Morris 1989; Finkelhor 1984; Pryor 1996; Sgroi 1989).

According to the 1984 Symposium of the US Department of Justice (Naitove 1988), the belief of experts at that time was that there were basically two types of sex offenders: regressed and fixated. Early therapeutic programmes also operated along this line of reasoning (Giarretto 1982). A 'regressed' sex offender allegedly began abusing in adulthood and because of extreme stress and unavailability of their partners for sex or affection, they turned to their own children to establish a sexual relationship. My own observations of those who were directly involved in the treatment of sex offenders at that time was that offenders were indulged with a considerable amount of sympathy and therapists were easily deceived by them. It was believed that a 'fixated' offender had begun a pattern of sexual abuse as an adolescent. There seemed to be little awareness at that time that children were also sexually abusing each other (Cunningham and MacFarlane 1991). Other writers, however, began challenging the regressed–fixated dichotomy. While Summit (1980) more broadly described sex offenders, he later went on to describe the 'Child Sexual Abuse Accommodation Syndrome', which consisted of the deliberate and systematic grooming behaviour of sex offenders in selecting and desensitising vulnerable victims for sexual abuse (Summit 1983). Becker (1988) found that 49 per cent of incest offenders she studied were also interested in children outside the family. She stated that the onset of interest in deviant sexual behaviours in adolescents occurred in 60 per cent of offenders studied. Conte, Wolf and Smith (1989) interviewed twenty adult sex offenders about the processes whereby they selected, recruited and maintained children in a sexually abusive situation. The deliberate, blatant and systematic process of engaging vulnerable children to cooperate in their own abuse was made appallingly apparent.

Adult sex offenders, like adolescent sex offenders, typically are unable to empathise with their victims, or with others. They need to come to a deep sense of the damage they have done. They commonly feel self-pity that they have been caught far more than any remorse for what they have done to their victims, especially at the outset of treatment. They may exhibit a form of 'pseudo-denial' where they over-lament their crime, but are not sincere. They may attempt to convince others that they are sorry, but over-apologising is not necessarily empathy. Heavy use of denial and minimisation as a defence mechanism is common. Most offenders deny the abuse at the outset. In countries without diversion treatment programmes, they are even less likely to admit to what they have done. They may also insist that they did it only once or that they did not do it all, even where there is evidence to the contrary. Such an insistence needs to be consistently challenged, because it is highly unlikely. They are also likely to minimise the harm they have done to their victim(s), even alleging that small children wanted them to do it and liked it. A major advantage of group work with other offenders is that they are very good at confronting one another. They are able to see through the deceitful manoeuvres, because they have been so good at it themselves. They often make far better therapists in this respect than trained professionals.

Adult sex offenders are victims of a variety of abuses themselves. Becker (1988), who carried out research with the National Institute of Mental Health in the United States, described sex offenders as coming from backgrounds of sexual victimisation, physical victimisation, parental or peer violence, dysfunctional families, use of pornography, dysfunctional peer relationships and possible brain dysfunction. She pointed out, however, that many people with such a background do not sexually abuse children. Wolf (1989) substantiated Becker's claims in his study of over 300 sex offenders, finding that 44 per cent were either direct victims of sexual abuse, or had witnessed sexual abuse; 30 per cent suffered physical abuse as children and another 37 per cent observed it on a regular basis. All offenders in the study were from severely dysfunctional families. It is important to note, contrary to popular belief, that not all of them were sexually abused. Offenders were psychologically tested and a very high percentage were diagnosed with personality disorders under the DSM III-R categories of Antisocial Personality Disorder, Narcissistic Personality Disorder, Histrionic Personality Disorder and Borderline Personality Disorder (American Psychiatric Association 1987). Wolf found that sex offenders typically had lowered inhibitions because of their own histories of abuse. Approximately 50 per cent of the offenders studied also sexually abused children outside of their home and were involved in other kinds of violent behaviour.

Treatment issues in working with adult sex offenders

Sex offenders typically either do not want to recall their past histories of abuse, or are likely to use it as an excuse for sexually abusing children. Any such rationalisation needs to be rigorously and consistently challenged. Providing empathetic support for offenders in working through their own trauma is important, but helping them to see that they consciously *chose* to abuse other children is essential for them to learn to take responsibility. In the programmes where I worked, it was believed that offenders should work through their feelings about their own abuse histories as part of their treatment.

Because they tend to be emotionally immature and childlike, adult sex offenders typically exhibit poor impulse control and compulsive behaviour. They also tend to have arrested sexual development. They are usually very emotionally dependent on others, including their partners and children, and look to their children to provide them with affection rather than the other way round. They are likely to suffer from overwhelming feelings of inadequacy and display a high degree of passivity and passive-aggressive behaviour in order to maintain a sense of control over others. They are very capable of deceiving and manipulating others, and are often so charming and convincing that even seasoned therapists can be deceived. It may be necessary constantly to check out their stories with other mental health professionals such as social workers, probation officers or other therapists involved with their family members.

During treatment, sex offenders should not be allowed to have contact with their children, unless closely supervised. Even then, a meeting may be psychologically traumatic for the child. In the programmes where I worked, whenever any evidence surfaced that any of the offenders had contacted their children against a court order and the rules of the programme, the suspicion was immediately relayed to appropriate professionals for further investigation. If it was found that the offenders had attempted in any way to contact their children, they faced the possibility of being expelled from the programme and sent to prison. Only after a year or two of intensive individual and group therapy were offenders able to visit their children, after several other therapists had assessed that they were indeed taking total responsibility for the abuse. The programmes where I worked required that each offender write a letter to his victim apologising and stating clearly that it was not the child's fault. Such letters would be read to therapy groups where the group assessed how sincere they were. Unless it became clear that the offender really meant it, he had to continue working on the letter as a therapeutic tool and was not allowed to send it to the child. In the mean time, the child was likely to be in ongoing individual and group therapy as well, coming to terms with the fact that the abuse was not his or her fault.

As discussed in Chapter 7 on adolescent sex offenders, many adult offenders have problems with alcohol and drug dependency and need to be in specific treatment for such addictions as part of their overall therapy. A good deal of sexual abuse occurs while under the influence of alcohol and/or drugs. Sex offenders will use the fact that they were drunk or 'high' as another excuse for the abuse, and even deny remembering it.

The tendency of sex offenders to be loners and isolated from others was noted in Chapter 7. Problems abound not only with peers, but also in relationships with their partners. This is largely due to a poor sense of themselves and extremely low self-esteem. Such isolation feeds into the 'cycle of abuse' whereby they can indulge in their feelings of self-pity, self-hatred and fantasies of sexual abuse. Difficulties with anger management are common and need specialised treatment, again with cognitive-behavioural approaches. Constant use of cathartic approaches where offenders are encouraged to express their anger can become self-reinforcing, and such anger expression in a group setting can result in verbal and emotional abuse toward other group members or the therapist in the name of 'good therapy'. They need to recognise verbal and emotional abuse and learn to express themselves in more constructive ways.

There are many issues involved in working with sex offenders and such work is complex and requires long-term treatment. Programmes in which I was involved believed that as long as two to three years was necessary, but some offenders needed much more than that. The man's self-loathing is magnified by being known as a 'sex offender', and should he be in a prison setting, the hostility of other inmates is well known because their hierarchy of morality defines sexual abuse as a greater offence than murder. An offender is quite likely to be physically, sexually and mentally abused if other inmates learn why he is in prison. His self-esteem obviously becomes even more deficient. Many prisons have high security offender units where sex offenders are kept together. A major problem with this approach is that, while it may protect them from abuse from other inmates, it provides a fertile ground for them to share their sexual fantasies with each other, increasing their fantasy repertoire. It is little wonder that when they are eventually released from prison after having no control over their lives and where they are highly unlikely to have received therapy, so many quickly return to sexually abusing children.

Because a sex offender has become so adept at not allowing himself to feel anything, approaches which elicit emotional responses and expression are valuable. Helping him to express sadness, anxiety and anger in a healthy way is important to the therapeutic process. He needs to become more aware of his feelings and to be reassured constantly that it is all right to experience any emotion. The problem lies in learning to be responsible for what he does about his feelings. Many behaviours may not be acceptable, but feelings simply are and bear no judgement.

A major goal of treatment is to get the offender genuinely to take total responsibility for his sexual relationship with a child. He needs to admit and believe sincerely that he has seriously harmed a child or children. He must, at some point, have owned up to all of the specific acts he has done. Caution is needed in this area and group work is not the place for sharing sexual details. Going into detail about sexual acts in a group feeds into the fantasies of other offenders and is counterproductive. Repeatedly telling the details of the abuse leaves no emotional impact. I have heard offenders glibly list all of the details of what they did to a child with absolutely no emotional connection to what they are saying. An offender needs to be able to identify the forms of coercion he used with a child, whether it was verbal threats, physical abuse, or bribery with sweets, treats, money and/or alcohol or drugs. He needs to be able to describe how he created or took advantage of opportunities, such as taking the child shopping, waiting until the mother had gone to work, and so on.

The sexual abuse of a child has a horrendous effect on other family members whether it be the mother, other siblings and other relatives. The offender needs to realise what an effect his abusive behaviour has had on the rest of the family and ultimately to make amends in whatever way possible. Because of fear of the family's reaction, many adult survivors of sexual abuse have disclosed their abuse to me for the first time, never daring to tell anyone in the family because they might be hurt. Survivors will often suffer in silence rather than hurt everyone else, fearing they will 'blow the family apart'. In quite a few instances, this does happen and the survivor is blamed for telling anyone, rather than the offender being appropriately confronted and action taken. The secret is perpetuated – a cloak of silence under which the offender continues to operate, destroying the lives of one or more children.

Cycle of sexual abuse

In cognitive-behavioural work with sex offenders, a behavioural feedback loop has been identified which clarifies the thought processes likely to lead to an episode of sexual abuse. One thought, feeling or behaviour leads to another, beginning with extremely low self-esteem to expectations of rejection and criticism, to withdrawal and isolation, to lack of assertiveness, to sexual fantasies involving children, to masturbation, to grooming of the victim, to acting out the sexual abuse, to momentary guilt which is pushed away with distraction and rationalisation, and back to more low self-esteem. Many therapists have found it useful to help offenders identify these phases and to find ways of breaking the cycle by introducing more productive ways of thinking, feeling and behaving.

Use of art in counselling adult sex offenders

Very little has been published on the use of art in therapeutic work with sex offenders, especially adult sex offenders. Naitove (1982) illustrated how the use of magazine collage enabled offenders to see their issues more clearly. Themes of isolation and denial were typical. The artwork also provided more information and insight into working with adult sex offenders in general. Words alone can deceive, but what is actually graphically presented with art materials is frequently a different story. One of the benefits of the use of artwork is that it serves as a tool to detect denial and minimisation. McCourt (1994) presents a case study of non-directive work with an adult sex offender utilising a variety of two-dimensional art materials. She convincingly relays how the spontaneous creative process alone is therapeutic, but does not address the cognitive-behavioural aspects of treatment, nor any focus on getting the offender to stop abusing children.

Another effective use of art materials is the power of images to evoke emotions. Sex offenders are adept at shutting off their feelings, but frequently when they see images they have painted or drawn, they are no longer able to suppress their emotions and in some instances may break down and cry. This requires a great deal of sensitivity on the part of therapists, because men tend to experience the expression of emotion as a weakness; many offenders were severely abused as children if they cried, thus learning to suppress their anger and sadness. Learning to experience all of their feelings in a healthy and integrated way is always a major treatment goal. Peer feedback is likely to be taken more seriously than that of therapists who are seen as authority figures. It is useful to encourage other group members to give feedback and express feelings about each other's artwork. It is important for the therapist not to take over the group and have it become one-to-one therapy. On the other hand, when an intervention or confrontation is needed, it is important to seize upon the opportunity.

The use of artwork can help these men to understand their own childhood and family issues in an attempt to help them gain some insight into where they learned to abuse children sexually. Their extremely low self-esteem had its origins in their dysfunctional families. They need to understand that they did not deserve whatever abuse they received themselves. In many instances they were either severely physically or sexually abused, or observed it happening to others. Emotional abuse is also a major part of their background. On the other hand, it is important not to allow them to wallow in self-pity in order to justify what they have done, thereby absolving them of responsibility. A careful balance of gaining insight and understanding and taking full responsibility for their own behaviour is absolutely essential. There are many ways that art materials can help offenders more clearly to understand themselves and their families.

Group work using art in counselling adolescent and adult sex offenders

Time management is always an issue in therapeutic work, and especially in group work where art materials are used. Most groups allow an hour and a half. In my experience, the first twenty minutes or so was usually sufficient to allow themes to emerge from verbal discussions. When a significant theme emerged, I would suggest that group members create a piece of artwork to elaborate on that theme (Liebmann 1986; Waller 1993). I brought a case of basic art supplies including felt-markers and oil pastels with me each week. A supply of art papers was kept on the premises. I found that twenty to thirty minutes usually allowed sufficient time for an art project. Sometimes group members finished well before that time. In order to manage time, it was helpful to remind them at the mid-point of the art-making process how much time they had left. The remainder of the session was used for talking, and sharing contents of the artwork. In some instances, therapeutic programmes have specific therapeutic goals to be addressed within a module of time (e.g. ten weeks). In such a structure, themes can be decided on in advance to provide a more directive format.

Because the impact of visual representation in artwork can evoke very strong feelings which previously have been suppressed, the group provided an ideal situation for listening to each other and to begin to develop empathy. It was especially important to encourage those in the group to give each other feedback and support. While adolescent sex offenders typically distracted themselves from any painful feelings by acting-out behaviour, adult offenders were likely to show no emotion at all.

Offenders may initially resist being involved in the art process by stating that they cannot draw, or that they do not want to participate. This resistance may come from deep-seated low self-esteem and fear of what others think, or be a way to attempt to initiate a power struggle with the therapist. It is helpful to offer reassurance that it is not an art class, but is intended for them to learn more about themselves. I often humorously ask them if they have seen any modern art exhibits, which usually sets them at ease. It is helpful to have the expectation that they will do the best they can. Feelings of hesitance are to be acknowledged and supported, not argued with. Beginning with magazine collage or cartooning often creates a less threatening medium. The wide variety of art media previously discussed in this book can be used with adult offenders.

Group rules

It is important at the outset of a group to have members make up a list of rules with which all participants are required to comply. Alcohol or drug use should not be condoned during therapy. If anyone comes to the group with alcohol on his breath, appears spaced-out or high (talking rapidly, etc.), he needs to be confronted and limits need to be set. He may need a referral for treatment of alcohol or drug abuse. Other rules to be made and enforced are being on time, attending regularly and showing respect for each other by no allowance of 'offender behaviour'. This should be clearly defined with the help of group members and consists of any behaviour which is hurtful, disruptive or abusive to others.

Case example: Group work with adolescent sex offenders

Because of the similarities in issues of both adolescent and adult sex offenders, I have chosen to present two case examples representing work with both age groups of offenders in the same chapter. The first case example describes how art therapy was used with a group of adolescent sex offenders with whom I worked prior to moving to Britain (Hagood 1991b, 1994b). The boys in this group lived in various situations, some at home, some in residential treatment centres and some in foster homes. The group sessions, however, were held on separate premises which were rented by the treatment programme where I worked, and the boys came from a variety of locations in the immediate area. A male therapist who had previously done a considerable amount of counselling with delinquent boys, including young sex offenders, was my co-therapist. It was mutually agreed that we would work together in combining verbal counselling approaches and art therapy. The duration of time spent with these boys was ten months. The length of each weekly session was one hour and twenty minutes and the average group consisted of seven boys with ages ranging from 11 to 17 years of age.

Because I had previously worked with a number of troubled adolescent boys, I found it surprisingly easy to like these boys. I had previously worked with a large number of survivors of sexual abuse, and had indeed experienced angry feelings toward sex offenders in general. Because I did not work with any of these boys' victims, and realised how like their victims these boys actually were, I was able to view them similarly to other sexually abused children. It was nevertheless important not to become too sympathetic and forget their sexual offences.

Treatment programmes typically consisted of providing these boys with weekly sessions of individual therapy, group therapy and family therapy when families were available. Treatment staff met each week to discuss the work done in groups and to consult with individual therapists who also worked with these boys. This made it possible to check out inconsistencies in what these boys said in the group with other staff members in order to minimise the occurrence of deception. The group was structured with rules established by the therapists and group members alike. It was agreed that there would be no destruction of anyone else's artwork. Issues of confidentiality were discussed and what was shared within the group was not to be told to anyone outside of the group. However, it was also explained to the boys that what happened in the group and the artwork would be discussed with other therapists in the programme who were involved in their treatment in order to help them better. Rules about behaviour during group sessions were established and enforced. These behaviours consisted of arriving late, missing sessions, physical or verbal abuse toward other members of the group, and the use of alcohol and/or drugs prior to coming to the group.

Thorough discussions with the boys regarding any possibilities of future sex offending was essential in order to hopefully prevent its reoccurrence. The main group rules regarding re-offending were:

1. That each boy would under no circumstances offend again.
2. That any future offences would have to be reported.
3. That there would be consequences of any re-molesting such as further sentencing, longer probation or, if old enough, prison.

Within the group rules and structure, however, much latitude was given to encourage open sharing of feelings between members of the group, to allow for a natural unfolding of issues, and to work with the dynamics of the group as they occurred. As issues emerged, we encouraged the boys to depict them with coloured drawings and to share them with each other. Newsprint and coloured markers were used throughout these group sessions. Unfortunately, this created considerable limitations in the possibilities for the uses of art therapy with a greater variety of media. Many other uses of art materials are possible with this population such as paints, magazine collage, sugar paper, clay and oil pastels, to name but a few. However, due to time constraints and the situation of borrowing someone else's office for the sessions, it was necessary to choose art materials to allow for portability and minimal clean-up.

My approach with these boys was a mix of directive and non-directive. A theme was given for drawings as they spontaneously emerged in the group. After the drawings were completed, each boy shared what was depicted in his artwork. The other boys were encouraged to comment and to give feedback. As a result of the artwork, feelings frequently emerged which had previously been blocked and an opportunity was created to help the boys develop empathy for each other. As questions were asked, more verbalisation of problems and feelings unfolded. These boys had learned to suppress their feelings at a very early age because they were abused themselves. Physical abuse, emotional abuse and/or sexual abuse were commonly experienced in their early development. In order to survive, their emotions became blunted and little empathy was displayed toward each other. Art therapy was used in a cathartic way to help these boys ventilate their anger, pain and sadness. The artwork was a major advantage in that it elicited feelings that these boys were so adept at concealing, or even allowing themselves to experience.

Special problems arose during these therapeutic sessions such as poor attention span, hyperactivity, changing the subject and distracting behaviour such as rocking and banging chairs, especially when discussing anxiety-producing subjects. Interestingly, these behaviours tended to diminish during the art-making process. These boys were very adept at showing little emotional connection to what they verbalised. They learned to present to the group what they thought would impress the therapist and enable them to leave the group sooner. Time was spent helping the boys to learn to negotiate, to be assertive instead of aggressive or passive, and to realise that acting the opposite of what people wanted was not a free choice. By rebelling, they were not free to choose either. It was essential to focus on the positive qualities that each boy possessed and to attempt to help him to eliminate behaviours which were self-defeating as well as extremely harmful to others.

Artwork sometimes reflected blatant sexually explicit material in what appeared to be an attempt to shock us as therapists, especially in the early stages of the sessions. The boys expended a considerable amount of energy in testing group rules and our patience. In previous work with troubled adolescent boys, I had learned that much of this testing was an effort to drive me away lest they become emotionally attached to me and then abandoned. One boy asked me if I was going to leave him 'like everyone else had done'. Developing a trusting and predictable relationship with these boys was essential. It was important for therapists not to miss group sessions without telling the boys ahead of time in order to minimise their feelings of abandonment. Some professionals in American treatment programmes advocated repeated and detailed disclosures in the group of the actual molestation. It was found, however, that this fed into sexual fantasies, which usually precipitated sexual offending, and thus was not encouraged in this group. For this reason, explicit sexual artwork was also discouraged.

Gaining a sense of empowerment over offending behaviour was the most important therapeutic issue. It was emphasised that each boy had total responsibility for not sexually offending and any offending behaviour could not be blamed on anyone else. Blaming parents, the victim or the system for their own offences simply was not tolerated. One boy in the group illustrated his fears of re-molesting and needing someone else to stop him from doing so (Figure 8.1). This boy needed to learn to master his own sense of control and to build in mechanisms to keep him from re-offending. It is believed that molesting other children is a re-enactment of the offender's own victimisation and a power issue ('get back'). Sexually abusing another child provides temporary relief of

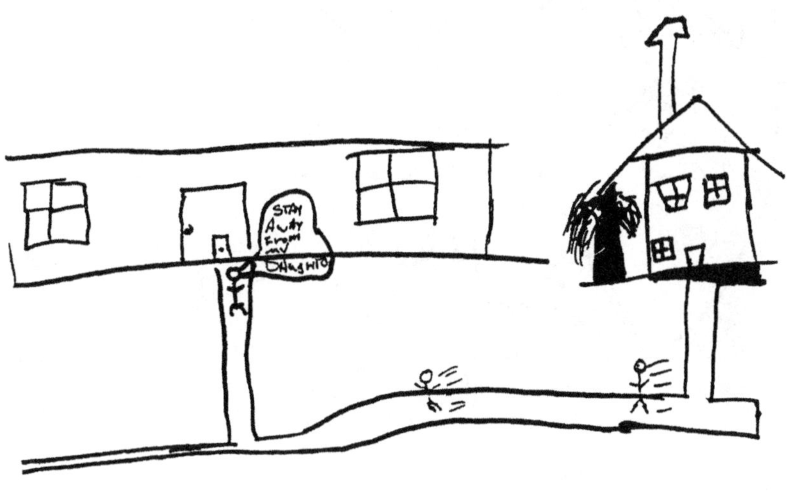

Figure 8.1 'Keep Your Daughter Away from Me'

negative feelings and becomes self-reinforcing and addictive. It was discussed and reinforced that there were options available if tempted to re-offend, such as contacting the therapist or other designated persons for support and agreeing not to be alone with any younger child – ever.

There was a tendency for these boys to isolate themselves from other people. They were asked to create a picture illustrating what they typically did during a 24-hour period of time. Figure 8.2 illustrates an analysis of time management by one of the young offenders. He depicted boredom with nothing in life to do but work, chores, sleep and occasional time spent with music and parties. The purpose of this exercise was to help these boys to gain insight as to how they had set themselves up for isolation and depression which are known precursors to sex offending.

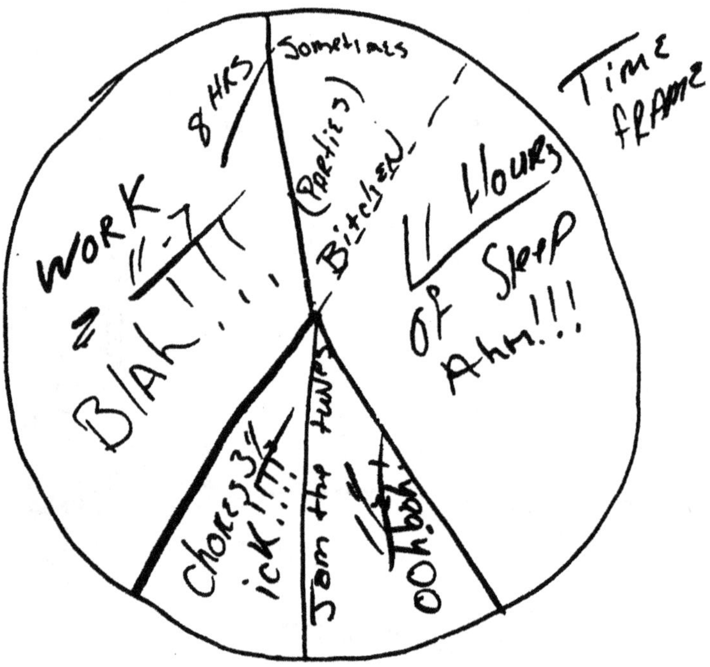

Figure 8.2 'Time Management and Isolation'

The boys were asked to make a picture about how they felt about being in the group. Resistance to being in the group and the desire to escape dealing with issues of sexual abuse were illustrated in Figure 8.3, entitled 'I Think of Driving Away'. This boy expected to be reprimanded for not wanting to be in the group, but instead was congratulated for his honesty. Much to his surprise, it was supportively acknowledged that his desire not to be there was understandable and that it was indeed difficult to talk about sexual abuse.

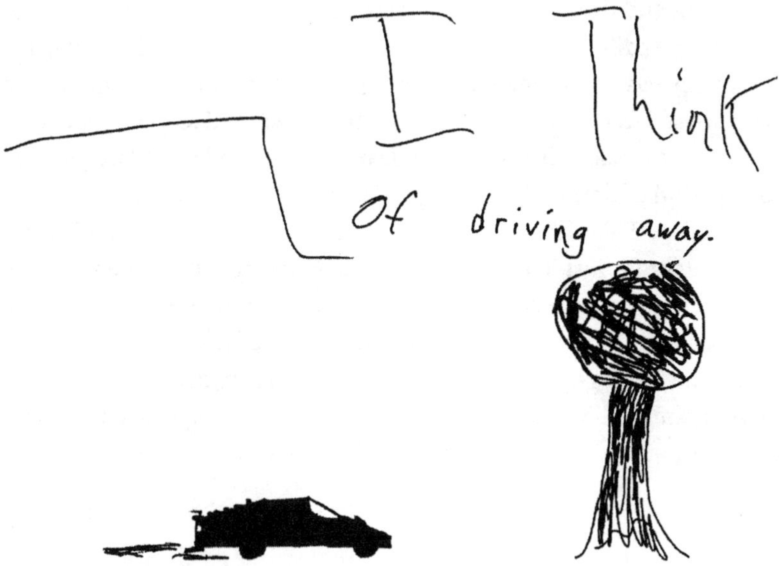

Figure 8.3 'I Think of Driving Away'

Missing therapy sessions for reasons that were untrue occurred from time to time. One boy missed a session and told the group the following week that he had been ill. I personally had seen him waiting the week before for a bus just outside the location where the group was held. He had lied to his foster parents that he was going to therapy, but went somewhere else instead. This incident provided an opportunity to confront him about his lying and deceitful behaviour. Group members were encouraged to express how it felt to them to have been lied to. Needless to say, they did not like it and expressed that it made them feel stupid to have believed him and they could no longer trust him. When supported, the boy was able to admit that he had been lying.

In working with this group, I quickly learned that being deceived by sex offenders is common until a therapist becomes more experienced with this population. These boys are experts at deceit and manipulation. As I learned to listen to my gut reaction when stories did not add up, as well as to look for inconsistencies in what was said and what was actually depicted in the artwork,

I was deceived less frequently. I learned that these boys often felt angry toward therapists if they could easily manipulate them. They needed limit-setting and firm, but gentle, confrontation. Too much sympathy made therapists vulnerable to this manipulation. Balancing being supportive, caring and empathetic with consistent and firm limit-setting was essential. Feedback from peers frequently was more readily heard. My co-therapist and I worked together as catalysts, but the group was encouraged to be doing most of the therapy. Children who have been abused frequently adopt a stance that is referred to in therapeutic circles as a 'victim position'. This is an attitude resulting from learned helplessness over a long period of time and these boys tended to perceive the world from a victim's perspective. They felt little control over their environment and believed that negative things just 'happened' to them. Working with these young people to help them to become more assertive and to see how they set themselves up for many of their difficulties was an ongoing part of therapy.

As trust was gradually developed in the group, defences softened and the boys became willing to be more open. The artwork began to change and themes of abandonment, loneliness and current problems emerged. Figure 8.4 clearly

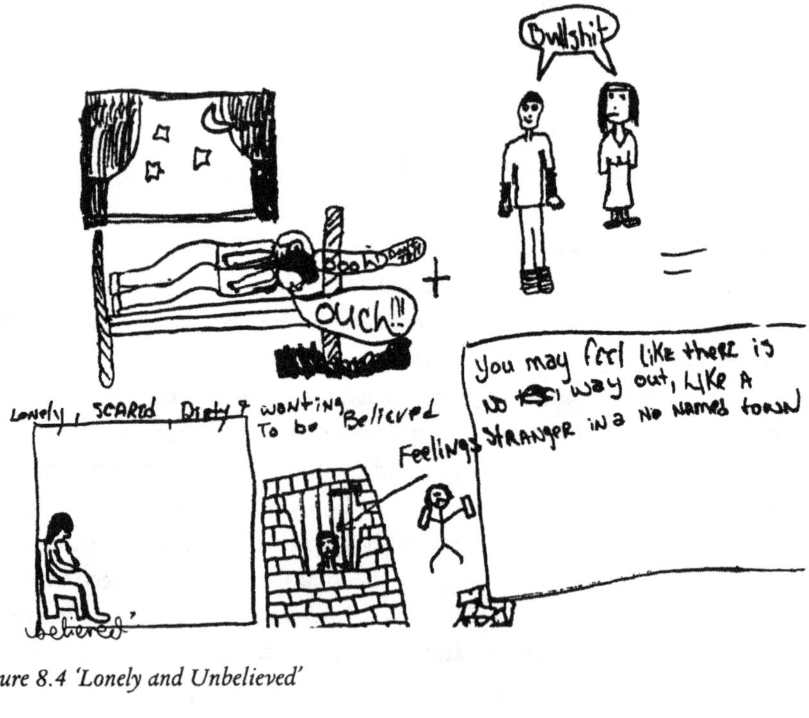

Figure 8.4 'Lonely and Unbelieved'

depicts a boy's own victimisation as a child and his parents' refusal to believe that he himself had been sexually abused. He portrayed himself locked inside a brick wall feeling lonely, scared, dirty and disbelieved. As he spoke about the drawing, he broke into tears and expressed his feelings very openly in the group for the first time. The other boys began their distracting behaviour and were unable to be supportive. The remainder of the session was used in working with them to hear what the boy was saying and to begin learning to empathise.

Relationships with girls were typically fraught with difficulties. One very attractive boy in the group appeared to be able to relate to girls only through promiscuous sex. Extremely low self-esteem, fear of rejection and problems with social skills tend to create a fear of relationships with girls (Katz 1990). Another boy in the group was invited to attend a high school dance by an attractive cheerleader. We encouraged him to accept the invitation hoping he might develop healthier age-appropriate relationships. His self-esteem was so low that even though he was a very likeable and handsome boy, he was unable to accept the invitation.

Other symptoms of low self-esteem were apparent in the boys in this group and put-downs were made to themselves as well as to each other. Unfortunately such low self-esteem made it easier to gratify sexual needs with younger children. Some of these boys had sexually offended while child-minding instead of spending their spare time in appropriate relationships with peers. Difficulties in developing relationships with each other were demonstrated as the boys created a large mural together on the topic of 'Friends'. Most of the images reflected concerns with money, drugs and other superficial values with little evidence of the camaraderie usually involved in healthy friendships. Another attempt was made to bring these boys together as a cohesive group was made by having them do a fantasy mural imagining they were taking a trip into outer space together. Hyper-sexuality was expressed as the boys focused only on their individual rocket ships, which were replete with explicitly phallic images. There was little interaction with each other during the process.

Because of poor impulse control, depression and isolation, as well as negative circumstances in which these boys found themselves, it was important to be alert for signs of suicidal ideation. One boy in the group consistently chose only black for all of his drawings. I consulted with his counsellor at the residential treatment centre where he lived and in fact the boy had been verbalising suicidal feelings. Using artwork for diagnosis is fraught with difficulties and can be misleading. Clues, however, often appear which alert the art therapist to carry out further verbal assessment. Images of wrist slashing, dead people, graveyards and whirlpools, and consistent use of black, brown, grey and dark blue, are frequently seen in the artwork of suicidal people. If such symbols appear in an adolescent offender's artwork, it cannot be automatically assumed that he is suicidal, but such images should serve as an indicator and further assessment is needed.

There tended to be a considerable amount of ignorance regarding accurate sexual information as well as a multitude of misconceptions about sex and love. Their understanding of reproduction, birth control, sexually transmitted diseases, safe sex and personal responsibility for self and others was minimal, and for the most part erroneous. Much sexual knowledge had been learned from other children and involved street language. In therapeutic work, frank and open discussions about sex with accurate information were essential. These boys initially felt uncomfortable with me as a female therapist, but ended up respecting me as they listened to my perspectives about relationships with girls.

Abandonment by parents, whether physical, emotional or both, was a theme recurring in the artwork of these boys. Figure 8.5 illustrates efforts by one boy to reach out to his parents with love, only to be rejected. This boy had been

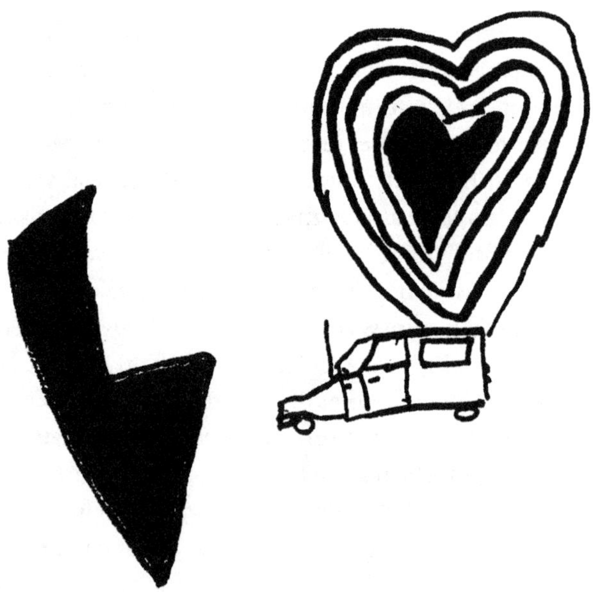

Figure 8.5 'Abandonment'

promised repeatedly that his parents would take him home to live. He waited in constant hope and disappointment as he continued to be left in residential care.

The relationships of these adolescent sex offenders with their fathers were also explored. In one session, one boy constantly bragged to the group that everything at home was wonderful. In Figure 8.6 he depicted going fishing with his father. This boy had repeatedly told others that his relationship with his father was wonderful. When asked to talk about his picture, he said his father's back was turned to him and he began crying, revealing that he always felt emotionally shut out by his father.

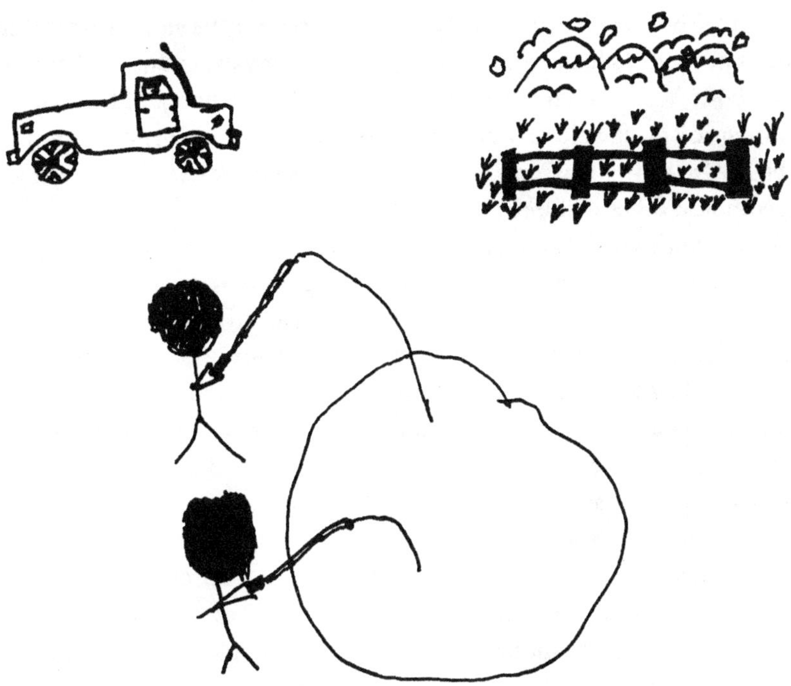

Figure 8.6 'My Dad and I Fishing'

It is not unusual to see sexual images incorporated into a good deal of artwork of young sex offenders (Liebmann 1994) and the boy should not be censored for this. The appropriateness of the setting, however, is an important factor. To display sexually explicit artwork in a school setting, for example, would create many problems and, again, it is a therapeutic issue for these boys to learn where certain behaviours are acceptable and why. I found that images appearing in the artwork of adolescent sex offenders often included blood, gore, sadistic and/or satanic themes. Phallic shapes incorporated into artwork is a phenomenon commonly seen in paintings and drawings of sexually abused children (Hagood 1992a), and these boys were no exception (see Chapter 9). Most of these boys listened to heavy metal music and it could have influenced the inclusion of satanic symbols in their drawings. Graffiti, which is normally enjoyed by teenage boys and sometimes used in art therapy, tended to encourage the use of these symbols. Blood and gore can serve as a defence against feelings and also may be an attempt to shock the therapist. Normal, nonabused boys go through phases in their development when they may draw such material (Uhlin 1979).

Therapeutic work with boys who have been victims of sexual abuse and have repeated the behaviour by molesting other children may be viewed as extremely difficult or as very challenging and rewarding. In my experience, it has been a mix of both. Within each one of these boys has been a hurt child who needed nurturing and much help to overcome the results of his own victimisation and to enable him to learn to manage his life in such a way that one hopes he would no longer molest other children.

As my work with this adolescent offenders' group drew to an end, I was convinced that art therapy was effective in helping these young sex offenders deal with their problems. At that time I was preparing for my move to Scotland. When the boys were told that adolescent sex offenders in Britain received little or no help, they were considerably upset. The use of art therapy supplemented counselling in a comfortable way and the boys in the group readily and easily accepted its use. They participated willingly and enthusiastically in creating the images which illustrated their dilemma, not only to us as therapists, but better still, more clearly to themselves.

Whether working in groups or individually, young sex offenders need to be able to recognise and identify patterns in their lives that led up to their offending behaviour or thoughts of offending. Examples have been discussed such as anger and frustration, sexual fantasies, problems at home, rejection by peers, feelings of isolation and low self-esteem. There is a need to address to what extent a background of childhood abuse existed, namely emotional, physical and/or sexual abuse, and to enable young offenders to work through their feelings about what happened. These boys need to become more self-aware. They need to learn better ways to meet their own needs and how to build in more positive and pleasurable activities for themselves. They need to be able to identify strengths and weaknesses and learn ways to build on those strengths.

Self-respect needs to be developed in order to learn to respect the rights of others. They need to value themselves as persons and distinguish that they are valuable, but their behaviour has been destructive both to themselves and to others. Both negative and positive attitudes regarding other people need to be identified and improved. Family dynamics need to be explored and a greater understanding of how those dynamics have contributed to the boy's situation. Feelings about parental relationships and those with significant others need to be expressed genuinely. Understanding how to have needs for affection and attention appropriately met by family members is extremely valuable to minimise the likelihood of further offences. Peer relationships need to be explored in a similar fashion. Feelings of helplessness, fear, confusion, anger, guilt, being different, betrayal and being exploited are important to address.

These boys need to learn to take total responsibility for any sexual relationship they have had with a child or other children and to become genuinely aware that such abuse was harmful to their victim(s). Learning empathic skills are essential to treatment. There is a need to focus on experiencing and expressing feelings because these boys have often become numb and hardened. This is an essential step to learning to empathise with others and to understand how their victim(s) must have felt. They need to be able to own up to what they did and to be able to verbalise the methods of coercion used, both physical and psychological. Insight is needed as to how the abuse was set up with the *deliberate* intent to abuse a child. An understanding of how the abuse was rationalised and minimised is also essential. Awareness of the validity of laws and public reactions to sexually abusive behaviour is also important.

Case example: Group work with adult sex offenders

The group consisted of eight to ten men ranging from ages 23 to 45 who had been charged with sexual offences against children. These men had been thoroughly screened for no prior history of violence or other criminal offences. The programme where I worked at that time had developed a treatment approach whereby group work was done in ten-week intervals. At the end of each ten-week period, offenders were assessed and it was decided whether they were ready to move to a more advanced group. Groups were a mix of men who had been in treatment for one or more years along with newcomers to the programme. The offenders who had already received a certain amount of treatment were extremely helpful in confronting the newer men with their denial, minimisation and deceitfulness because they recognised it whenever it occurred better than the therapists could. Therapists who are eager to help these men can be easily misled until they gain a great deal of experience.

Contrary to my fears, these men were courteous, pleasant and friendly within the group context. They appeared as ordinary men and were from a variety of occupations ranging from ranchers and mechanics to business and professional men. It became readily apparent why sex offenders are not easily recognised. Several of these men were very religious, attending church regularly. As the group progressed, however, two of the offenders became sexually flirtatious with me at the end of group sessions and it was necessary to set a firm boundary. The men were extremely plausible in everything they said and it was extremely difficult not to believe them. Only when other offenders confronted them, or when contrary information was learned from other professionals, was I able to realise how easy it was to be deceived. I became much less gullible as time went on.

These men were interested and willing to use art in the group process. My co-therapist was a clinical psychologist with considerable experience in forensic work who enthusiastically joined in introducing art themes at various points of the session. It became apparent in working with these offenders that in many instances what they verbally denied appeared blatantly in their artwork. They had learned to deceive others verbally, but did not seem to have an awareness of how much would be revealed in their artwork. A good example of this phenomenon was when group members were asked to draw a picture of a sex offender. One offender who regularly came to the group dressed in a business suit drew an accurate picture of himself without realising it. The hairstyle and facial features were very much like his own, even down to the exact colour of the neck tie he was wearing. When he completed the drawing, however, he stated to the group: 'This is what a sex offender looks like – I am so glad I am not like him.' Whether the other group members noticed the similarity or not is unknown because none of them commented on it. Another offender drew a picture of a child molester as ugly and distorted, entitling it 'Monster Molester' (Figure 8.7). In discussing the drawings more thoroughly, it emerged that being named a sex offender, while necessary, also fed into their extremely low self-esteem and self-hatred. They knew full well what society felt about them.

In a subsequent meeting, the topic evolving at the beginning of the session from the men in the group was about relationships with their partners. One offender drew a picture of himself with his wife and told the group that all of their problems were solved (since the previous week) and that they were now getting along beautifully. The drawing, however, depicted long sharp finger-

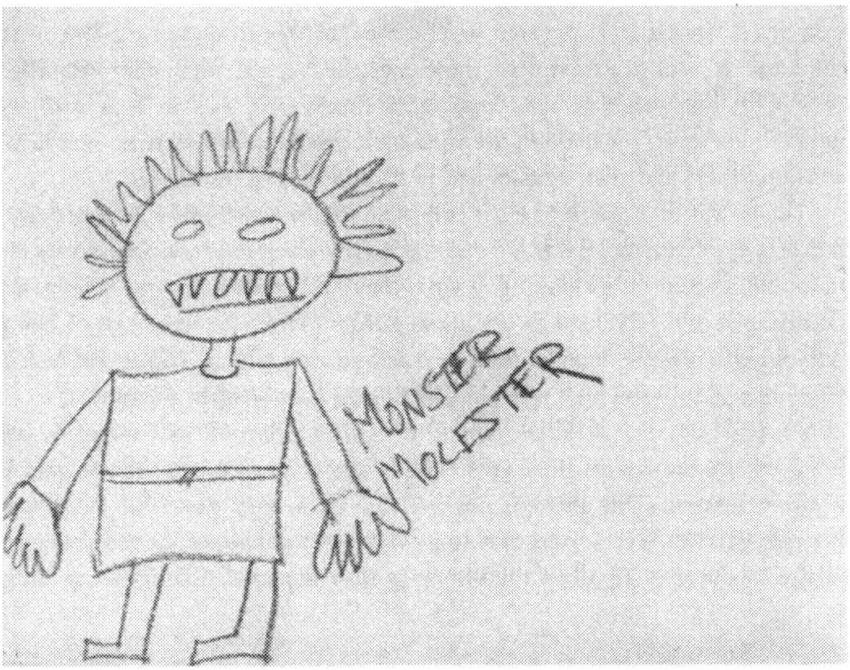

Figure 8.7 'Monster Molester'

nails from both partners which appeared far from amicable. The breakdown of these offenders' relationships with their wives or partners was a theme arising in many of the sessions. We decided to ask them to create a picture of what 'Love' meant. It was clear that their concept of love was extremely shallow and included platitudes such as 'Love means never having to say you're sorry', which, in hindsight, described the attitude of an abusive sex offender quite accurately. It became apparent that these offenders were adept at telling us therapists whatever they thought we wanted to hear. If a problem was pointed out, it was not uncommon for them to return the next week and claim that it was already solved even though it had existed for years. They would often ask what the group was going to address in the following weeks, but we learned not to tell them anything, and instead asked them what *they* intended to address in the group. A common dynamic with those who abuse others is that of feeling fear and subsequently passing it on to their victim. The offenders were asked to do artwork around the theme of 'Fear'. One offender simply wrote the word 'God', while another one wrote 'Court'. Many of these men were active churchgoers, typically subscribing to rigid and authoritarian belief systems, and could recite the Bible very accurately. Their interpretations of religion, however, often sounded distorted and appeared to lock them further into their dysfunctional thinking. It was apparent that these men had come from very disturbed childhood backgrounds and these were shared and explored. It was not unusual, however, for them to use their own history of abuse as an excuse for abusing others and such a belief had to be continually challenged.

The power of artwork to elicit emotions and to make problems more clear was very apparent, and it was not unusual to have these men cry, perhaps for the first time, as a result of looking at what they had created. In one session, my co-therapist and I decided to use visual imagery to evoke memories of being only 6 years old. We actually used a relaxation tape with a 'Trip to the Beach' vignette and told the men prior to listening to it to imagine themselves to be only 6 years old. It was rather humorous to see a group of eight sex offenders lying on the floor with their eyes closed following a twenty-minute guided imagery session. This proved, however, to be a very powerful technique, because afterwards they were able to produce very detailed coloured drawings of their memories. In all of the drawings they depicted themselves as being

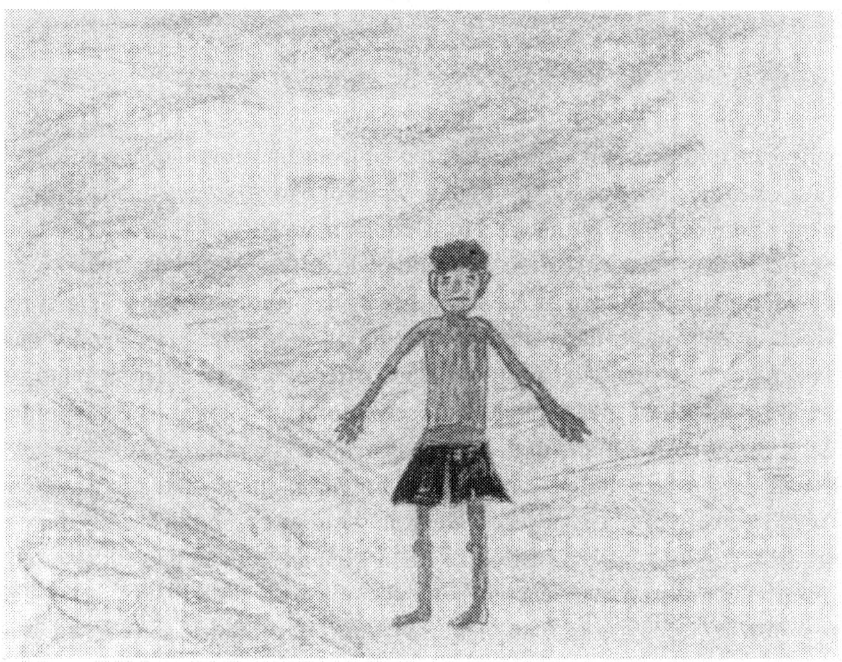

Figure 8.8 'Angry and Alone'

lonely, feeling abandoned and in some instances angry. One group member had grown up in a minister's family where he strictly had to 'Honour the Sabbath'. He described going to the beach with his family on Sunday and being told that if he went into the water above his knees, he would be committing a sin, because he would be 'Breaking the Sabbath'. If he broke his father's 'commandment' he would be beaten severely with a belt until the blood ran. It was amazing to hear that he believed he fully deserved the beating. Another man in the group drew himself in bright red standing all alone on the beach (Figure 8.8). He stated that the red showed the anger he still remembers feeling. Themes of loneliness continued to emerge in subsequent art sessions. Another offender drew himself alone in the corner with his peers all playing together without him. He aptly entitled the picture 'Lost and Unimportant to the World...No Understanding' (Figure 8.9).

As the group cohesiveness developed and trust in the therapists increased, the men in the group gradually became more candid and honest about what they had done. They were slowly able to take more responsibility for what they had done to their daughters and their denial and minimisation began to lessen.

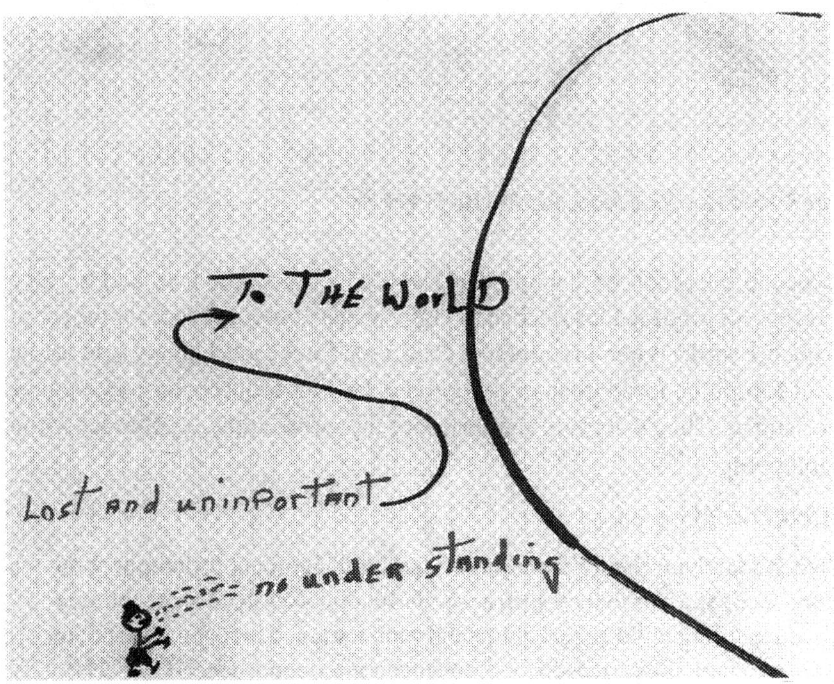

Figure 8.9 'Lost and Unimportant to the World...No Understanding'

One offender, for example, clearly drew a picture of himself reaching out with 'Love' to his daughter, who was only 4 years old. When he began talking about the drawing, he broke down and cried, saying: 'Oh, my God – I gave her much more than she bargained for!' (Figure 8.10).

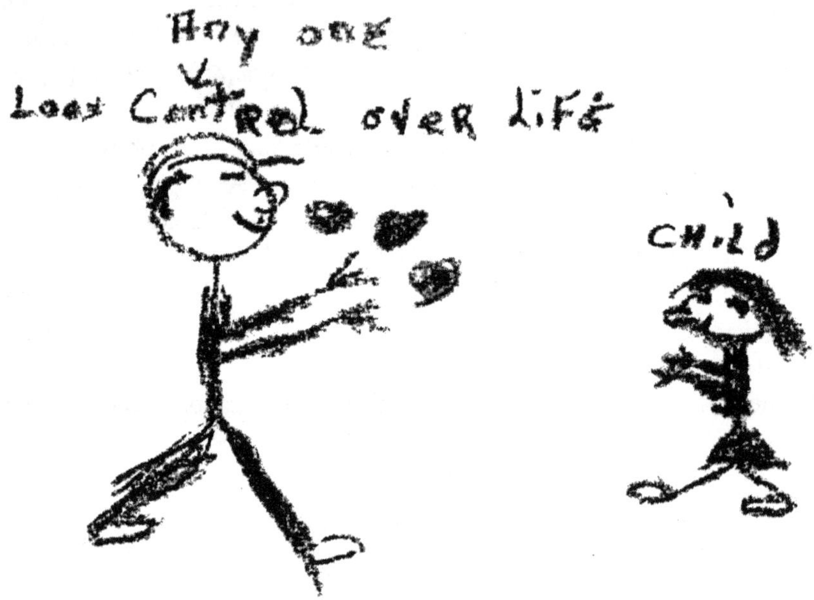

Figure 8.10 'I Gave Her More than She Bargained for'

The men in the group were aware that I would be moving to Scotland to carry out research into drawings relative to child sexual abuse and to train others in therapeutic work. When I returned to California from a preliminary visit to the United Kingdom, I told them of the extreme lack of resources for treatment of sex offenders. They were very supportive of my move, and one offender wrote the following:

> Dear Friends,
>
> When Maralynn first told me she was going to Scotland, I thought about how lucky she was to have such a wonderful opportunity to share information regarding child sexual abuse and molestation. Then when Maralynn told me about the current status of treatment programs there, I realized how lucky I was to be involved in treatment here in the United States.

> I molested a child, a 13-year-old boy about five years ago. I finally was able to place myself in treatment. It was not easy, in fact, it was, and still is, the most difficult thing I have ever done. I realize that there are many who advocate incarceration for all offenders, and it's possible that incarceration may be the partial answer for some offenders, and the only answer for others. But my feelings based on the last several months of being involved with treatment groups, is that incarceration, in the absence of therapy, will not be effective in changing the behavior of offenders, and therefore does little to protect the children once the offender has 'served his sentence' and is released. The fact is that I can envision incarceration *without* therapy to actually generate a person who is *more* likely to offend by feeding his inadequacies and feelings of powerlessness.
>
> Best of luck to all of you. I hope that we all soon will see the day that child sexual abuse is indeed a part of our history, and not our future.

This offender was in the early stages of treatment and had a long way to go. He tended at that stage to view therapy in terms of what *he* was getting out of it and still did not demonstrate a serious-enough concern for what he had done to his victim(s). He was a warm, friendly, well-educated and plausible man, but was caught shortly before writing this letter looking for another target for abuse in a public place where adolescent boys were likely to be. This letter clearly illustrates how convincing and cunning these abusers can be. It is hoped, however, that with continued treatment, he will ultimately be able to manage his behaviour and no longer abuse other children. It was easy to see why sex offenders are rarely suspected of the abuse they committed. The therapist needs to be continually on guard for such deception and the focus of treatment needs to be on how child sexual abuse will *not* be repeated.

Summary

I found it particularly surprising that working with adult sex offenders was not as frightening as I had expected. It was extremely important, however, not to be working with any of their victims at the same time. While I still react with disgust and anger when I listen to survivors' stories, it was somehow possible to focus on these men as survivors as well, rather than letting such feelings get in the way. On the other hand, I openly expressed such feelings to these men when it was appropriate to do so.

These men had been thoroughly screened for treatability in a nearby medical prison before entering therapy. While they exhibited the usual denial and minimisation at the outset, I do not believe that the therapeutic process was particularly easy for them. In fact, I knew of offenders who had been offered treatment, but declined, preferring to do their prison sentence than to go through the rigours of treatment. It was an emotionally painful and difficult experience for them to deal with their own childhood trauma, which they had never discussed with anyone. It became increasingly clear how they had come to learn to repress their emotions and to feel powerless and in need to have control over others. It would have been impossible for them to have any degree of self-esteem given their childhood experiences. Most had a role model in one or both parents for abusive and controlling behaviour. These men were emotionally very immature for their age, typical of sexually abused children. I found many of their issues to be little different from those of adult survivors of sexual abuse, with the obvious exception of their abusive behaviour toward others and having committed the heinous crime of child sexual abuse. Any abusive behaviours or attitudes were continually challenged. Some were gradually able to develop more empathy toward their peers in the group and to consider the reality of the damage they had done to their victims.

There are no easy answers in working in the area of child sexual abuse, and this is especially true when it comes to offender treatment. Basic therapeutic issues and goals along with characteristics of adult sex offenders have been addressed in this chapter. A case presentation of group work with adolescent sex offenders was included to lead into the example of work with adult offenders. The overlap and similarity of issues and themes in the artwork of both the adolescents and adults in these two groups was apparent. I would encourage others who do a considerable amount of work in the area of child sexual abuse to consider spending some time working with offenders in order to gain a greater understanding of the dynamics of such a tragic phenomenon.

CHAPTER 9

Diagnosis or Dilemma

Artwork by Sexually Abused Children

Clinicians who use art in therapeutic work with sexually abused children often see characteristics in their drawings which appear to be related to a history of sexual abuse. Many, however, do not seriously consider the child's developmental stage and how it also may influence characteristics in the artwork. As has been reiterated throughout this book, it is extremely important to understand how child development can affect interpretations of children's drawings. Without such an understanding, features in children's artwork may be misunderstood and the therapist may jump to the wrong conclusions. In our zeal to protect these children, it is easy to look for signs of sexual abuse in their artwork, hoping for evidence to provide such protection. We can forget, however, that to make false allegations of sexual abuse based on misinterpreting children's artwork can create disastrous consequences not only for the children, but also for their families. We can also lose our credibility as clinicians if we report suspicion of sexual abuse based on children's artwork alone, unless the child has *clearly* disclosed such information.

The literature has presented a variety of so-called indicators of sexual abuse observed in children's artwork. Because clinicians typically see only disturbed children, it is easy to conclude that what some children paint or draw is due to having been sexually abused or indicates some other psychological symptom. As discussed in Chapter 2, drawings by a 3-year-old child may be considerably different from drawings by a child one year younger, or even two years older. Drawings by a 6-year-old child and a 12-year-old child are even more different. Children's drawings not only change radically as they get older, but also can change significantly from day to day. Many art therapists and other mental health professionals have studied drawings by sexually abused children sincerely hoping to find clues that might better enable them to protect these children. There have been, however, considerable problems in research methodology in the majority of studies. Most investigations to date have commonly used matched comparison groups covering a wide age range, but have not controlled specifically for the ages of the children studied.

These observations inspired me to carry out research into drawings of ordinary children with no known history or suspicion of sexual abuse (Hagood 1999). I wanted to learn whether any of these so-called 'sex abuse indicators' ('SAI's) appeared in drawings of children who had not been sexually abused, as well as how they might be related to the child's level of cognitive development. I also wanted to know whether there were features found in sexually abused children's artwork which did *not* appear in drawings by nonabused children. I believe it is essential to discriminate between features related to ordinary cognitive development and those which indeed may be a clue to possible sexual abuse.

Background and history

American psychologists, counsellors, art therapists and others working with sexually abused children began incorporating the use of art in therapeutic work in the late 1970s and early 1980s. This created the possibility of using drawings as evidence to assist in the protection of such children (Cohen-Liebman 1994, 1995). While the use of art therapy with sexually abused children is now being developed by some British art therapists (Murphy, in press; Sagar 1990), to my knowledge there are no publications regarding the utilisation of artwork of sexually abused children as legal evidence in Britain to date. The overall use of art in assessment and diagnosis has been generally discouraged in the training of art therapists in the United Kingdom (Waller and Gilroy 1992; Woddis 1986).

On the other hand, research into characteristics of artwork of sexually abused children has been carried out in the United States by American art therapists and other mental health professionals with the hope of using children's drawings as a diagnostic tool to detect sexual abuse. American art therapists are increasingly testifying on behalf of sexually abused children using their artwork as evidence (Cohen-Liebman 1994, 1995). The use of such evidence, however, is largely based on the experience and qualifications of the art therapists, relying on their 'expertise'.

In recent years clinicians working with sexually abused children have increasingly reported observations that certain characteristics appeared peculiar to these children's artwork. In the late 1970s and early 1980s little systematic research had been carried out to substantiate these assumptions and the literature relied largely on anecdotal accounts. None at that time included comparisons with children who had no history of sexual abuse. By the mid-1980s, comparative studies began to emerge, but graphic indicators in drawings were compared with somewhat poor results between groups of sexually abused children and those who were in psychiatric treatment for other emotional problems. A major problem was that the latter comparison groups were likely to be contaminated with the possibility that emotionally disturbed subjects could also be victims of undisclosed sexual abuse. Comparisons including ordinary children judged to be nonabused began to appear in 1987. In investigations involving nonabused children, there has been almost unanimous neglect in the close observation of the influence of normal development on characteristics of children's drawings.

Review of the literature

As discussed earlier, Edith Kramer (1971, 1975, 1979) was a major contributor to the field of art therapy as a profession in both the United States and the United Kingdom. She bridged her understanding of psychoanalysis with her background in art education. An illustration of how her background in the Freudian concepts of childhood sexuality influenced her interpretation of children's artwork is reflected in her case study of a 9-year-old child named 'Samantha'. Kramer (1979) described the child's drawings as repeatedly depicting genitalia and believed that the child had *not* been sexually abused because her artwork was well organised. Kramer gave a graphic description of more sexual details in this particular case that are known to be related to child sexual abuse (e.g. the act of fellatio and sexualised behaviour toward other children), but dismissed them as 9-year-old Samantha's attempt to use her artistic talent 'in the service of taming and civilising her sexuality' and that some process of 'sublimation' must be at work as well as a metaphorical 'intercourse' with her doctor. Kramer wrote:

> Although their bodies were strangely condensed and sexualized, their faces belonged to real persons – her doctor and herself, and later on her siblings. The sexual play enacted with these images seems tender rather than aggressive, serene rather than climactic. This seems to indicate that the experiences which found expression on Samantha's sculptures had actually been tender rather than crudely sexual ones. It seems unlikely that she had been sexually abused. When children who have been so treated communicate these experiences in the art the work is rarely well organized; chaotic and fragmented work prevails. Samantha's work is bizarre but well integrated. We can rather assume that Samantha's primitive mentality made her perceive any positive relationship in sexual terms. She evidently

> conceived of her relationship to Dr. M as a kind of intercourse. (Kramer 1979, p.114)

Kramer further developed her argument about Samantha's work as an attempt to 'impose a private kind of organization upon a chaotic inner world buffeted by archaic libidinal and aggressive strivings' (p.117). While she dismissed the possibility of sexual abuse in Samantha's case, her description of the child's artwork contained repeated suggestions not only of intercourse, but also of fellatio and sexual acts with other children. The child's artwork appears to contain sexual knowledge well beyond the ordinary sexual curiosity of a normally developing nonabused 9-year-old child.

Kramer attributed much of the development of her theoretical framework to her reliance on Freudian psychoanalytic theory, but she also stated: 'My understanding of child development in art and of methods of teaching art to children owes much to Victor Lowenfeld' (Kramer 1979, p.xv). Lowenfeld (as discussed in Chapter 2) clearly described drawing characteristics which were typical at various stages of children's cognitive development, relating them to Piaget's theory. While Kramer broadly discusses developmental tasks from a Freudian perspective, she does not appear to consider expected characteristics of children's artwork specific to cognitive development. After a thorough review of Kramer's writings (1971, 1975, 1979) there was *no* discussion of these stages of development directly related to specific drawing features in the artwork of the children whose case studies were presented.

I began my art therapy training in 1980 under the supervision of Dr Donald Uhlin, art therapist and art educator, at California State University in Sacramento. He was the primary inspiration for me to pursue research into the artwork of sexually abused children. Uhlin (1979) illustrated examples of paintings, drawings and sculptures created by adolescents who were known to have been sexually abused. The artwork included the scribbling out of the body, distorted illustration of the body, the exclusion of hands or the lower part of the body. These were all interpreted to symbolise self-obliteration, poor body image, helplessness or sexual arousal respectively, according to Uhlin, who used accepted analytic interpretations of such characteristics. Clay sculptures of human heads created by victims of sexual abuse often portrayed exaggerated facial features such as bulging eyes and exceptionally large noses resembling replicas of engorged sexual organs.

Clara Jo Stember (1980) was one of the first American art therapists to use art therapy extensively with sexually abused children. She found that drawings sometimes revealed the possibility of sexual abuse. She frequently used scribble drawings and sometimes lifelike male genitalia were depicted in the scribbles. Stember also observed that these children often created disorganised drawings, clown images and people with no mouth. Horizontal scribbling frequently changed to vertical scribbling and then as therapy progressed, drawings became more organised. Such characteristics, however, were only generally discussed without focusing on the age levels of these children and how the child's cognitive development might also have affected the artwork. For example, it is normal for very young children to use horizontal and vertical scribbling before they progress to more sophisticated attempts to name and draw objects (Lowenfeld and Brittain 1987). Stember did, however, briefly mention age-inappropriateness as a feature of sexually abused children's drawings. She made a considerable contribution in leading the way for the use of art therapy in helping these children emotionally resolve their trauma. She stated:

> Art therapy is a way of using art materials to help damaged people form a supportive alliance that permits expression of their emotions... Sexually abused children need appropriate ways to ventilate their anger, hostility, fear, and other feelings that may be inhibited or repressed. Painting the fantasies of the mind can be the first externalization, the first way of bringing healing and growth to occur. (Stember 1980, p.59)

Jean Goodwin (1982) developed a Draw-the-Perpetrator task and observed that children refused to draw about sexual abuse as frequently as they refused to talk about the event. She stated that frequently the victim crossed out repeated attempts to draw the perpetrator, drew a figure with an obvious phallus, or finally gave up. Goodwin found the use of drawings helpful in evaluating sexual abuse with children under 12. She did not find as much success, however, in using drawings with adolescents. She concluded:

> Such drawings, by themselves, are not sufficient to make a diagnostic decision. It is the child's increasing sense of being able to communicate and her experience of being understood that are helpful to the clinician in reconstructing what is happening in the family. The discovery of a workable avenue of communication is also helpful in reducing the anxiety of a child whose enmeshment in family secrets has often blocked verbal means of asking for help. (Goodwin 1982, p.55)

As a result of her observation of children's art-making in clinical sessions, Goodwin (1982) subsequently carried out nineteen consecutive interviews with girls aged 5 to 16 who were suspected incest victims. She claimed that the drawings were of diagnostic value in understanding the child's fears and anxieties, her view of her family and her self-image. Goodwin observed what appeared to be images of male phalluses incorporated into more 'acceptable' objects such as trees. Goodwin described the artwork of a girl 8 years old depicting a dream in which she was camping inside a zipped-up tent with a phallic-appearing tree intrusively overlapping the tent. Some children again drew the perpetrator with an obvious phallus, but identified it as a 'decoration' or said it was 'nothing'. I have also frequently observed this phenomenon in working with sexually abused children.

Silvercloud (1982) listed several features she observed in clinical work with sexually abused children. Their drawings frequently included characteristics such as stab marks, crossed-out windows, heavy lines, red houses, phallic shapes and highly sexualised drawings. She made no attempt to discuss the effects of age relative to the children's drawings. Like Stember (1980), she saw the value of using art media to help children work through their feelings. In my research, it was quite common for younger nonabused children to draw red houses and heavy lines. Again I believe it is dangerous to assume that any of these characteristics are indicative of sexual abuse until more systematic research is carried out.

Silvercloud stated:

> Art expression, as a projective tool, is a great aid to free association. It opens doors to blocked memories, ideas and emotions. The unconscious, where all information is potentially accessible, gives clues, mostly allegorical, to whatever issues are currently troublesome. When expressed visually, these clues become verbalized more naturally. The harmful event stored in the memory as an image, is recalled and externalized as an image, and then is put into words. The artwork, however crude, transmits the message unmistakably and is less threatening to the client than is talking face to face. Such graphic indicators are invaluable when working with the sexually abused (whether they are children or are adults who were abused as children) when powerlessness and betrayal magnify the harmful effects of the physical violation of space and person. (Silvercloud 1982, p.86)

Wohl and Kaufman (1985; Kaufman and Wohl 1992) wrote two popular American books addressed to clinicians who use art in their therapeutic work with children. The books are filled with lengthy accounts of children's drawings and interpretations relative to sexual abuse. Particular attention is focused on drawings of children from homes where both physical and sexual abuse have occurred, and sweeping analytic interpretations are made. One example of such interpretations by Kaufman and Wohl (1992) is as follows:

> ...we observe a strange thinning of the hair at the crown. This phenomenon is one which has not been documented elsewhere, but it is one that the authors have seen as a detail frequently present in the Person of sexually abused youngsters. As such, we believe it may be a significant indice of sexual trauma. (p.63)

Another typical interpretation by Kaufman and Wohl (1992) about 'tree' drawings of sexually abused children is as follows:

> Elmer's inability to adequately defend against the flooding of his inner tensions is projected by the number of clouds present on both renderings (Jolles 1971). The very existence of this hole, or scar, indicates an earlier trauma, suggesting a possible reason for Elmer's agitation. Last, we cannot help but notice the thin and transparent roots which look pitifully incapable of stabilizing a tree of that size. They connote how tenuously Elmer is maintaining his grasp of reality and just how flimsy his hold on it may be. (p.61)

Elmer is a 7-year-old child and there is no mention of the developmental aspects of the quality or content of his drawing, much less what the boy himself had to say. The basis for Kaufman and Wohl's tree interpretations is the work of Hammer (1958), which relies on interpretations from Buck's (1948) House–Tree–Person Test (HTP) developed using drawings of adult psychiatric populations. The test was subsequently standardised on adults with extremely low intelligence (called imbeciles at that time) who allegedly thought like children. It was then argued that such interpretations could be generalised to children's drawings.

It is interesting that the title of Kaufman and Wohl's (1992) second book is *Casualties of Childhood: A Developmental Perspective on Sexual Abuse Using Projective Drawings.* A very brief discussion of cognitive development reflected in children's drawings comprises only two pages of the entire book and is presented in a vague and unsystematic manner. 'Age-inappropriateness' is then mentioned only sporadically throughout the book. Kaufman and Wohl typically carried out their interpretations metaphorically and did not work with nonabused children. The major problem with this approach is that one can establish whatever one likes to support a particular view.

Riordan and Verdel (1991) reiterated the importance of the use of children's drawings in diagnosing child sexual abuse, in particular by school counsellors who allegedly would need little training in art to use drawing instruments such as the Draw-A-Person Test (DAP) (Harris 1963) or the Kinetic-Family-Drawing (KFD) (Burns 1982). They listed various characteristics of human figure drawings which purported to be indicative of symptoms commonly experienced by children who had been sexually abused. They claimed, for example, that an overemphasised, elongated neck indicated difficulty in maintaining control of sexuality, and that a nose overemphasised by size or linear contrast indicated 'phallic preoccupation'. These conclusions were drawn from a review of the work of Stember (1980), Yates, Beutler and Crago (1985), Wohl and Kaufman (1985), Buck (1977) and Di Leo (1973). Riordan and Verdel also stated that the most important features included in drawings of sexually abused children were the genitals themselves, but nevertheless were primarily relying on similar analytic assumptions as do those whose work they reviewed. The effects of cognitive development again were not considered.

In the above publications based primarily on psychoanalytic interpretations and projective drawing instruments, developmental phases of these children's creations are discussed only superficially, if at all. Drawings appear to be somewhat wildly analysed, and interpretations commonly used in such approaches for adults are generalised to the assessment of drawings of young children. There are undoubtedly considerable problems in the use of psychoanalytic interpretations (Hagood 2000e) as well as projective drawing tests relative to drawings of sexually abused children (Hagood 2000b).

Systematic studies of features of drawings of sexually abused children

Attempts have been made to carry out systematic research into drawings of sexually abused children. For example, Johnston (1979) evaluated drawings by ten sexually abused children aged from 5 to 11 using the KFD and judged that the drawings revealed dysfunctional family systems. Two of the ten children included representations of the male sex organ. Isolation was said to be manifested by the drawing of the family members in separate compartments on the paper and role reversal was metaphorically interpreted in drawings where the child made him or herself larger than the mother figure. Johnston (1979) made no attempt to evaluate the validity of the KFD before using it. Considerable weaknesses in this instrument are not addressed (Dunn 1972). She did not take into consideration developmental aspects of the drawings, even though the age range was considerable. While Johnston's study involved too few children over too wide an age range, it nevertheless was one of the earliest writings relative to unusual features in drawings of sexually abused children.

Kelley (1984) examined 120 pictures drawn by ten sexually abused children between the ages of 3 and 10. Analysis showed that, of the self-portraits drawn,

20 per cent portrayed prominent genitalia, 40 per cent placed an added emphasis on the pelvic region, 43 per cent emphasised the upper portion of their bodies and 30 per cent drew themselves without hands. The only discussion of developmental aspects of the children's drawings was Kelley's claim that 'pictures drawn in the earlier stages of treatment are often below expected developmental levels. However, during later phases children often draw more age-appropriate pictures' (p.426). There was no attempt to back up such a statement empirically. Kelley (1985) later noted certain characteristics in drawings of sexually abused children. Shading of parts of the body, focus on genitals, omission of upper extremities and emphasis on the mouth were some of the features she discussed relative to their drawings of the human figure. She argued that paediatric nurses should take these aspects of children's drawings into consideration when they use art to help sexually abused children to communicate. Unfortunately, in both the above studies she made no comparisons with drawings made by nonabused children.

The first significant study to appear in art therapy literature in the United States was that of Cohen and Phelps (1985), who compared sets of drawings of 166 children, with a very wide age range of 4–18 years. Of these, 89 subjects were known to have been sexually abused and 77 subjects were children who were being treated for other emotional problems. While statistically significant differences were found in the frequency of rated graphic indicators between the two groups on both the HTP and the KFD, by the admission of the investigators, considerable problems with poor inter-rater reliability made the results inconclusive. The rating scale contained vague descriptions and illustrations of what was to be scored and it is not surprising that there were such problems with obtaining reliability. The comparison group consisted of psychiatrically hospitalised children and it was suggested that the use of a 'normal' comparison group should be incorporated into future studies. The only accounting for development was in matching groups for age. It was therefore not possible to determine if differences were due to a history of sexual abuse or as a matter of development.

Yates *et al.* (1985) compared drawings of eighteen girls who were incest victims and seventeen girls who were disturbed, but not incest victims. The age range (considerably broad for such a small sample) of the first group was 3.5 to 17 years old, and the age range of the second group was 4 to 17 years old. The list of characteristics to be rated were derived from the clinical literature and consisted of fifteen dimensions. The only item of a developmental nature was 'degree of immaturity', which likewise was not defined. Nowhere in the paper did the authors define what characteristics in children's drawings indicated the above symptoms and how they were scored or interpreted.

In the mid-1980s most systematic studies into drawings of sexually abused children thus far were those of American art therapists Sidun (1986) and D. A. Chase (1987). They developed a coding manual based on existing literature on artwork of sexually abused children at that time. Many items on the coding manual appear to be based on psychoanalytic theory, such as canes, cigarettes and so on, with the Freudian belief that they were 'phallic symbols' (Freud 1953). Sidun rated and compared Human-Figure-Drawings (HFD) (Koppitz 1968) of 30 known sexually abused adolescents with drawings of 30 adolescents who had been treated for emotional disturbance with no known history of sexual abuse. The age range for all subjects was 13–17 years and one drawing was collected for each subject. Sidun hypothesised that the abused group would draw more 'oversexualised and undifferentiated figures', more 'indicators of anxiety' and more 'indicators of poor self-esteem'. These 'indicators' were very loosely defined and no statistically significant differences were found in measuring any of these features.

It was further hypothesised by Sidun that drawings of the sexually abused group would contain a greater frequency of wedges, phallic-like objects and circles than drawings of the nonabused group, again based on common Freudian interpretations. A greater number of such characteristics was found in artwork of the sexually abused group. When these characteristics were analysed independently, however, the only characteristic found to be statistically significant was the use of 'enclosed circles'. Sidun analytically interpreted these circles as indicative of 'oral regression' (Sidun, personal communication, April 1989). It was further concluded in Sidun's study that the strongest graphic indicators seen as red flags for possible sexual abuse in adolescence were omitted hands, omitted fingers, head only, enclosed circles and heavy line pressure. It is interesting to note that these features are all commonly seen in drawings of much younger children (Kellogg 1969; Lowenfeld and Brittain 1987; Naglieri 1988). Another graphic indicator that Sidun expected from drawings of sexually abused subjects was exaggeration of trouser flies. Nonabused adolescents actually drew trouser flies more often than did the abused group. The investigator reasoned that adolescence is a natural time for heightened concern about sexuality and therefore not specific to abused subjects. Here is an example of a so-called indicator of sexual abuse which appeared to be more associated with normal development.

D. A. Chase (1987), a colleague of Sidun's, introduced a comparison group of normal nonabused children into her research design when she compared the HFDs and KFDs of 34 female subjects, aged 5–16, who were victims of incest with those of 26 matched emotionally disturbed subjects and 34 matched subjects with no known adjustment disorders. Chase used the same scoring manual for HFDs as was used in Sidun's (1986) study with adolescents. The scoring manual was specially designed for both studies to measure 'indicators of sexual abuse', but as mentioned above, items appeared loosely defined which could make judgement very difficult. Nonetheless, Chase argued that significant differences were found in that drawings of sexually abused children were 'less mature' than those of nonabused children and adolescents, as well as 'less mature' than children who were emotionally disturbed. 'Maturity' was judged by scores on the Koppitz HFD, with the human figure drawings of the sexually abused subjects containing fewer details specific to the drawing of the human figure. Results showed that there were significant differences in developmental levels as measured by Koppitz's scale, with sexually abused children scoring at a lower level than did the other groups.

The findings in my research (Hagood 1999, 2000d) supported those of both Sidun and Chase in that many features purported to be linked with sexual abuse were more likely to appear in drawings of younger nonabused children. As nonabused children grew older, they were much less likely to draw such features (see Figure 9.1, p.239).

Hibbard *et al.* (1987) compared drawings of 57 children with an alleged history of sexual abuse (narrowing the age range to ages 3–7) with the drawings of 55 nonabused children matched for age, sex, race and socio-economic background. While the age range of children in this investigation was narrower than in previous studies, there nevertheless are considerable differences between drawings by 3-year-old children and those by 7-year-old children. Hibbard *et al.* failed to address this issue by not controlling for specific age differences. Subjects were also asked to make two drawings from the Goodenough–Harris DAP (Goodenough 1926; Harris 1963), one of each sex, and to complete a human figure outline of a person. All drawings were scored for the inclusion of five body parts: eyes, navel, vulva/vagina, penis and anus. Five (8.7%) of the sexually abused children drew genitalia and only one (1.8%) of the nonabused children did so. Genitalia appeared in drawings by the youngest children (ages 3, 4 and 5). The authors concluded that few children drew genitalia, but that those who did were likely to have been sexually abused. The results were summarised by stating that sexually abused children were 6.8 times more likely to draw genitalia than were comparison children. Given the small percentages in each group, this summary is highly misleading.

Hibbard and Hartman (1990a) later replicated the earlier study (Hibbard *et al.* 1987). They compared drawings of matched groups of 109 children alleged to have been sexually abused with those of 109 children who had been screened to determine that there was no known history of sexual abuse. They again collected from each subject two drawings of a person (a man and a woman) in the same session, as well as two completion drawings, one an outline of a large 'mature' person and one an outline of a smaller 'immature person'. Comparison groups matched for age, sex, race and level of education consisted of children ranging from ages 3 to 8 (mean age 5.2 years). The developmental maturity of these children was measured by the Goodenough–Harris DAP (Harris 1963) and the Peabody Picture Vocabulary Test (PPVT) (Dunn and Dunn 1981). Hibbard and Hartman found that 6 out of 109 (5.5%) allegedly sexually abused children drew genitalia on the completion drawings. Only one child (0.9%) in the nonabused group did so. Again, these percentages are far too small to conclude that genitalia in children's drawings are indcative of sexual abuse.

Drachnik (1994) claimed that depiction of the tongue was a graphic symbol of sexual abuse. She reviewed anthropological and art historical information that might support the idea of the tongue as a symbol of sexual abuse. She retrospectively examined drawings of 263 children between the ages of 2.5 and 18 years which she had collected over 15 years. Of these children 57 had been identified as having been sexually abused with 12 having been identified as suspected victims. Children under age 4 were eliminated, leaving the age range at 4–18 years, and of the remaining 43 children with a history of sexual abuse, the drawings by 14 children displayed one or more tongues. Of the 12 suspected victims, 3 children drew tongues as well. Of the remaining 194 children in her study not known to have been sexually abused, only 2 drawings contained a protruding tongue. Unfortunately there was no attempt to work out any statistical analysis. Drachnik rightly cautioned against the automatic assumption that sexual abuse has occurred when children depicted tongues and argued for the need for further investigation. She did not, however, account for the ages at which the appearance of tongues occurred to consider the possible effects of development. Drachnik's findings, however, were supported by the analysis of my collection of 306 Man, Woman and Self drawings by nonabused children in that *no* tongues were drawn by any of the nonabused children (Hagood 1999, 2000c).

While most of the previous writers who alleged that genitalia and other features were linked with sexual abuse did not attempt to control for age differences, others have considered the problem more directly from a developmental standpoint. Koppitz (1968) found, in her well-known developmental study of children's drawings, that HFDs of normal children aged 5–12 rarely included genitalia. Conclusions were based on the drawings of over 1800 school children. In examining body parts drawn by 5 to 12-year-old 'normal' school children, Koppitz reported that only 2 of 925 girls (one 7 years of age and one 9 years of age) and 9 of 931 boys (six 5 years of age and one each 6, 7 and 9 years of age) included genitalia. Koppitz developed a list of 'emotional indicators' which she claimed occurred more frequently in children with a history of psychological disturbance. While she did not control for sexual abuse specifically, she informally linked certain features with sexual abuse or sexual preoccupation, examples being legs pressed together and genitals.

Di Leo (1973) also studied children's drawings from a developmental perspective and noted after reviewing thousands of children's figure drawings that the representation of genitalia was rare. He reasoned that when it did occur it was because the child had been made more aware of the sex organs due either to surgery or to seduction by older adults or children. Di Leo also believed that the generalised neglect of genitalia in drawings of the vast majority of children from diverse environments suggested that it may be due to the sexual latency which, according to psychoanalytic theory, prevailed during early childhood. He noted that girls' drawings showed evidence of sexual and social awareness at an earlier age than did boys' drawings.

The findings in the research I carried out did not support any of the previous writers' contention that drawing genitalia was necessarily an indicator of sexual abuse (Hagood 1999, 2000f). In the 306 Draw-A-Persons, 6 out of 34 ordinary primary school children (17.7%) with no known history of sexual abuse drew genitalia, which is a higher frequency than that reported in drawings of sexually abused children by the above writers. Contrary to the claims of previous writers, the frequency of genitalia increased as the children grew older. (See further discussion in this chapter.) It is important to note that many of these writers made their observations as far back as the mid-1970s. Easy access to sexual material has continually increased since that time in the form of films, videos, television and the Internet, which is likely to influence how much children include genitalia in their artwork.

Burgess *et al.* (1981) believed that sexual abuse should be suspected in children whose drawings markedly shifted from age-appropriate figures to disorganised objects and showed repeated sexual figures. However, these conclusions were not systematically validated. Kelley (1985) observed that pictures drawn by sexually abused children in the early phases of therapy frequently appeared below expected developmental levels, but that during the later stages of therapy, children drew more age-appropriate pictures. She did not state how long the children had been in therapy, nor address the possibility that these changes might also be due to cognitive developmental growth over the course of therapy. She did not use any standardised test or systematically present any scores representing the developmental levels of these children.

Burgess (1988) carried out a retrospective study on two very small groups of children, aged 3–7, matched for age, ethnicity, family structure and gender. One group consisted of nine children with a history of sexual abuse and the other group was made up of eight children with no known history of sexual abuse or age-inappropriate sexual behaviour. Children in the latter group were exposed to the stressful events of visiting the dentist for dental care education. Drawings were collected from all children in the study with the following topics: favourite weather, self now, self younger, the family doing something, the event, a house and tree, and a free drawing. Drawings were scored for 43 characteristics, the definitions of which were loosely described. Details of the data are presented in such a confusing and contradictory manner that any conclusions are highly questionable.

Burgess further claimed, contrary to most researchers, that nonabused children actually created drawings at a lower level of development than did the sexually abused children. She argued that it was possibly due to the abused children in her study being from a higher socio-economic level. Upon closer examination, however, of the drawing assessment instrument designed by the investigator and her colleagues, there were only two measures of developmental level, which were: '...are the drawings (a) age-appropriate (organised), or (b) regressed for age (disorganised)?' There was no formal attempt to determine actual developmental levels for the children by using any form of standardised instrument, nor any description as to what 'disorganised' and 'organised' actually meant. Burgess argued 'that omission of body parts indicate that the abused children feel violated and vulnerable' with no apparent basis for such an interpretation. She then counter-argued that the very same characteristics in nonabused children's drawings are representative of the child's developmental achievement, leaving the reader with a considerable amount of confusion.

Hibbard and Hartman (1990b) found no statistically significant differences in Koppitz's emotional indicators in drawings of sexually abused children compared with nonabused children, even though they previously had found significant differences in scores on the Peabody Picture Vocabulary Test (Dunn and Dunn 1981) with nonabused children scoring higher (Hibbard and Hartman 1990a). A focus of this study was to examine test–retest reliability of Koppitz's scoring of emotional indicators. Subjects ranged in age from 5 to 8 years. One group comprised 65 children suspected of having been sexually abused and the other group was made up of 64 children who had been screened for any concerns about sexual abuse. The children were asked to make two drawings of a person. On the second drawing, a picture of a person of the sex opposite to the first drawing was requested. The results were that there were few clinically significant differences between groups and no statistically significant differences were found for emotional indicators.

Methodological problems

In the above presentation of the findings of various investigators, it has become apparent that numerous methodological problems have created considerable difficulties. Problems with consistent use of matched groups, lack of precise operational definitions of items to be scored on scoring charts resulting in poor inter-rater reliability, use of instruments with poor validity and reliability, and publication of inaccurate or questionable statistics were among the problems observed. Studies comparing drawings of nonabused and sexually abused children using matched groups did not seriously take into account differences in drawing abilities at each age level assessed, e.g. drawings by 3-year-old children versus 8-year-old children or even 15 year olds. Items such as no pupils in eyes, no mouth, no neck, transparencies, no hands, heavy lines and so on were frequently calculated. As discussed in Chapter 2, differences in drawing characteristics between children vary considerably as they mature. Specific ages where these characteristics were likely to begin occurring were not a consideration. Frequencies measured the total quantities of certain characteristics occurring in each comparison group, regardless of the age of the child. This is an especially important issue for studies of drawings of sexually abused children where certain features in drawings are assumed to be linked with sexual abuse.

Trowbridge (1995) reviewed the literature on drawings of sexually abused children and argued that the *strong* point in the methodology of the research carried out thus far was the use of matched groups. It seems clear, however, in taking a closer look at the articles reviewed above, that the use of matched groups has created considerable problems with studying children's drawings, with no provision for controlling for age. Isaac and Michael (1985) argued that

'Matching has many disadvantages and is now generally discouraged' (p.86) and 'the technique of matching subjects to form pairs for later comparison tends to create more control problems than it solves. Therefore, the matching technique is coming under increasing criticism' (p.99). The research I carried out did not use matched groups, but controlled for age, and the findings were considerably different than those of many previous studies.

Variability of children's drawings on a day-to-day basis, discussed at length by Rhoda Kellogg (1969), has not been accounted for in most studies, much less variations likely to occur over longer periods of time. Kellogg found in her collection of over 1 million children's drawings that a child's rendition of the human figure changed considerably when drawn on a daily basis. Rubin, Shacter and Ragins (1983) similarly found considerable variations in drawings created at different times, and that these variations also increased and decreased at certain age levels of the children whose drawings were studied, with the highest variability occurring among 8 year olds.

Measurements of mental maturity made with instruments which are known and respected for their validity and reliability, such as the WISC, Stanford-Binet, Ravens and picture vocabulary scales, e.g. the British Picture Vocabulary Scale (BPVS) (Dunn, Dunn and Whetton 1982) and the PPVT (Dunn and Dunn 1981), were not used to measure the effects of mental maturity on children's drawings in most of the literature discussed above, other than as criteria for matching groups, with the exception of Hibbard and Hartman (1990a, 1990b).

Another major problem in studies of drawings of sexually abused children has been poor verbal definitions of items to be rated and unclear illustrations of items to be scored (D.A. Chase 1987; Sidun 1986). Discussions on how scoring charts were designed and validated are not presented. The result has been poor inter-rater reliability and highly questionable validity of the results presented. The development of good rating methods requires designing clearly defined scoring charts which have been tested several times for their reliability prior to scoring any drawings in the study.

'Sex abuse indicators' associated with normal child development

Unfortunately, it was not possible to obtain sufficient data from sexually abused children either from the United States or the United Kingdom for involvement in the doctoral research which I conducted at Edinburgh University. The focus, therefore, was exclusively on drawings of nonabused children. It was found that approximately one-third of the features listed in the literature as being associated with sexual abuse were linked with the level of development of the child (Hagood 1999, 2000d). The research was a longitudinal study of 306 drawings of normal, nonabused children from ages 5 to 10. Data were collected at three six-month intervals and analysed to determine whether and to what extent characteristics alleged to be linked with sexual abuse might appear in drawings of nonabused children. The drawings were first scored using the Naglieri (1988) Draw-A-Person Test, which is based on the work of Goodenough (1926) and Harris (1963). The scoring chart is comprised of certain characteristics expected at various stages of development. These tend to become more complex and detailed as the child matures. (Hagood, 2000a) Scores measuring the level of cognitive development typically increase with age and over time. Figure 9.1 illustrates how Naglieri scores on the drawings of nonabused children increased with age.

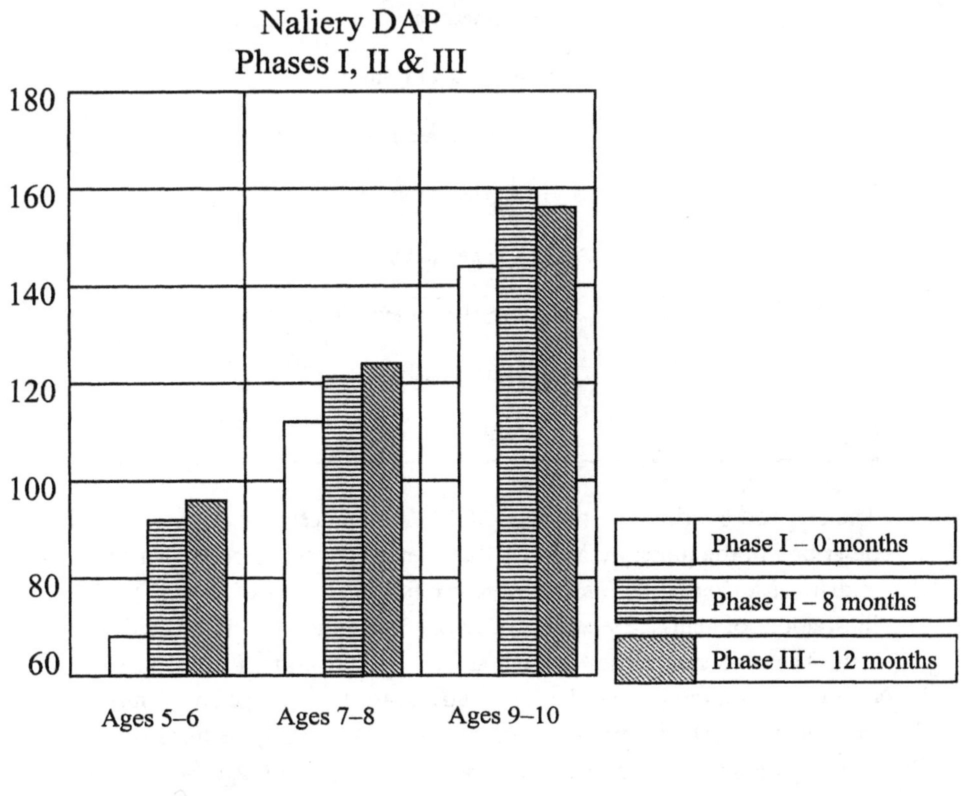

Figure 9.1 Children's drawings: Developmental scores increasing with age

The analysis of the data identified fourteen different characteristics which have been repeatedly listed in the literature as being linked with sexual abuse to be associated with ordinary cognitive development (Table 9.1) (Hagood 2000d).

Table 9.1 'Sex abuse indicators' as features of normal development
Hands absent
Head disproportionately smaller
Neck absent
Eyes with crossed pupils
Legs apart
One finger disproportionate
Linear nose
Legs pressed together
Phallic arms
Exaggerated full lips
Puppet mouth
Large circular eyes
Head detached
Phallic-like nose

The Hagood Scoring Chart (Hagood 1999) was designed to include features described in the literature alleging that they were associated with a history of sexual abuse. Verbal definitions were carefully worked out as well as pictorial illustrations of items to be scored. Inter-rater reliability was established at 95 per cent. These characteristics named 'sex abuse indicators' ('SAI's) actually decreased as children grew older. The study controlled for age and demonstrated that many so-called 'sex abuse indicators' were actually features of younger children's drawings and their appearance decreased with age (see Figure 9.2).

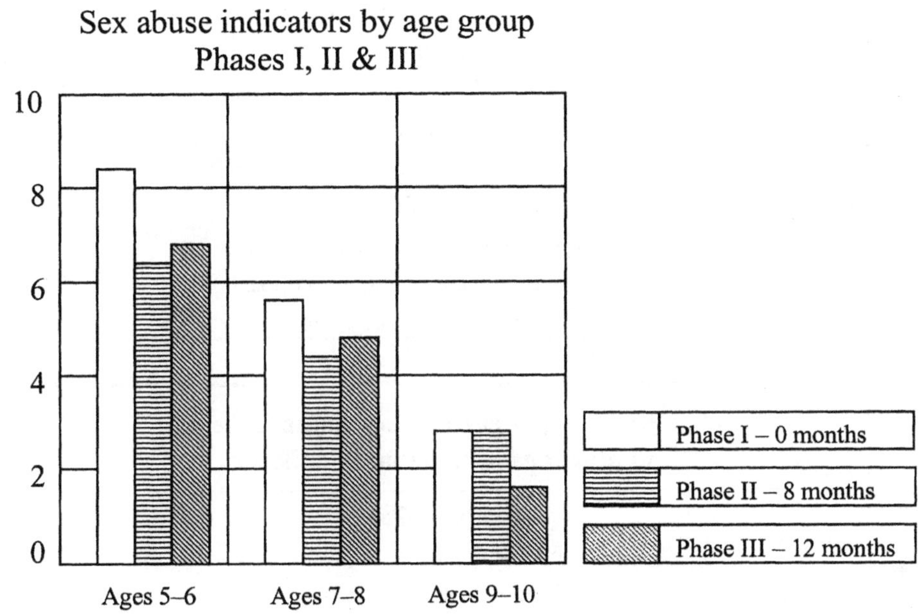

Figure 9.2 Children's drawings: 'Sex abuse indicators' decreasing with age

Non-occurring and rarely occurring 'SAI's in nonabused children's drawings

It is important to point out that nearly two-thirds of the so-called 'sex abuse indicators' found in the literature were *not* found in drawings by nonabused children at all or appeared so rarely that it was probably due to chance (less than 5%) (Hagood 1999, 2000c). These features are listed in Tables 9.2 and 9.3.

Table 9.2 Non-occurring 'sex abuse indicators' in drawings of nonabused children
Head absent
Head only, or head and neck only
Triangular neck
Legs repeatedly redrawn (more than two legs)
Phallic-shaped legs
Tongue protruding
Complete absence of facial features
Crossed-out, shaded-out or scribbled-out face
Entire person or body crossed out or scribbled out
Trunk drawn from waist up only

Table 9.3 Rarely occurring 'sex abuse indicators' in drawings of nonabused children
Eyes as wedges
Eyes with angular pupils
Eyes with vertical pupils
Hands hidden
Hands with no fingers
Phallic-shaped hair
Neck disproportionately long
Minimal genital area
No mouth
Mouth wide open
Jagged lip line
Mouth turned downward
Teeth exaggerated
Question-mark nose
Clown instead of person

Further direct comparison of these results with drawings by children with a known history of sexual abuse is needed to clarify further to what extent any of these features indeed are indicators in considering whether a child may have been sexually abused.

Appearance of genitalia in nonabused children's drawings

Out of 306 drawings of 34 nonabused children, male genitalia appeared in drawings by 6 nonabused children, some appearing more than once on different drawings (Table 9.4). Genitalia also appeared more frequently in drawings by older nonabused children (Table 9.5).

Table 9.4 Frequency of genitalia appearing in drawings of nonabused children

No. of drawings	No. of children	Frequency of drawings of genitalia per child
3	3	1
4	2	2
3	1	3

Total number of drawings with genitalia = 10

Total number of children = 6

Percentage of children (N = 34) = 17.7%

Table 9.5 Frequency of genitalia appearing in drawings of nonabused children related to age

Subject	Age of child	Frequency
1	5	1
2	7	2
3	8	1
4	9	3
5	9	2
6	10	1

Sublimation of genitalia into artwork

The phenomenon of subliminal images of male genitalia occurring in the paintings, drawings and sculptures of young sexually abused children may also be a characteristic arousing suspicion of sexual abuse (Hagood 1992a, 1994a; Uhlin 1979). To depict anatomically correct male genitalia with an ability for realism far beyond developmental appropriateness seems an unusual phenomenon and needs further investigation. The child commonly names the phallic image something else such as a tree, a rainbow, a cloud, a heart and so on (see case example in Chapter 4). The naming of these phalluses as some other object could be due to three explanations. One possibility might be that the phallus as the traumatic object is unconsciously portrayed. The second possibility might be that the child is conscious of what he or she has drawn but attempts to disguise this knowledge. I observed, for example, a 6-year-old child who had been sexually abused begin a drawing with what appeared to be a life-sized male phallus. She looked to see what my reaction was and then methodically drew over it, transforming it into dark clouds. Another 5-year-old child suspected of having been sexually abused drew a so-called cloud which was shaped as male genitalia and kept asking me to look at it, wanting to know how I liked it, as if she were trying to tell me something. The third possibility might be that the therapist's own projections are at play, and there is no connection with sexual abuse at all.

Additional problems in assessment of children's drawings

Sweeping statements are frequently made about children's drawings without considering several phenomena (Hagood 1992a, 1994a). One of these is the effects of immediate prior events. It is essential to consider what has gone on in the child's life immediately prior to doing artwork. In my pilot work for the research with 4-year-old children, for example, I noticed that all of the children drew large daisies in their pictures. When I asked them about it, I was informed that they had been painting daisies in their nursery school the day before.

A second consideration must be the effects of therapeutic treatment versus ordinary developmental maturing during the process of therapy. It is easy to assume that changes in children's artwork which indicate more maturity are due to therapy, but in actual fact may be due to normal developmental maturation which would have occurred without therapy. For example, a child may draw legs apart at the initial phase of therapy, but later draws them together. This could be due to resolution of the trauma of sexual abuse, or to mental development, or both.

A third consideration is the phenomenon of projection. We must always be aware that we can project into children's drawings what *we* see, not what the child might intend. It is important to obtain a description from the child wherever possible. When a clinician suspects sexual abuse, it is easy to project 'evidence' into children's drawings, seeing genitalia everywhere. The problem in working with sexually abused children is that these children are very often unable to verbalise such a trauma, and it is easy for an over-anxious clinician to read more into the artwork than may actually be there. On the other hand, it is equally easy to overlook clues that may indeed indicate that sexual abuse could have occurred.

A fourth consideration for those of us who have been psychoanalytically trained is that we must be on guard against making interpretations of artwork that may be appropriate for adults, but not for children. I would question whether psychoanalytic symbols commonly used with adult patients can be assumed to mean the same thing when working with children. For example, interpretations commonly made by users of the HTP (Buck 1948) which apply to adults' drawings are not necessarily appropriate for drawings by young children.

Future research into artwork of sexually abused children

This chapter has reviewed the literature on the use of children's artwork to identify possible sexual abuse. It has discussed the strengths and weaknesses of various studies and highlighted considerations for future research in this area. Methodology in such studies needs to be refined considerably. The focus has been primarily on artwork involving drawings of the human figure. It is apparent that continuing research is needed in investigating ways that children's artwork might be used in the detection of sexual abuse. Further comparisons between nonabused children and those known to have been sexually abused need to be carried out. It is apparent that those who use artwork with sexually abused children need a greater awareness of what ordinary nonabused children paint, draw and sculpt to minimise erroneous allegations of sexual abuse.

Research comparing the processes of art-making of sexually abused and nonabused children has not been carried out to date. Observations that sexually abused children tend to sublimate genitalia into their paintings, drawings and sculptures have not been investigated. It may be possible that nonabused children likewise exhibit this phenomenon in their art-making and further comparisons need to be made.

A more specific focus on the use of the Draw–A–Family Test (Hulse 1952), KFD (Burns 1982) or the HTP Test (Buck 1948) in detecting child sexual abuse has not been included in this chapter. Data have been collected from nonabused children using these three tests, and will be analysed and written up in the future. Further investigation of the validity and reliability of these tests and comparisons between sexually abused and nonabused children would be a valuable contribution to our body of knowledge.

It is important to emphasise at this point that the features listed in Tables 9.2 and 9.3 remain to be investigated further. The development of more valid and contemporary projective instruments using children's drawings is also essential. Methodologically sound studies must be developed and continue to be carried out to understand differences in drawings of nonabused and sexually abused children. Meanwhile we are faced with the task of adequately protecting the children with whom we come into contact.

Summary

The British Psychological Society has expressed its concerns regarding the ability of psychologists to assess child sexual abuse lest psychologists have their own 'Cleveland' (Howitt 1990). The dilemma in using children's drawings as indicators of possible sexual abuse is apparent. Caution and common sense cannot be overemphasised as clinicians increasingly treat children who are alleged to have been sexually abused. Many variables must be taken into account. Some indicators listed in the literature as characteristics of drawings of sexually abused children are frequently seen at various stages of development in the ordinary nonabused child. They also may appear in drawings of children with other emotional problems, perhaps suffering from forms of abuse other than sexual. It is also questionable whether analytic interpretations used in working with adults or older children can be generalised to younger children's drawings. Knowing events which may have occurred immediately prior to seeing a child may help clarify why the child depicted certain elements in his or her drawing. Listening to what the child has to say about a drawing, painting or sculpture is important, but one must take into account the reluctance of most children to disclose sexual abuse. The child may be trying to communicate indirectly and be unable to describe verbally what could be happening.

At the present time, it has been consistently demonstrated that drawings alone cannot be used as evidence that sexual abuse has occurred. Perhaps as we continue to refine our search for clues to possible sexual abuse in children's artwork, courts will begin to take such evidence more seriously. In reviewing existing literature on drawings of sexually abused children, it is understandable why they have been reluctant to do so. It is hoped that, with time, the use of children's artwork will become increasingly valuable in detecting sexual abuse and we will become better equipped to protect children from the long-term psychologically damaging effects of such abuse.

Epilogue

I have attempted to pull together what knowledge and clinical experience I have acquired since 1983 in my work in the area of child sexual abuse. I have felt extremely privileged to be instrumental in passing this knowledge on to others working in this difficult area, both in my writing and teaching. I have observed the evolution and ever-increasing knowledge that has been gained in the understanding of the dynamics of child sexual abuse. Many other professionals with whom I have worked over the years, including art therapists, counsellors, psychologists and psychiatrists, have shared their knowledge and expertise with me through personal communication. I am also indebted to those numerous professionals who have added to my knowledge through their literature, research, teaching, and conference presentations. I have endeavoured to acknowledge their work throughout this book.

The tragedy of childhood sexual abuse is one that continues to occur. Awareness of its incidence is ever-increasing, as well as reporting of suspected cases. A major problem continues to be not only of obtaining adequate protection for these children, but also that of gaining adequate and cost-effective treatment. In the United Kingdom there is a severe shortage of psychologists and treatment on the National Health Service is difficult to obtain, with many long waiting lists. In the United States, managed care programmes and increasing problems with litigation against therapists working with survivors of sexual abuse have unfortunately made obtaining therapy more difficult. Private therapy is expensive and those on both sides of the Atlantic who are covered by private insurance companies are likely to be covered only for short-term work. Many more people are obtaining training in counselling, psychotherapy and art therapy. It has been my observation, however, that they often receive inadequate skills to address the many and severe problems suffered by those who have been sexually abused. I hope that this book will help them and other mental health professionals to broaden those skills.

I have tried to challenge art therapists on both sides of the Atlantic to consider more closely how they interpret children's drawings and to refine their approaches to research. In my view, art therapists, particularly in the United Kingdom, need a wider scope of theoretical models, along with a greater awareness of the *many* therapeutic issues involved in working with both child and adult survivors of sexual abuse. My views will undoubtedly raise a considerable amount of debate, but I consider that to be very healthy.

My purpose in pointing out methodological difficulties in research into drawings by sexually abused children carried out by art therapists and others is not one of criticism, but of encouragement to continue to refine art therapy research in the future. There is a need to eliminate and minimise these methodological problems in order to resolve more clearly the question of whether and to what extent we can use children's drawings in the detection of sexual abuse or other trauma. Art therapists typically come from a fine art background and prefer to use more intuitive and phenomenological approaches to research. This may be appropriate for some investigations, but for the practice of using children's drawings for sexual abuse investigation, more rigorous methodology needs to be learned and applied.

Some may feel that my inclusion of working with adolescent and adult sex offenders was inappropriate for a book claiming to be about 'survivors'. I believed it to be extremely important to realise how victimised these offenders also have been, not as an excuse, but to provide a greater understanding of their horrendous acts against children. I hope that my experiences in using artwork in their therapeutic process will prove beneficial to others who work with sex offenders, both adolescent and adult. I have found my understanding of the dynamics of sex offenders to be immensely useful in working with adult survivors who consistently blame themselves for what has happened. Helping them to realise that their abusers were totally responsible, and why, has helped them to overcome their profound sense of guilt.

The incorporation of artwork into the therapeutic process is not one to be taken lightly. This is particularly true when working with survivors of sexual abuse. Judith Rubin (1984), a well-known child art therapist, cautions those who use art with children:

> Art is a powerful tool – one which, like the surgeon's, must be used with care and skill if it is to penetrate safely beneath the surface. Using media with those who are significantly handicapped or disturbed (even without analysis of process or product) requires an understanding not only of art, but also of the world of those with whom one is working. The use of art

> with all kinds of children or families as a symbolic communicative medium is a clinically-demanding task, which carries with it both a tremendous potential and an equally great responsibility. (p.298)

The fact that over these many years so many children and adults have trustingly shared their experiences with me, both verbally and in their artwork, attests to their determination to overcome their many difficulties. I have felt privileged to be a part in their journey toward personal growth and psychological health. It is reasonable, however, to expect that many will continue to struggle with considerable psychological difficulties which could not be overcome within the short-term therapy limitations within which we were required to work. I hope, however, that they will feel empowered to reach out for further treatment should they need to. This is particularly my hope for those children whom I saw, but sadly was unable to see protected from further abuse. People continually ask me how I can cope with working in such a difficult area. My answer is simply the incredible reward of seeing so many survivors go on to live much happier and healthier lives.

References

Agee, V.L. (1979) *Treatment of the Violent Incorrigible Adolescent.* Lexington, MA: Lexington Books.

Ainscough, C. and Toon, K. (1993) *Breaking Free: Help for Survivors of Child Sexual Abuse.* London: Sheldon Press.

Alexander, P.C. (1985) 'A systems theory conceptualization of incest.' *Family Process 24,* 79–88.

American Art Therapy Association (1999) *AATA Newsletter,* summer, 3. Available from American Art Therapy Association, 1202 Allanson Road, Mundelein, IL 60060–3808, USA.

American Psychiatric Association (1980) *Diagnostic and Statistical Manual of Mental Disorders* (3rd edn). Washington, DC: APA.

American Psychiatric Association (1987) *Diagnostic and Statistical Manual of Mental Disorders* (3rd edn – revised). Washington, DC: APA.

American Psychiatric Association (1994) *Diagnostic and Statistical Manual of Mental Disorders* (4th edn). Washington, DC: APA.

American Psychiatric Association (1997) *Diagnostic and Statistical Manual of Mental Disorders* (4th edn – revised). Washington, DC: APA.

Anderson, F.E. (1995) 'Catharsis and empowerment through group claywork with incest survivors.' *The Arts in Psychotherapy 22,* 5, 403–427.

Art Therapy Credentials Board (1994) *Certification Examination in Art Therapy: Bulletin of Information.* Mundelein, IL: American Art Therapy Association.

Aulich, L. (1994) 'Fear and loathing: Art therapy, sex offenders, and gender.' In M. Liebmann (ed) *Art Therapy with Offenders.* London: Jessica Kingsley Publishers.

Austin, V. (1980) 'The art of synthesis: Working with borderlines.' *Proceedings of the Eleventh Annual Conference of the American Art Therapy Association,* 23–26.

Axline, V.M. (1969) *Play Therapy* (revised edn). New York: Ballantine.

Baker, A.W. and Duncan, S.P. (1985) 'Child sexual abuse: A study of prevalence in Great Britain.' *Child Abuse and Neglect 9,* 457–467.

Baldwin, J.M. (1898) *Die Entwicklung des Geistes beim Kinde und bei der Rasse* [*Mental Development in the Child and by Race*]. Berlin.

Barnes, E. (1893) 'A study of children's drawings.' *Pedagogical Seminary 2,* 451–463.

Beattie, M. (1987) *Codependent No More.* New York: Harper and Row.

Beck, A.T. (1976) *Cognitive Therapy and the Emotional Disorders.* New York: International Universities Press.

Becker, J.V. (1988) *Intervening in Child Sexual Abuse: Learning from American Experience.* Proceedings of Child Sexual Abuse Conference, Social Paediatric and Obstetric Research Unit, University of Glasgow, June.

Becker, J.V., Kaplan, M.S., Cunningham-Rathner, J. and Kavoussi, R. (1986) 'Characteristics of adolescent incest perpetrators: Preliminary findings.' *Journal of Interpersonal Violence 1,* 1, 5–96.

Bentovim, A. (1993) 'Treatment services for sexually abused children and families: Forwards, backwards, and standing still.' *Child Abuse Review 2*, 3, 196–202.

Bentovim, A., Elton, A., Hildebrand, J., Tranter, M. and Vizard, E. (1988) *Child Sexual Abuse within the Family.* London: John Wright.

Berliner, L. (1995) 'Commentary on "Incest revisited: Delayed post-traumatic-stress-disorder in mothers following the sexual abuse of their children."' *Child Abuse and Neglect 19*, 10, 1311–1312.

Betensky, M. (1973) *Self-Discovery through Self-Expression.* Springfield, IL: Charles C. Thomas.

Betensky, M.J. (1995) *What Do You See? Phenomenology of Therapeutic Art Expression.* London: Jessica Kingsley Publishers.

Blum, R.H. (1954) 'The validity of the Machover DAP technique: A study in clinical agreement.' *Journal of Clinical Psychology 10*, 120.

Bolton, F. and Morris, L. (1989) *Men at Risk.* London: Sage.

Bowen, M. (1978) *Family Therapy in Clinical Practice.* New York: Jason Aronson.

Breer, W. (1987) *The Adolescent Molester.* Springfield, IL: Charles C. Thomas.

Briere, J. (1984) 'The effect of childhood sexual abuse on later psychological functioning: Defining a "post sexual abuse syndrome".' Paper presented at the meeting of the Third National Conference on Sexual Victimization of Children, Washington, DC, April.

Briere, J. (1989) *Therapy for Adults Molested as Children.* New York: Springer.

Briere, J. (1992) *Child Abuse Trauma: Theory and Treatment of the Lasting Effects.* London: Sage.

Briere, J. and Runtz, M. (1987) 'Post sexual abuse trauma: Data and implications for clinical practice.' *Journal of Interpersonal Violence 2*, 367–379.

Brooke, S.L. (1995) 'Art therapy: An approach to working with sexual abuse survivors.' *The Arts in Psychotherapy 22*, 5, 447–466.

Brooks, B. (1983) 'Preoedipal issues in a postincest daughter.' *American Journal of Psychotherapy 37*, 1, 129–136.

Buck, J.N. (1948) 'The House–Tree–Person test.' *Journal of Clinical Psychology 4*, 151–159.

Buck, J.N. (1977) *The House–Tree–Person (H–T–P) Manual Supplement.* Los Angeles, CA: Western Psychological Services.

Burgess, A.W. (1988) 'Sexually abused children and their drawings.' *Archives of Psychiatric Nursing 2*, 2, 65–73

Burgess, A.W., McCausland, M.P. and Wolbert, W.A. (1981) 'Children's drawings as indicators of sexual trauma.' *Perspectives in Psychiatric Care 19*, 2, 50–59.

Burns, D.D. (1980) *Feeling Good: The New Mood Therapy.* Harmondsworth: Penguin.

Burns, R.C. (1982) *Self-Growth in Families: Kinetic Family Drawings, Research and Application.* New York: Brunner/Mazel.

Burns, R.C. and Kaufman, S.H. (1970) *Kinetic Family Drawings (KFD). Psychological Assessments.* London: Abnormal Psychology CRM Books.

Buros, O.K. (ed) (1972) *The Seventh Mental Measurements Yearbook* (vol. 1). Highland Park, NJ: Gryphon Press.

Burt, C. (1921) *Mental and Scholastic Tests.* London: P.S. King and Son.

Butler-Sloss, E. (1988) *Report of the Inquiry into Child Abuse in Cleveland 1987.* London: HMSO.

Campbell, A. (1993) *Out of Control. Men, Women and Aggression.* London: Pandora (HarperCollins).

Canavan, M.M., Meyer, W.J. and Higgs, D.C. (1992) 'The female experience of sibling incest.' *Journal of Marital and Family Therapy 18*, 129–142.

Cane, F. (1951) *The Artist in Each of Us.* New York: Pantheon.

Cantwell, H.B. (1988) 'Child sexual abuse: Very young perpetrators.' *Child Abuse and Neglect 12*, 579–582.

Capacchione, L. (1991) *Recovery of Your Inner Child.* London: Simon and Schuster.

Carozza, P.M. and Heirsteiner, C.L. (1982) 'Young female incest victims in treatment stages of growth seen with a group art therapy model.' *Clinical Social Work Journal 10*, 3, 165–175.

Carson, R.C. and Butcher, J.N. (1992) *Abnormal Psychology and Modern Life.* New York: HarperCollins.

Case, C. and Dalley, T. (eds) (1990) *Working with Children in Art Therapy.* London: Routledge.

Chase, D.A. (1987) 'An analysis of human figure and kinetic family drawings of sexually abused children and adolescents.' *Dissertation Abstracts International* (University Microfilms no. 87–10434), Ann Arbor, MI.

Chase, T. (1987) *When Rabbit Howls.* New York: Jove.

Chassequet-Smirgel, J. (1970) 'Feminine guilt and the Oedipus Complex.' In J. Chassequet-Smirgel *et al.* (eds) *Female Sexuality.* Ann Arbor, MI: University of Michigan Press.

Chissick, R. (1993) 'She never said no.' *New Woman* February, 68–71.

Cohen, F.W. and Phelps, R.E. (1985) 'Incest markers in children's artwork.' *The Arts in Psychotherapy 12*, 265–283.

Cohen-Liebman, M.S. (1994) 'The art therapist as expert witness in child sexual abuse litigation.' *Art Therapy 11*, 4, 260–265.

Cohen-Liebman, M.S. (1995) 'Drawings as judiciary aids in child sexual abuse litigation.' *The Arts in Psychotherapy 22*, 5, 475–483.

Conn-Caffaro, A. and Caffaro, J.V. (1993) 'Sibling affairs: The impact of abuse on sibling relationships.' *California Therapist,* July/August, 51–61.

Conte, J.R. and Schuerman, J.R. (1988) 'The effects of sexual abuse on children: A multidimensional view.' *Journal of Interpersonal Violence 2*, 380–390.

Conte, J.R., Wolf, S. and Smith, T. (1989) 'What sexual offenders tell us about prevention strategies.' *Child Abuse and Neglect 13*, 293–301.

Coulborn-Faller, K. (1995) 'Children's interview statements and behaviors: Role in identifying sexually abused children.' *Child Abuse and Neglect 19*, 1, 71–82.

Cunningham, C. and MacFarlane, K. (1991) *When Children Molest Children.* New York: Safer Society Press.

Dalley, T. (ed) (1984) *Art as Therapy: An Introduction to the Use of Art as a Therapeutic Technique.* London: Tavistock.

Deblinger, E., McLeer, S.V., Atkins, M.S., Ralphe, D. and Foa, E. (1989) 'Post-traumatic stress in sexually abused, physically abused, and nonabused children.' *Child Abuse and Neglect 13*, 403–408.

De Jong, A.R. (1989) 'Sexual interactions among siblings and cousins: Experimentation or exploration?' *Child Abuse and Neglect 13*, 271–279.

Di Leo, J.H. (1973) *Children's Drawings as Diagnostic Aids.* New York: Brunner/Mazel.

Drachnik, C. (1994) 'The tongue as a graphic symbol of child sexual abuse.' *Art Therapy 11*, 1, 58–61.

Dunn, J.A. (1972) 'The Draw-A-Person Test.' In O.K. Buros (ed) *The Seventh Mental Measurements Yearbook* (vol. 1). Highland Park, NJ: Gryphon Press.

Dunn, L.M. and Dunn, L.M. (1981) *Manual for the Peabody Picture Vocabulary Test – Revised.* Circle Pines, MN: American Guidance Service.

Dunn, L.M., Dunn, L.M. and Whetton, C. (1982) *The British Picture Vocabulary Scale.* Windsor: NFER-Nelson.

Dworetzky, J.P. (1984) *Introduction to Child Development* (2nd edn). New York: West.

Edwards, B. (1979) *Drawing on the Right Side of the Brain.* Los Angeles: J.P. Tarcher.

Edwards, S. (1998) 'Incorporating a trauma model into the assessment/therapy of adolescents and adults experiencing mental health problems.' *Proceedings of the Twelfth International Congress of Child Abuse and Neglect.* Auckland, New Zealand, September.

Ellis, A. and Harper, R.A. (1975) *A New Guide to Rational Living.* North Hollywood, CA: Wilshire.

Erikson, E. (1950) *Childhood and Society.* New York: Norton.

Faller, K.C. (1988) *Child Sexual Abuse: An Interdisciplinary Manual for Case Management and Treatment.* New York: Columbia University Press.

Fehrenback, P.A., Smith, W., Monastersk, C. and Deisher, R. (1986) 'Adolescent sex offenders: Offender and offence characteristics.' *American Journal of Orthopsychiatry 36,* 2, 225–233.

Finkelhor, D. (1979) *Sexually Victimized Children.* New York: Free Press.

Finkelhor, D. (1980) 'Sex among siblings: A survey of the prevalence, variety, and effects.' *Archives of Sexual Behavior 9,* 171–194.

Finkelhor, D. (1984) *Child Sexual Abuse: New Theory and Research.* New York: Free Press.

Finkelhor, D. (1987a) 'The trauma of child sexual abuse: Two models.' *Journal of Interpersonal Violence 2,* 348–365.

Finkelhor, D. (1987b) 'The sexual abuse of children: Current research reviewed.' *Psychiatric Annals: Journal of Continuing Psychiatric Education 17,* 4, 233–237.

Finkelhor, D., Williams, L.M. and Burns, N. (1988) *Nursery Crimes.* London: Sage.

Finney, L.D. (1990) *Reach for the Rainbow: Advanced Healing for Survivors of Sexual Abuse.* New York: Putnam.

Freidrich, W.N., Beilke, R.L. and Urquiza, A.J. (1988) 'Children from sexually abusive families: A behavioral comparison.' *Journal of Interpersonal Violence 2,* 4, 391–402.

Freidrich, W.N., Urquiza, A.J. and Beilke, R.L. (1986) 'Behavior problems in sexually abused young children.' *Journal of Pediatric Psychology 11,* 45–57.

Freud, S. (1896) *The Aetiology of Hysteria.* In *The Standard Edition of the Complete Psychological Works of Sigmund Freud,* vol. III. London: Hogarth.

Freud, S. (1953) *The Interpretation of Dreams. Standard Edition,* vols. IV and V. London: Hogarth.

Gardner, H. (1980) *Artful Scribbles: The Significance of Children's Drawings.* New York: Basic Books.

Gerber, J. (1994) 'The use of art therapy in juvenile sex offender specific treatment.' *The Arts in Psychotherapy 21,* 5, 367–374.

Gersten, J.C. (1978) 'Kinetic family drawings.' In O.K. Buros (ed) *The Eighth Mental Measurements Yearbook.* Highland Park, NJ: Gryphon Press.

Giarretto, H. (1982) 'A comprehensive child sexual abuse treatment program.' *Child Abuse and Neglect 6,* 263–278.

Gil, E. (1987) *Children Who Molest: A Guide for Parents of Young Sex Offenders.* Walnut Creek, CA: Launch Press.

Gil, E. (1988) *Treatment of Adult Survivors of Sexual Abuse.* Rocklin, MD: Launch Press.

Gil, E. (1992) *Outgrowing the Pain Together: A Book for Spouses and Partners of Adults Abused as Children.* New York: Dell.

Gil, E. and Johnson, T.C. (1993). *Sexualized Children.* Rockville, MD: Launch Press.

Golomb, C. (1990) *The Child's Creation of a Pictorial World.* Berkeley, CA: University of California Press.

Goodenough, F.L. (1926) *Drawings as Measures of Intellectual Maturity.* New York: Harcourt Brace.

Goodwin, J. (1982) *Sexual Abuse: Incest Victims and Their Families.* London: John Wright.

Goodwin, J., McCarthy, T. and DiVasto, P. (1981) 'Prior incest in mothers of abused children.' *Child Abuse and Neglect 5,* 87–95.

Gordon, R.A. and Manning, T. (1991) '1990–91 membership survey report.' *Art Therapy 8,* 2, 20–29.

Groth, A.N. (1977) 'The adolescent sex offender and his prey.' *International Journal of Offender Therapy and Comparative Criminology 21,* 249–254.

Groth, A.N., Hobson, W.F., Lucey, K.P. and St. Pierre, J. (1981) 'Juvenile sex offenders: Guidelines for treatment.' *International Journal of Offender Therapy and Comparative Criminology 25*, 3, 265–272.

Groth, A.N. and Loredo, C.M. (1981) 'Juvenile sex offenders: Guidelines for assessment.' *International Journal of Offender Therapy and Comparative Criminology 25*, 1, 31–39.

Groth, A.N., Longo, R. and McFadin, B. (1982) 'Undetected recidivism among rapists and child molester.' *Journal of Crime and Delinquency 28*, 450–458.

Hagood, M.M. (1990) 'Art therapy research in England: Impressions of an American art therapist.' *The Arts in Psychotherapy 17*, 75–79.

Hagood, M.M. (1991a) 'Group art therapy with mothers of victims of sexual abuse.' *The Arts in Psychotherapy 18*, 17–27.

Hagood, M.M. (1991b) *The Use of Art Therapy in Working with Adolescent Sex Offenders: A Handbook.* London: British National Library.

Hagood, M.M. (1992a) 'Diagnosis or dilemma: Drawings of sexually abused children.' *British Journal of Projective Psychology 37*, 1, 22–33.

Hagood, M.M. (1992b) 'Status of child sexual abuse in the United Kingdom and implications for British art therapists.' *Inscape*, spring, 27–33.

Hagood, M.M. (1994a) 'Diagnosis or dilemma: Drawings of sexually abused children.' *Art Therapy 11*, 1, 37–42. Reprinted by permission, *British Journal of Projective Psychology.*

Hagood, M.M. (1994b) 'Group art therapy with adolescent sex offenders.' In M. Liebmann (ed) *Art Therapy with Offenders.* London: Jessica Kingsley Publishers.

Hagood, M.M. (1999) 'The development of children's drawings with reference to possible indicators of sexual abuse.' Doctoral dissertation, University of Edinburgh. *Dissertation Abstracts International 60* (04B), Publication no. 9922274.

Hagood, M.M. (2000a) 'The use of the Naglieri Draw-A-Person Test ot measure cognitive development.' Manuscript submitted for publication.

Hagood, M.M. (2000b) 'Projective theory and drawings of sexually abused children.' Manuscript submitted for publication.

Hagood, M.M. (2000c) '"Sex Abuse Indicators" not appearing in drawings of nonabused children: Need for further investigation.' Manuscript submitted for publication.

Hagood, M.M. (2000d) 'Sex abuse indicators in drawings of nonabused children as features of normal cognitive development.' Manuscript submitted for publication.

Hagood, M.M. (2000e) 'Psychoanalytic theory relative to drawings of sexually abused children.' Manuscript submitted for publication.

Hagood, M.M. (2000f) 'Genitalia and other anatomical sexual features in drawings of sexually abused children.' Manuscript submitted for publication.

Hagood, M.M. (2000g) 'Cognitive development and drawings of sexually abused children.' Manuscript submitted for publication.

Hagood, M.M. (in press) *The Use of Art in Counselling.* London: Jessica Kingsley Publishers.

Hammer, E.F. (1958) *Clinical Application of Projective Drawings.* Springfield, IL: Charles C. Thomas.

Harris, D.B. (1963) *Children's Drawings as Measures of Intellectual Maturity: A Revision and Extension of the Goodenough Draw-A-Man Test.* New York: Harcourt Brace/Jovanovich.

Haugaard, J.J. and Reppucci, N.D. (1988) *The Sexual Abuse of Children: A Comprehensive Guide to Current Knowledge and Intervention Strategies.* London: Jossey-Bass.

Herman, J. and Hirschman, L. (1980) 'Father–daughter incest.' *Sexual Abuse of Children: Selected Readings*, 65–75. (DHHS Publication no. OHDS 78-30161). Washington, DC: US Government Printing Office.

Herman, J., Russell, D. and Trocki, K. (1986) 'Long-term effects of incestuous abuse in childhood.' *American Journal of Psychiatry 143*, 10, 1293–1296.

Hibbard, R.A. and Hartman, G. (1990a) 'Genitalia in human figure drawings: Childrearing practices and child sexual abuse.' *Pediatrics 116*, 5, 822–828.

Hibbard, R.A. and Hartman, G. (1990b) 'Emotional indicators in human figure drawings of sexually victimized and nonabused children.' *Journal of Clinical Psychology 46*, 2, 211–219.

Hibbard, R.A., Roghmann, K. and Hoekelman, R.A. (1987) 'Genitalia in children's drawings: An association with sexual abuse.' *Pediatrics 79*, 129–136.

Hiebert-Murphy, D. (1998) 'Emotional distress among mothers whose children have been sexually abused: The role of a history of child sexual abuse, social support, and coping.' *Child Abuse and Neglect 22*, 5, 423–435.

Hildebrand, J. and Forbes, C. (1987) 'Group work with mothers whose children have been sexually abused.' *British Journal of Social Work 17*, 285–304.

Howitt, D. (1990) 'Expert opinion: Risky sexual abuse diagnosis.' *The Psychologist 3*, 15–17.

Hulse, W. (1952) 'Childhood conflict expressed through family drawings.' *Journal of Projective Techniques 16*, 66–79.

Iehe, W. (1989) *Sibling Abuse: Hidden Physical, Sexual and Emotional Trauma.* Lexington, MA: Lexington Books.

Ireland, M.S. and Brekke, J. (1980) 'The mandala in group psychotherapy: Personal identity and intimacy.' *The Arts in Psychotherapy 7*, 217–231.

Isaac, S. and Michael, W.B. (1985) *Handbook in Research and Evaluation* (2nd edn). San Diego, CA: EDITS.

Ivey, A.E. and Simek-Downing, L. (1980) *Counseling and Psychotherapy: Skills, Theories and Practice.* Englewood Cliffs, NJ: Prentice-Hall.

Jacobson, H. (1994) 'Abreacting and assimilating traumatic dissociated memories of MPD patients through art threrapy.' *Art Therapy 11*, 1, 48–52.

Jaffe, A. (1979) *C. G. Jung: Word and Image*, Bollingen Series XCVII: 2. Princeton, NJ: Princeton University Press.

Johnson, T.C. (1989) 'Female child perpetrators: Children who molest other children.' *Child Abuse and Neglect 12*, 219–229.

Johnston, M.S.K. (1979) 'The sexually mistreated child: Diagnostic evaluation.' *Child Abuse and Neglect 3*, 943–951.

Jolles, I. (1971) *A Catalogue for the Qualitative Interpretation of the House–Tree–Person (H–T–P).* Los Angeles: Western Psychological Services.

Jones, A. and Schechter, S. (1992) *When Love Goes Wrong.* New York: HarperCollins.

Jourard, S. (1971) *The Transparent Self* (2nd edn). New York: Van Nostrand Reinhold.

Joyce, P. (1997) 'Mothers of sexually abused children and the concept of collusion: A literature review.' *Journal of Child Sexual Abuse 6*, 2, 75–92.

Jung, C.G. (1933) *Modern Man in Search of a Soul.* New York: Harcourt Brace.

Jung, C.G. (1935) *Collected Works* (*The Transcendent Function*) (vol. 8), par. 168. Princeton, NJ: Princeton University Press.

Jung, C.G. (1973) *Mandala Symbolism. Collected Works of Carl Jung* (vol. 9), Part I. Princeton, NJ: Princeton University Press.

Kalff, D.M. (1980) *Sandplay.* Boston, MA: Sigo Press.

Katz, R.C. (1990) 'Psychosocial adjustment in adolescent child molesters.' *Child Abuse and Neglect 14*, 567–575.

Kaufman, B. and Wohl, A. (1992) *Casualties of Childhood: A Developmental Perspective on Sexual Abuse Using Projective Drawings.* New York: Brunner/Mazel.

Keller, R.A., Cichinelli, L.F. and Gardner, D.M. (1989) 'Characteristics of child sexual abuse treatment programs.' *International Journal of Child Abuse and Neglect 13*, 361–368.

Kelley, S.J. (1984) 'The use of art therapy with sexually abused children.' *Psychosocial Nursing 22*, 12, 12–18.

Kelley, S.J. (1985) 'Drawings: Critical communications for sexually abused children.' *Pediatric Nursing 11*, 421–426.

Kellogg, J. (1978) *Mandala: Path of Beauty.* Towson, MD: Mandala Assessment and Research Institute.

Kellogg, R. (1955) *What Children Scribble and Why.* San Francisco, CA: Golden Gate Nursery School.

Kellogg, R. (1969) *Analyzing Children's Art.* Palo Alto, CA: National Press Books.

Kelly, G.A. (1955) *The Psychology of Personal Constructs* (vols 1 and 2). New York: Norton.

Kempe, R.S. and Kempe, C.H. (1978) *Child Abuse.* London: Fontana.

Kempe, R.S. and Kempe, C.H. (1984) *The Common Secret: Sexual Abuse of Children and Adolescents.* New York: W.H. Freeman.

Kendall-Tackett, K.A., Williams, L.M. and Finkelhor, D. (1993) 'Impact of sexual abuse on children: A review and synthesis of recent empirical studies.' *Psychological Bulletin 113*, 164–180.

Kernberg, O. (1975) *Borderline Conditions and Pathological Narcissism.* New York: Jason Aronson.

Kerschensteiner, D.C. (1905) *Die Entwickelung der Zeichnerischen Begabung* [*The Development of Drawing Talent*]. Munich: Gerber.

Kilgore, L.C. (1988) 'Effect of early child sexual abuse on self and ego development.' *Social Casework 69*, 4, 224–230.

Klein, M. (1948) 'The importance of symbol formation in the development of the ego.' In *Contibutions to Psychoanalysis* London: Hogarth.

Klein, M. (1949) *The Psycho-Analysis of Children* (2nd edn). London: Hogarth and Institute of Psychoanalysis.

Klepsch, M. and Logie, L. (1982) *Children Draw and Tell: An Introduction to Projective Uses of Human Figure Drawings.* New York: Brunner/Mazel.

Knibbe, C. (1990) 'Treating sexually abused children using art therapy.' *Canadian Art Therapy Association Journal 5*, 1, 18–26.

Knopp, F.H. (1982) *Remedial Intervention in Adolescent Sex Offenses: Nine Program Descriptions.* Syracuse, NY: Safer Society Press.

Koppitz, E.M. (1968) *Psychological Evaluation of Children's Human Figure Drawings.* New York: Grune and Stratton.

Koverola, C., Pound, J., Heger, A. and Lytle, C. (1993) 'Relationship of child sexual abuse to depression.' *Child Abuse and Neglect 17*, 393–400.

Kramer, E. (1971) *Art Therapy in a Childen's Community.* New York: Schocken.

Kramer, E. (1975) *Art as Therapy with Children.* New York: Schocken.

Kramer, E. (1979) *Childhood and Art Therapy: Notes on Theory and Application.* New York: Chocken.

Kroth, J.A. (1979) *Child Sexual Abuse.* Springfield, IL: Charles C. Thomas.

Krug, R.S. (1989) 'Adult male report of childhood sexual abuse by mothers: Case descriptions, motivations and long-term consequences.' *Child Abuse and Neglect 13*, 111–119.

Kwiaktowska, H. (1978) *Family Therapy and Evaluation through Art.* Springfield, IL: Charles C. Thomas.

Landgarten, H.B. (1981) *Clinical Art Therapy· A Comprehensive Guide.* New York: Brunner/Mazel.

Landgarten, H.B. (1987) *Family Art Psychotherapy: A Clinical Guide and Case Book.* New York: Brunner/Mazel.

Larose, M.E. (1987) 'The use of art therapy with juvenile delinquents to enhance self-esteem.' *Art Therapy 4*, 3, 99–104.

Lawlor, M. (1993) 'Assessment of the likelihood of primary school teachers believing children's disclosures of sexual abuse.' *Child Abuse Review 2*, 174–184.

Lawson, C. (1993) 'Mother–son sexual abuse: Rare or underreported? A critique of the research.' *Child Abuse and Neglect 17*, 261–269.

Lerner, H.G. (1989) *The Dance of Anger*. New York: HarperCollins.

Leuner, H. (1969) 'Guided affective imagery (GAI): A method of intensive psychotherapy.' *American Journal of Psychotherapy 23*, 4–22.

Levens, M. (1994) 'The use of guided fantasy of art therapy with survivors of sexual abuse.' *The Arts in Psychotherapy 21*, 2, 127–133.

Levenstein, S. (1904) *Kinderzeichnungen biz Zum 14ten* [*Children's Drawings up to the Age of 14*]. Leipzig: Lebensjahr.

Levick, M.F., Safran, D.S. and Levine, A.J. (1990) 'Art therapists as expert witnesses: A judge delivers a precedent-setting decision.' *The Arts in Psychotherapy 17*, 49–53.

Lichtwark, A. (1887) *Die Kunst in der Schule* [*Art in School*]. Leipzig.

Lieberman, S. (1979) 'Transgenerational analysis: The genogram as a technique of family therapy.' *Journal of Family Therapy 1*, 51–65.

Liebmann, M. (1986) *Art Therapy for Groups: A Handbook of Themes, Games, and Exercises*. London: Routledge.

Liebmann, M. (1990) '"It just happened": Looking at crime events.' In M. Liebmann (ed) *Art Therapy in Practice*. London: Jessica Kingsley Publishers.

Liebmann, M. (1994) *Art Therapy with Offenders*. London: Jessica Kingsley Publishers.

Linehan, M.M. (1993) *Cognitive-Behavioral Treatment of Borderline Personality Disorder*. London: Guilford Press.

Linesch, D.G. (1988) *Adolescent Art Therapy*. New York: Brunner/Mazel.

Linesch, D.G. (1992) *Art Therapy with Families in Crisis*. New York: Brunner/Mazel.

Llewelyn, S. (1994) 'Trauma, child sexual abuse and survival.' *The Psychologist 7*, 4, 171.

Loftus, E.F. (1993) 'The reality of repressed memories.' *American Psychologist 48*, 518–537.

Longo, R. (1982) 'Sexual learning and experience among adolescent sexual offenders.' *International Journal of Offender Therapy and Comparative Criminology 26*, 31.

Longo, R. (1986) 'The impact of sexual victimization on males.' *International Journal of Child Abuse and Neglect 10*, 411–414.

Loredo, C. (1982) 'Sibling incest.' In S. Sgroi (ed) *Handbook of Clinical Intervention in Child Sexual Abuse*. Lexington, MA: Lexington Books.

Lowenfeld, M. (1979) *The World Technique*. London: Allen and Unwin.

Lowenfeld, V. (1939) *The Nature of Creative Activity*. London: Routledge and Kegan Paul.

Lowenfeld, V. and Brittain, W. (1957) *Creative and Mental Growth*. New York: Macmillan.

Lowenfeld, V. and Brittain, W. (1982) *Creative and Mental Growth* (7th edn). New York: Macmillan.

Lowenfeld, V. and Brittain, W. (1987) *Creative and Mental Growth* (8th edn). New York: Macmillan.

Lukens, H. (1896) 'A study of children's drawings in the early years.' *Pedagogical Seminary 4*, 79–110.

Luquet, G.H. (1913) *Les Dessins d'un Enfant: Etude Psychologique* [*Children's Drawings: A Psychological Study*]. Paris: Librarie Felix Alcan.

Luquet, G.H. (1929) 'L'evolution du dessin enfantin' [The development of children's drawings]. *Bulletin of Binet Society 29*, 145–163.

McCourt, E. (1994) 'Building up to a sunset.' In M. Liebmann (ed) *Art Therapy with Offenders*. London: Jessica Kingsley Publishers.

MacFarlane, K. and Waterman, J. (eds) (1986) *Sexual Abuse of Young Children*. New York: Guilford Press.

Machotka, P., Pittman, F. and Kalman, F. (1967) 'Incest is a family affair.' *Family Process 6*, 98–116.

Machover, K. (1949) *Personality Projection in the Human Figure.* Springfield, IL: Charles C. Thomas.

Machover, K. (1953) 'Human figure drawings of children.' *Journal of Projective Techniques 17*, 85–91.

McLeer, S.V., Dixon, J.F., Henry, D., Ruggiero, K., Escovitz, K., Niedda, T. and Scholle, R. (1998) 'Psychopathology in non-clinically referred sexually abused children.' *Journal of the American Academy of Child and Adolescent Psychiatry 37*, 12, 1326–1333.

McNeilly, G. (1983) 'Directive and non-directive approaches in art therapy.' *The Arts in Psychotherapy 10*, 4, 211–219.

Mahler, M., Pine, F. and Bergman, A. (1975) *The Psychological Birth of the Human Infant.* London: Hutchinson.

Malchiodi, C. (1990) *Breaking the Silence: Art Therapy with Children from Violent Homes.* New York: Brunner/Mazel.

Malchiodi, C. (1998) *Understanding Children's Drawings.* London: Jessica Kingsley Publishers.

Mark, B. (1980) 'Hospital treatment of borderline patients: Toward a better understanding of problematic issues.' *Journal of Psychiatric Nursing and Mental Health Services,* 25–31.

Marrion, L.V. (1990) 'Art therapists' approaches to the treatment of guilt and body image distortion in sexually abused girls, ages 4, 8, and 13. 'Unpublished doctoral dissertation, University of Victoria, BC, Canada.

Marshall, W., Jones, R., Ward, T., Johnston, B. and Barbaree, H. (1991) 'Treatment outcome with sex offenders.' *Clinical Psychology Review 11*, 465–485.

Martin, D. (1977) *Battered Wives.* New York: Pocket Books.

Masson, J.M. (1984a) 'Freud and the seduction theory.' *Atlantic Monthly,* February, 33–60.

Masson, J.M. (1984b) *The Assault on Truth: Freud's Suppression of the Seduction Theory.* New York: Farrar, Straus and Giroux.

Masterson, J.F. (1976) *Psychotherapy of the Borderline Adult.* New York: Brunner/Mazel.

Masterson, J.F. (1988) *The Search for the Real Self.* New York: Free Press.

Mearns, D. and Thorne, B. (1992) *Person-Centred Counselling in Action.* London: Sage.

Miles, T. (1989) 'Child abuse move as cases rise again.' [London] *Observer,* 9 April, 6.

Miller, A. (1984) *For You Own Good: Hidden Cruelty in Child Rearing and the Roots of Violence.* New York: Farrar, Staus and Giroux.

Miller, A. (1990) 'The search for the true self.' In J. Abrams (ed) *Reclaiming the Inner Child.* Los Angeles: J.P. Tarcher.

Minuchin, S. (1974) *Families and Family Therapy.* Cambridge, MA: Harvard University Press.

Missildne, W.H. (1963) *Your Inner Child of the Past.* New York: Simon and Schuster.

Mrazek, P.B. and Kempe, C.H. (1981) *Sexually Abused Children and Their Families.* Oxford: Pergamon Press.

Murphy, J. (1998) 'Art therapy with sexually abused children and young people.' *Inscape 3*, 1, 10–16.

Murphy, J. (in press) *Art Therapy in the Treatment of Sexually Abused Youngsters.* London: Routledge.

Murray, H.A. (1943) *Thematic Apperception Test.* Cambridge, MA: Harvard University Press.

Naglieri, J.A. (1988) *Draw-A-Person: A Quantitative Scoring System.* San Antonio, TX: Psychological Corporation and Harcourt Brace/Jovanovich.

Naitove, C.E. (1982) 'Arts therapy with sexually abused children.' In S. Sgroi (ed) *Handbook of Clinical Intervention in Child Sexual Abuse.* Lexington, MA: D.C. Heath.

Naitove, C.E. (1988) 'Arts therapy with child molesters: An historical perspective on the act and an approach to treatment.' *The Arts in Psychotherapy 15*, 151–160.

National Center on Child Abuse Prevention Research (1994) *Current Trends in Child Abuse Reporting and Fatalities: The Results of the 1993 Annual Fifty State Survey.* Chicago: National Committee for Prevention of Child Abuse.

National Children's Home (1990) *Survey of Treatment Facilities for Abused Children and of Treatment Facilities for Young Sexual Abusers of Children.* London: Department of Health.

National Children's Home (1992) *The Report of the Committee of Enquiry into Children and Young People Who Abuse Other Children.* London: NCH Publications.

Naumburg, M. (1953) *Psychoneurotic Art Its Function in Psychotherapy.* New York: Grune and Stratton.

Naumburg, M. (1987) *Dynamically Oriented Art Therapy.* Chicago: Magnolia Street.

Nelson, R.M. (1992) 'Why I'm every mother's worst fear.' *Redbook,* April, 85–116.

Ney, P.G. and Peters, A. (1995) *Ending the Cycle of Abuse: The Stories of Women Abused as Children and the Group Therapy Techniques that Helped Them Heal.* New York: Brunner/Mazel.

Nez, D. (1991) 'Persephone's return: Archetypal art therapy and the treatment of a survivor of abuse.' *The Arts in Psychotherapy 18,* 2, 123–130.

Oaklander, V. (1978) *Windows to Our Children: A Gestalt Therapy Approach to Children and Adolescents.* Moab, UT: Real People Press.

Pasto, T. (1965) *The Space-Frame Experience in Art.* New York: A.S. Barnes.

Pattison, C. (1992) 'Child sexual abuse: Integrating work with victims, their families, and perpetrators.' *Child Abuse Review 5,* 3, 16–17.

Pavlov, I.P. (1927) *Conditioned Reflexes.* Trans. and ed. by G.V. Anrep. London: Oxford University Press.

Peacock, M.E. (1991) 'A personal construct approach to art therapy in the treatment of post sexual abuse trauma.' *American Journal of Art Therapy 29,* 100–109.

Perls, F. (1969a) *Gestalt Therapy Verbatim.* Moab, UT: Real People Press.

Perls, F. (1969b) *In and Out of the Garbage Pail.* Moab, UT: Real People Press.

Perry, B.D. (1996) *Maltreated Children's Experience: Brain Development and the Next Generation.* New York: W.W. Norton.

Perry, B.D. (1997) 'Incubated in terror: Neurodevelopmental factors in the cycle of violence.' In J. Osofsky (ed) *Children, Youth and Violence: The Search for Solutions.* New York: Guilford Press.

Perry, B.D., Marcellus, J., Pollard, R., Blakley-Harris, T. and Hanley, D. (1998) 'Physiological measurements in the assessment of maltreated children: The physical impact on the developing brain.' *Proceedings of the Twelfth International Congress on Child Abuse and Neglect.* Auckland, New Zealand.

Pervin, L.A. (1984) *Personality* (3rd edn). New York: John Wiley and Sons.

Piaget, J. (1926) *The Language and Thought of the Child.* New York: Harcourt Brace.

Piaget, J. (1953) *The Origin of Intelligence in the Child.* London: Routledge and Kegan Paul.

Piaget, J. and Inhelder, B. (1969) *The Psychology of the Child.* London: Routledge and Kegan Paul.

Pierce, L. and Pierce, R. (1987) 'Incestuous victimization by juvenile sex offenders.' *Journal of Family Violence 2,* 351–364.

Porter, E. (1986) *Treating the Young Male Victim of Sexual Assault.* Syracuse, NY: Safer Society Press.

Powell, L. and Faherty, S.L. (1990) 'Treating sexually abused latency age girls: A 20 session treatment plan utilizing group process and the creative arts therapies.' *The Arts in Psychotherapy 17,* 35–47.

Pryor, D.W. (1996) *Unspeakable Acts. Why Men Sexually Abuse Children.* New York: New York University Press.

Putnam, F.W. (1989) *Diagnosis and Treatment of Multiple Personality Disorder.* London: Guilford Press.

Putnam, F.W. (1993) 'Dissociative disorders in children: Behavioral profiles and problems.' *Child Abuse and Neglect 17,* 39–45.

Putnam, F.W., Guroff, J.J., Silberman, E.K., Barban, L. and Post, R.M. (1986) 'The clinical phenomenology of multiple personality disorder: Review of 100 recent cases.' *Journal of Clinical Psychiatry 47*, 285–293.

Read, J. (1998) 'Abuse histories of psychiatric inpatients: To ask or not to ask?' *Psychiatric Services 49*, 3, 355–359.

Rhyne, J. (1984) *The Gestalt Art Experience.* Chicago: Magnolia Street.

Rhyne, J. (1987) 'Gestalt art therapy.' In J.A. Rubin (ed) *Approaches to Art Therapy.* New York: Brunner/Mazel.

Ricci, C. (1894) 'L'arte de bambini.' *Pedagogical Seminary 3*, 302–307.

Richmond, J. (1977) 'Art therapy and group process.' *The Arts in Psychotherapy 4*, 5–9.

Riordan, R. and Verdel, A. (1991) 'Evidence of sexual abuse in children's art products.' *School Counselor 39*, 117–121.

Rogers, C. (1939) *Clinical Treatment of the Problem Child.* Boston, MA: Houghton-Mifflin.

Rogers, C. (1942) *Counseling and Psychotherapy.* Boston, MA: Houghton-Mifflin.

Rogers, C. (1951) *Client-Centred Therapy.* Boston, MA: Houghton-Mifflin.

Rogers, C. (1961) *On Becoming a Person.* Boston, MA: Houghton-Mifflin.

Rorschach, H. (1932) *Psychodiagnostik* [*Psychodiagnostics*]. Bern: Hans Huber.

Ross, C.A., Norton, G.R. and Wozney, K. (1989) 'Multiple personality disorder: An analysis of 236 cases.' *Canadian Journal of Psychiatry 34*, 413–418.

Roth, E.A. (1987) 'A behavioral approach to art therapy.' In J.A. Rubin (ed) *Approaches to Art Therapy.* New York: Brunner/Mazel.

Rouma, G. (1913) *Le Language Graphique de l'Enfant* [*The Child's Graphic Language*]. Paris: Misch. et Thron.

Rubin, J.A. (1973) 'Mother–child art sessions: Part I, Treatment in the clinic.' *American Journal of Art Therapy 4*, 165–181.

Rubin, J.A. (1978) *Child Art Therapy: Understanding and Helping Children Grow through Art.* New York: Van Nostrand.

Rubin, J.A. (1984) *The Art of Art Therapy.* New York: Brunner/Mazel.

Rubin, J.A. (1987) *Approaches to Art Therapy: Theory and Technique.* New York: Brunner/Mazel.

Rubin, J.A., Shacter, J. and Ragins, N. (1983) 'Intra-individual variability in H-F-D's: A developmental study.' *American Journal of Orthopsychiatry 53*, 654–667.

Russell, D.E.H. (1986) *The Secret Trauma: Incest in the Lives of Girls and Women.* New York: Basic Books.

Ryan, G. (1988) *Victim to Victimizer: Re-Thinking Victim Treatment.* Available from Kempe National Center for Prevention and Treatment of Child Abuse and Neglect, 1205 Oneida Street, Denver, CO 80220.

Ryce-Menuhin, J. (1992) *Jungian Sandplay. The Wonderful Therapy.* London: Routledge.

Sagar, C. (1990) 'Child sexual abuse.' In C. Case and T. Dalley (eds) *Working with Children in Art Therapy.* London: Routledge.

Satir, V. (1967) *Conjoint Family Therapy* (revised edn). Palo Alto, CA: Science and Behavior Books.

Satir, V. (1972) *Peoplemaking.* Palo Alto, CA: Science and Behavior Books.

Serrano, J.S. (1989) 'The arts in therapy with survivors of incest.' In H. Wadeson, J. Durkin and D. Perach (eds) *Advances in Art Therapy.* New York: Wiley.

Sgroi, S.M. (1982) *Handbook of Clinical Intervention in Child Sexual Abuse.* Lexington, MA: D.C. Heath.

Sgroi, S.M. (1989) *Vulnerable Populations* (vols 1 and 2). Lexington, MA: Lexington Books.

Shields, S.S. (1991) 'Mothers of incestuously abused children in group art therapy.' In H.B. Landgarten and D. Lubbers (eds) *Adult Art Psychotherapy: Issues and Applications.* New York: Brunner/Mazel.

Shorr, M., Speed, M. and Bartlet, C. (1966) 'Syndrome of the adolescent child molester.' *American Journal of Psychiatry 122*, 783–789.

Sidun, N.M. (1986) 'Graphic indicators of sexual abuse in adolescent Draw-A-Person tests.' Unpublished doctoral dissertation, Illinois School of Professional Psychology, Chicago, IL.

Sidun, N.M. and Rosenthal, R.H. (1987) 'Graphic indicators of sexual abuse in Draw-A-Person tests of psychiatrically hospitalized adolescents.' *The Arts in Psychotherapy 14*, 25–33.

Silvercloud, B. (1982) 'Using art to express the unspeakable: A tool for intervention and therapy with the sexually abused.' *Proceedings of the Thirteenth Annual Conference of the American Art Therapy Association.* Philadelphia, PA.

Silverstone, L. (1997) *Art Therapy: The Person-Centred-Way* (2nd edn). London: Jessica Kingsley Publishers.

Simonds, S.L. (1992) 'Sexual abuse and body image: Approaches and implications for treatment.' *The Arts in Psychotherapy 19*, 289–293.

Skinner, B.F. (1953) *Science and Human Behavior.* New York: Free Press.

Slegelis, M. H. (1987) 'A study of Jung's mandala and its relationship to art psychotherapy.' *The Arts in Psychotherapy 14*, 301–311.

Smith, W.R. (1988) 'Delinquency and abuse among juvenile sex offenders.' *Journal of Interpersonal Violence 3*, 4, 400–413.

Snets, A.C. and Cebula, C.N.M. (1987) 'A group treatment program for adolescent offenders: Five steps toward resolution.' *International Journal of Child Abuse and Neglect 11*, 247–254.

Speltz, A.M. (1990) 'Treating adolescent satanism in art therapy.' *The Arts in Psychotherapy 17*, 147–155.

Spring, D. (1985) 'Symbolic language of sexually abused, chemically dependent women.' *American Journal of Art Therapy 24*, 13–21.

Spring, D. (1993) *Shattered Images: Phenomenological Language of Sexual Trauma* Chicago, IL: Magnolia Street Publishers.

Stember, C.J. (1978) 'Existential art therapy: The Clara Jo Stember model.' In A. Burgess and L. Holmstrom (eds) *Rape: Crisis and Recovery.* Bowie, MD: Brady.

Stember, C.J. (1980) 'Art therapy: A new use in the diagnosis and treatment of sexually abused children.' In *Sexual Abuse of Children: Selected Readings* (DHHS Publication no. OHDS 78-301261). Washington, DC: US Government Printing Office.

Stern, M.J. and Meyer, L. (1980) 'Family and couple interactional patterns in cases of father/daughter incest.' In *Sexual Abuse of Children: Selected Readings* (DHHS Publication no. OHDS 78-301261). Washington, DC: US Government Printing Office.

Stern, W. (1908) *Spezielle Beschreibung der Ausstellung Freier Kinderzeichnunger aus Breslau* [*Special Description of the Exhibition of Children's Free-Hand Drawing from Breslau*]. Berlin: Bericht uber den kongress fur kinderforschung.

Sully, J. (1895) *Studies of Childhood.* New York: D. Appleton.

Summit, R. (1980) 'Sexual abuse of children: A clinical spectrum.' In *Sexual Abuse of Children: Selected Readings.* (DHHS Publication no. OHDS 78-301261). Washington, DC: US Government Printing Office.

Summit, R. (1983) 'The child sexual abuse accommodation syndrome.' *Child Abuse and Neglect 7*, 177–193.

Thomas, G.V. and Silk, A.M.J. (1990) *An Introduction to the Psychology of Children's Drawings.* London: Harvester Wheatsheaf.

Thomas, J. (1981) Child Sexual Abuse Victim Assistance Project, Research Foundation of Children's Hospital, Washington, DC. Personal communication cited in A. Groth and C. Loredo (1981) 'Juvenile sexual offenders: Guidelines for assessment.' *International Journal of Offender Therapy and Comparable Criminology 25*, 31–39.

Ticen, S. (1990) 'Feed me ... Cleanse me ...: Sexual trauma projected in the art of bulimics.' *Art Therapy 7*, 1, 17–21.

Trikett, P.K. and Putnam, F.W. (1993) 'Impact of child sexual abuse on females: Toward a developmental, psychobiological integration.' *Psychological Science 4*, 81–87.

Trowbridge, M.M. (1995) 'Graphic indicators of sexual abuse in children's drawings: A review of the literature.' *The Arts in Psychotherapy 22*, 5, 485–493.

Tsalikis, M. (1998) 'Understanding the symbol: The therapeutic and assessment use of drawing with traumatised children.' *Proceedings of the Twelfth International Congress on Child Abuse and Neglect.* Auckland, New Zealand, September.

Tyndall, C.I. (1997) 'Current treatment strategies for sexualy abused children.' *Journal of Aggression, Maltreatment and Trauma 1*, 1, 277–291.

Uhlin, D.L. (1979) *Art for Exceptional Children.* Dubuque, IA: Wm C. Brown.

Vander Mey, B.J. (1988) 'The sexual victimization of male children: A review of previous research.' *Child Abuse and Neglect 12*, 61–72.

Verworn, M. (1907) 'Kinderkunst und urgeschichte' [Child art and early history]. *Korrespondenz der Deutschen Anthropologischen Gesellschaft* [*Correspondence of the German Anthropological Society*] *27*, 42–46.

Wadeson, H. (1980) *Art Psychotherapy.* New York: John Wiley and Sons.

Waller, C.A. (1992) 'Art therapy with adult female incest survivors.' *Art Therapy 9*, 3, 135–138.

Waller, D. (1993) *Group Interactive Art Therapy.* London: Routledge.

Waller, D. and Gilroy, A. (1992) *Art Therapy: A Handbook.* Buckingham: Open University Press.

Wang, C.T. and Daro, D. (1998) *Current Trends in Child Abuse Reporting and Fatalities: The Results of the 1997 Annual Fifty State Survey.* Chicago: National Committee to Prevent Child Abuse. (Retrieved 10 April 1999 from the World Wide Web: http//childabuse.org/facts.html)

Ward, T., Hudson, S.M., Johnston, L. and Marshall, W.L. (1997) 'Cognitive distortions in sex offenders: An integrative review.' *Clinical Psychology Review 17*, 479–507.

Winnicott, D.W. (1971) *Playing and Reality.* London: Tavistock.

Woddis, J. (1986) 'Judging by appearances.' *The Arts in Psychotherapy 13*, 2, 147–149.

Wohl, A. and Kaufman, B. (1985) *Silent Screams and Hidden Cries: An Interpretation of Artwork by Children from Violent Homes.* New York: Brunner/Mazel.

Wolf, S. (1989) 'Sex offender research.' Paper presented at the Third National Conference on the Sexual Victimisation of Children, Reading University, England.

Wyss, D. (1966) *Depth Psychology: A Critical History.* London: George Allen and Unwin.

Yalom, I. (1975) *The Theory and Practice of Group Psychotherapy.* New York: Basic Books.

Yates, A., Beutler, L.E. and Crago, M. (1985) 'Drawings of child victims of incest.' *Child Abuse and Neglect 9*, 183–189.

Yates, M. and Pawley, K. (1987) 'Utilizing imagery and the unconscious to explore and resolve the trauma of sexual abuse.' *Art Therapy 4*, 1, 36–41.

Index

Abuse-focused therapy (*see* Trauma model)
Abuse-reactive behaviour, 21, 81–84, 86, 174, 177, 183, 190 (*see also* Sexualised behaviour and Sexual abuse by children)
Adolescent sex offenders, 174–194
  abandonment by parents, 181, 212
  abuse as children, 185, 206
  acting out behaviour of, 179, 206
  delinquent behaviour of, 183
  denial and minimisation of, 196–198, 202
  family dynamics of, 181 (*see also* Family dysfunction)
  feelings of, 176, 206
  groupwork with, 188, 203–215 (*see also* Adolescent sex offenders, use of art with)
  ignorance of sexual information, 180, 212
  involvement with babysitting, 184
  isolation of, 208, 218–219
  lack of empathy of, 184, 193, 197, 206
  onset of abusive behaviour by, 176, 193
  relationship problems of, 180, 182, 211, 213
  seductive behaviour of, 188
  sexual fantasies of, 214
  therapeutic issues of, 179–190
  use of art with, 190–193, 203–215 (*see also* Adolescent sex offenders, groupwork)
  violent behaviour of, 188
Adolescent use of art, 64, 70
Adult sex offenders, 84, 120, 123, 128
  anger management for, 200
  as victims of abuse, 196, 198
  characteristics of, 196–198
  childhood issues of, 202
  cognitive-behavioural approaches with, 177–178, 200, 202
  conning and manipulation by, 123–129, 189–190, 209–210 (*see also* Adolescent sex offenders)
  contact with children, 199
  denial and minimisation by, 196–197, 221
  directive work with, 196
  emotional immaturity of, 199
  grooming behaviour or, 84 (*see also* Accommodation syndrome)
  groupwork with, 215–221
  lack of empathy of, 197
  loneliness and isolation of, 200, 219
  occupations of, 216
  passivity of, 199, 201
  personality disorders of, 198
  regressed and fixated, 197
  relationship problems of, 216–217
  responsibility for abuse, 195, 200–201
  sexual fantasies of, 201
  therapeutic issues of, 198–201
  threats by, 127, 155
Adult survivors of sexual abuse, 21–22, 74, 146–173
  case example of, 170–172
  characteristics of artwork of, 160
  clay sculptures of, 165
  developmental issues, 159–160
  drawings of, 164
  families of, 150
  feelings of, 149
  groupwork with, 158
  therapeutic issues of, 155
Alcoholics Anonymous, 126
Alcoholism, (*see* Alcohol/drug addiction)
Alcohol/Drug addiction, 19, 25, 126, 183–184, 199

American Art Therapy Association, 14–15, 54
Anger, 19, 80, 112, 115, 123, 149, 155–156
Anger management techniques, 184 (*see also* Cognitive-behavioural approaches)
Anxiety, 112, 149, 155, 186 (*see also* Fear)
Art materials, 39, 46, 66, 87–89, 93, 162–166 (*see also* Media)
  Destruction of, 39, 87–88
  For ages 2–4, 66
  For Ages 4–7, 68
  For ages 7–9, 68
  For ages 9–12, 69
  Storage of, 47, 88
Art process, 85–89
Art projects, 34, 47, 86, 89, 112
Art therapy
  definition of, 14–15
  training, 31, 54, 161
  with sexually abused children, 225–227
Artwork
  as evidence (*see* Evidence)
  characteristics in sexually abused children, 224, 226–237
  depicting progress, 91
  sexualised, 21, 104, 213, 225–226 (*see also* Genitalia)
Assertiveness, lack of, 123–124, 149 (*see also* Passivity)
Attention Deficit Hyperactive Disorder, 80, 186

Behaviour modification, 43, 82
Behaviour problems, 20, 76, 77, 82, 186–190, 206
Behaviour therapy, 33, 186
  using art, 42–43
Behavioural problems, 19, 76
  abusive behaviour, 85, 207 (*see also* Adult and Adolescent sex offenders)
  acting-out behaviour 80–81, 112, 179, 206 (*see also* Adolescent sex offenders)
  obnoxious behaviour, 38
Bipolar disorder, 171
Borderline personality disorder, 46, 125
Boundaries, 81
Brain scan technology, 22
British Association of Art Therapists, 12–15, 161
British Psychological Society, 13, 246

California State University, 11
Case examples
  dyadic work with a sexually abused child and her mother, 102–111
  groupwork with adolescent sex offenders, 205–215
  groupwork with adult sex offenders, 215–221
  groupwork with mothers of sexually abused children, 132–144
  groupwork with sexually abused children, 111–118
  individual work with an adult survivor of sexual abuse, 170–172
  individual work with a sexually abused child, 93–99
Cartooning, 40–41
Catharsis, 156
Chaotic mess making, 45
Child protection, 98, 105, 110
Child sexual abuse
  accommodation syndrome, 197
  incidence of, 16–18
  symptoms of, 18–22
Childhood memories, 30, 192
Children's drawings
  as measures of mental maturity, 238

early development of, 61–63
projection into, 244
research into (*see* Research into artwork of sexually abused children)
variability of, 238
Cleveland scandal, 12, 18
Clinical psychology, 13, 32, 161
Closed family systems, 138
Co-dependency, 127, 141
Cognitive developmental theory and children's artwork, 53, 60–66
Cognitive distortions, 177, 196
Cognitive therapy, 33, 43
Cognitive-behavioural approaches, 81–82
Collage, 30, 106, 113, 130, 136, 139, 163, 182, 204
Confidentiality of artwork, 88
Confrontation, 41, 196
of parents, 156
of sex offenders, 196 (*see also* Adult and Adolescent sex offenders)
Conning and manipulation, by offenders, 123–129, 189–190, 209–210, (*see also* Adolescent and Adult sex offenders)
Counselling and art therapy integrated, 29–31
Counselling psychologist, 13
Counselling skills, 35–37
Cultural differences, 16, 25–27, 54–55, 123, 146–148
Cycle of abuse, 178, 200–201

Damaged goods syndrome, 79, 92
Defence mechanisms, 185–186, 192 (*see also* Denial, Splitting, and Projection)
Denial, 124, 134, 196
Depression, 19–20, 25, 80, 112, 149, 155–156
depicted in artwork, 90, 211–212
Development of children's artwork, 57–59 (*see also* Cognitive developmental theory and children's artwork)
Developmental maturity, 21 (*see also* Adult survivors, developmental issues of)
Developmental theory relative to sexually abused children, 65
Dialectic behaviour therapy, 124
Dialogue painting, 136
Dichotomous thinking, 125, 186 (*see also* Splitting)
Directive versus non-directive approaches, 32–34, 89–90, 206
Disclosure of sexual abuse, 112, 120, 148–150, 154–155, 207
Dissociation, 19, 149
Dissociative Identity Disorder, 21, 153 (*see also* Multiple Personality Disorder)
Domestic violence, 126, 129, 150
Draw-A-Family Test, 55, 245
Draw-A-Man Test, 60
Draw-A-Person Test
Goodenough's, 60, 239
Harris', 60, 239
Machover's, 60
Naglieri's, 55, 239
Drawings as evidence, 16, 224
Dysfunctional family systems, 134–138 (*see also* Family dysfunction)

Eating disorders, 19, 25, 112, 125, 149, 155
Edinburgh University, 12–13, 238
Emotional support for therapists, 75
Empathic understanding, 37
Employee Assistance Programmes, 146
Evidence
artwork as, 16, 108–109
gaining of 75
Exhibition of artwork, 30, 88, 191

Expression of anger and self-reinforcement, 156 (*see also* Catharsis)
Expression of feelings, 30, 86, 89, 191–192, 200, 202, 218

False allegations of sexual abuse, 152
False memory syndrome, 151–152
Family art therapy, 31–32, 178, 181
Family dysfunction, 20, 25, 123, 127–131, 150
Family relationships, 114
Father-daughter incest, 149
Fear, 80
 of abandonment, 78, 125, 155
 of intimacy, 125
Female sex offenders, 121, 175, 195 (*see also* Mothers, sexually abusive)
Flashbacks, 19, 121, 149, 156

Gang age, 64, 69–70
Genitalia
 in artwork of sexually abused children, 104, 243
 in artwork of nonabused children, 243
 sublimation of in artwork, 243–244
Genograms, 131, 140–141 (*see also* Collages, Family dysfunction, Family relationships)
Gestalt art therapy, 31–32, 40–42
Goldsmiths' College, 12
Grooming by offenders, 148, 155 (*see also* Child sexual abuse, Accommodation syndrome)
Group counselling using art, 46–47 (*see also* Case examples)
Group interactive psychotherapy, 34
Group murals, 113, 169 (*see also* Mural making, Mandalas)
Group rules, 204–205
Group work, 30, 91
 cohesiveness, 30, 112, 113
 curative factors in, 47
 directive versus nondirective, 33
 with adolescents sex offenders (*see* Adolescent sex offenders)
 with adult sex offenders (*see* Adult sex offenders)
 with adult survivors of sexual abuse, 158
 with mothers of sexually abused children, 129–131 (*see also* Mothers of sexually abused children and Case examples)
 with sexually abused children, 111–117
Guided fantasy, 157, 160 (*see also* Visual imagery)
Guilt, 19, 79, 149, 155–156

Hagood scoring chart for "Sex Abuse Indicators" , 240
House-Tree-Person Test, 42, 55, 245
Human-Figure-Drawing Test (Koppitz), 60 (*see also* Draw-A-Person tests)
Humanistic approaches, 32

Impulse control, 81
Indicators of sexual abuse, 223 (*see also* 'Sex Abuse Indicators')
Individual work, 46
 with adult survivors (*see* Case examples)
 with mothers, 131–132
 with sexually abused children 92–93,
Inner Child metaphor, 158
Integration of counselling and art therapy, 14, 29
Interpretation, 54–57, 66
Intra-familial incest, 150
Investigative process, 74, 111

Jungian theory, 32, 54, 157–158

Kinetic-Family-Drawing, 42, 55, 140, 245

Leading questions, 75, 124
Learning disabilities, 149
Limit-setting, 75, 124, 186, 189, 210
Lone mothers, 129 (*see also* Mothers of sexually abused children)

Mandala, 12, 61, 91, 113, 137, 142–144, 166–167, 171
Marriage, Family, and Child Counselling, 11, 13, 32
Media, 29, 40, 48–50, 67, 86–88, 129–130, (*see also* Art materials)
Mothers of sexually abused children, 97, 110, 120
  denial of, 122, 124 (*see also* Defence mechanisms)
  family dynamics of,, 126–128, 134–135
  feelings of, 123–124
  feelings toward daughters, 123, 125, 127, 132–133, 140–142
  groupwork with, 129, 132–144
  history of victimisation of, 131–132
  individual work with, 131
  marital relationships of, 127
  mother-daughter bond, 128
  mother-daughter dyadic work (*see* Case examples)
  Occupational backgrounds of, 123, 132
  passivity of, 124
  protective abilities of, 124
  relationships with mothers, 128, 131, 141
  relationships with offenders, 129, 137–141
  scapegoating of, 120
  sexually abusive, 121 (*see also* Female sex offenders)
  socialisation skills of, 134
Multiple Personality Disorder, 20, 152–153, 155 (*see also* Dissociative Identity Disorder)
Mural-making, 102–103, 137, 169 (*see also* Mandalas)

National Health Service, 13, 21–22, 25–26, 30, 145–149
National Society for the Prevention of Cruelty to Children, 12
Nightmares, 20, 80, 121, 149, 167
Numbing of feelings, 182–183

Object-relations theory, 33, 44–46 (*see also* Psychoanalytic theory)
Observational feedback, 38, 85
Oedipal fantasies, 44–45
Open-ended questions, 85
Out of body experiences, 149 (*see also* Dissociation)
Outcome studies of treatment methods, 16

Panic disorders, 19, 149
Parentified child, 127
Parenting skills, 124
Partners of survivors of sexual abuse, 156
Passivity, 77, 155 (*see also* Adolescent and Adult sex offenders)
Perpetrators, 146–147 (*see also* Sex offenders)
Personal safety, 84
Person-centred art therapy, 31, 34–37
Person-centred counselling, 85, 34–37
  limitations of, 196
Phenomenological art therapy, 32, 39–40, 54
  phenomenological accounting, 40
  phenomenological discussion, 40
  phenomenological perceiving, 39
Phobias, 19, 148

Play therapy, 37–39, 85
Positive role model of therapist, 77
Post-Traumatic-Stress-Disorder, 18–20, 120, 126, 149 (*see also* Child sexual abuse, symptoms of)
Power struggles, 83, 101, 106, 203
Pre-Schematic stage, 63–64, 68
Problem-solving with art, 11, 130, 178, 190–191
Progress in therapy reflected in artwork, 90
Projection into children's drawings, 244
Pseudo-Naturalistic stage, 64
Psychiatric hospitalization, 150, 154
Psychoanalytic theory, 31, 32–33, 44–56
    limitations of, 178
Psychotic breakdown, 154 (*see also* Schizophrenia)
Puppets, 51, 68, 85, 94

Realness, genuineness, and congruence, 35
Reflecting, 83, 93
Regression, 87, 108, 162
Relationship difficulties, 19–20, 25, 112, 149
Research into
    artwork of sexually abused children, 230–237
    history of development of children's drawings, 57–60
    methodological problems in, 237–238
Reunification programmes, 121
Role-playing, 130

Sand tray therapy, 50, 94–96
Scary toys, 51
Schematic stage, 64, 68–69
Schizophrenia, 22, 149
Scribble drawing, 157
Scribbling stage, 62
Secretiveness of sexual abuse, 146
Self-disclosure of therapist, 37, 77–78
Self-esteem, 112, 123, 129, 136–137, 147, 179, 191, 203, 211
Self-harm, 80, 124, 191
Self-protection, 84, 187
Settings, 70–71
Sex identity confusion, 179
Sex offenders, 84, 122, 127 (*see also* Adult and Adolescent sex offenders)
    conning and manipulation by, 84
Sexual abuse
    by children, 174, 175 (*see also* Abusive-reactive behaviour)
    by females (*see* Female sex offenders)
    false allegations of, 75
    of males, 121
    societal attitudes towards, 76
    symptoms and psychological effects of, 18–21, 74, 149
Sexually abused children
    acting-out behaviour of, 76 (*see also* Behaviour problems and Abuse-reactive behaviour)
    feelings of, 79–82
    feelings toward mothers, 102
    groupwork with, 111–117 (*see* Case examples)
    individual work with, 92–99 (*see also* Individual work)
    obnoxious behaviour of, 38, 77 (*see also* Behaviour problems)
    seductive behaviours of, 84, 188 (*see also* Sexual behaviour problems of)
    sexual behaviour problems of, 19, 21, 82 (*see also* Abuse-reactive behaviour)
    socialisation skills of, 81, 134
    therapeutic issues of, 74–118
Sibling incest, 150
Splitting, 124, 186 (*see also* Dichotomous thinking and Defence mechanisms)

Stages of cognitive development in artwork, 60–65 (*see also* Cognitive developmental theory and children's artwork)
Stigmatisation, 122, 154
Substance abuse, 183 (*see also* Alcohol/drug addiction)
Suicidal ideation, 80, 121, 211–212
Suicide attempts, 124
Support for therapists, 78, 154
Symbolic play, 65
Symbolic resolution of conflicts, 30
Symbolism, 54, 157

Temper problems, 19 (*see also* Anger)
Thematic Apperception Test, 42
Theme-centred groups, 33–34 (*see also* Group art therapy, directive)
Therapeutic programmes, 21, 31, 79, 119, 175
Therapist as role-model, 77
Trauma model, 22–23
Triangulation, 140 (*see also* Family dysfunction)
Trust, 93–95

Unconditional positive regard, 36, 76
Unconscious, 66, 71–72, 185–186 (*see also* Defence mechanisms)

Vicarious traumatisation, 84
Victim mentality, 155
Visual imagery, 134, 139, 143

CPSIA information can be obtained
at www.ICGtesting.com
Printed in the USA
LVHW081604090921
697451LV00017B/491

9 781853 022289